The Days of

Also by Mary Beth Sartor Obermeyer:

The Biggest Dance
Big!

The Days of Song and Lilacs

Mary Beth Sartor Obermeyer

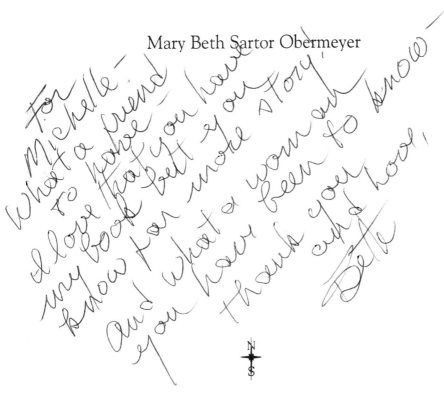

For Michelle —
What a friend
to have you have —
I love that you have
my book — bett you an
know for more story!
And what a woman to know —
you have been to know
thank you hool,
Beth

NORTH STAR PRESS OF ST. CLOUD, INC.

St. Cloud, Minnesota

ISBN 978-0-87839-580-0

First Edition, May 2012

Printed in the United States of America

Published by
North Star Press of St. Cloud, Inc.
P.O. Box 451
St. Cloud, Minnesota 56302

www.northstarpress.com

Dedication

In honor of the fiftieth anniversary of the film premiere of *The Music Man*.

To the Memories of the Music.

Of Mabel and Meredith. My Mother. And Mason City, in the time of *The Music Man*.

They say moments become important, stay with us when they affect our emotions, senses.

Those are the times I've remembered and write about, out of a school room, behind a stage, through the last gasps of Minstrelsy, circa 1954.

Scrapbooks from the era show my Mason City, Iowa, served up live entertainment like dessert, pre-television. The Fourths of July on the floating stage on Clear Lake melt into one sparkle time. And the quality hoopla at my house would crack any snow globe, as we tap-danced—literally—through the Iowa seasons.

Not as important to my story—I let a singer, a dancer, a whistler, an emcee drift time to time, from one show to another, but their feelings stay true. They were all in several shows, hard at work.

I change names of townspeople wherever I sense they might not, did not intend to go down in history saying their everyday thoughts in their stay-at-home house-dresses, sun-suits and flag costumes, in the rooms and fields my imagination provides them. Their thoughts—universal.

The important moments and passions filter through the pages and are true.

The struggle of neighbor Meredith Willson—his path to Broadway with his *The Music Man*—was handed to me as a living fairy tale by Mabel—the accompanist we had in common. Meredith's autobiographies and John Skinner's biography of the legend say it was so.

Mabel Kelso was brought to Mason City in 1913 by theater operator Tom Arthur and she and her husband first played in the stage orchestra of the Princess Theater. Next the couple was part of Joe Powers' orchestra at the Cecil Theater. Larry Fuller at the *Globe Gazette* wrote: "The orchestra was regarded as one of the best on the vaudeville circuit . . ."

But times changed and the Princess became the Strand. Vaudeville slowly lost its appeal. Mabel became staff pianist at KGLO, in their new studios on the upper floor of the Hotel Hanford.

But "her devotion to children will be the main reason she will be remembered, out of a lifetime furthering music," Fuller wrote. In her 50 years in Mason City Mabel played through silent movies, and stayed for the heyday of tap dancing, 1940s through the mid-1950s.

And yet Fuller wrote, 1967: "A great tradition has been built up around *Music Man*, the story of a fellow who 'brought music' to River City back in the early part of this century. But the passing of Mason City's 'music woman' last week brought relatively little comment outside those who knew her well."

She stars in my book.

TABLE of CONTENTS

Part III

Finding the Way

Part IV
The Miracle of Music:
The Music Seed

Prelude

"For a few moments music makes us larger than we really are, and the world more orderly than it really is. As our brains are thrown into overdrive, we feel our very existence expand and realize that we can be more than we normally are, and that the world is more than it seems. That is cause enough for ecstasy."

Music, the Brain and Ecstasy, Robert Jordain.

"Music stays in a body, even when much else is gone. The bones save it 'til last. This I know."

The Days of Song and Lilacs, Mary Beth Sartor Obermeyer.

Part I

Organizing the Rhubarb

MASON CITY, IOWA, 1954

Lilacs guard my yard. From my bedroom window. (Photo: Beth Obermeyer)

1

In Lilac Time

I t was a dazzling day on the playground, the sun all bright, the elm
seeds in a whir. I drew in one of those big breaths, the kind that
flutters up behind the forehead and makes one light.

I had not a clue that by day's end my heart would frost through.

By three o'clock, I declared the day a slam-bang. Tomorrow would
be the biggest day of the year, after all, the North Iowa Band Festival, right
through our town. Probably a hundred bands, as many queens. My mom
and I would go early, unfold our chairs, that was written in stone. And I'd
wave my arm off at Mr. Meredith Willson, our town music man, even
though he didn't know me from the next tap dancer—not yet. That would
be because the band festival didn't have any tap dancers. Just the big
stuff—bands, queens (one elected from each band) and some floats. But
when those bands marched by, their thunder rolled through and we were
all part of the show.

On I went, across Seventh Street towards home, leaving the jangle
and chime of the playground behind. I tucked between Mrs. Baird's hedge
and the church. The trees rattled, their buds opening to the wet green only
seen in spring. On I marched, mesmerized by my new red shoes, popping
one—then the other—from beneath my petticoat. And my first long skirt, it
tickled my knees. Twelve was a brand new age, after all.

Somewhere a lawn mower whirred away. All the while, the green
grass whizzed beneath. It was the first spring day of 1954, way more spring

than all those other little towns. Britt. Osage. Rudd. It was my world, my Mason City, and how it awaited.

On I bounced. From somewhere horns and drums set the scene—not surprising. The high school band pounded our town most every day. Their footprints were all over the place.

Soon my own steps searched for some grit, a sound for my dance. On I tapped, on the narrow path: a scrape—now a slide. An over the cracks, a bang on the bugs.

And start again. The best stuff always happened, when I wasn't even trying. I did my new combination over and over. I *could* use this step at Farmers' Round Up—that good. Or at Vivian's bridal shower. Or on the floating stage at Clear Lake on the Fourth of July.

I danced-out almost every single night. It was my job.

Soon I arrived at the end of the church wall. My back yard came towards me, a bump closer each step. I checked my behind—it sure wouldn't do if anyone saw. So I stopped my dance, scanned the alley, squinted. And the sun, it popped, like a flash bulb, all the way to the corners of my eyes.

But my next breath stopped, went bigger. I swallowed my music.

Because there they were, suspended in my lilac bushes, right along the edge of my yard. They were one with the branches. Their pin-curled hair lengthened and loosened in the breeze. Black, blond, brown, and red—it all mixed with the blossoms until it seemed their hair grew on the bush, too. Why the only sign of people beneath the billowing skirts was the saddle shoes and the big white bobby socks.

Those grown-up high-school girls probably just walked over from school to pick lilacs for the piano recital, without even telling their moms. My knees stiffened. Twelve years old was only sixth grade, after all. What? Did they hear me tap-dancing? Me and my big mouth, chanting away. One head swiveled.

"We can be here," she said, like it didn't even matter that this was my yard. "Sister Mary Franzeline called and asked your mother."

"I know," I said, bouncing right back. I wasn't sure which face talked. I kept my chin up. All I could think was the church basement, fragrant with the scent of good music, one and the same with these lilacs. But the big white teeth opened: "You look just like Alice Lon on the *Lawrence Welk Show*, dancing through with your big petticoat." No music in that voice.

4

Well. *Her* skirts flittered, too, about her legs. And her calves were all in a fuzz—the sunshine gave them a halo. Her mother wouldn't even let her shave her legs!

"The pattern's in *TV Guide*," I said. "That's where my mom found it. Yes, fifty yards of satin ribbon binding the edge. That way it doesn't itch."

"*Really.*"

By my next bounce I knew. *Ewww, that was not the right thing to say.* I'd wanted to keep up, answer fast. I was getting more different each step, all the dance and net. All I wanted was to just get along, get past them.

The big girl swayed her head and lowered. Her lilacs even waved and laughed. My breath swelled hot under my eyes. Those lilac trees were *my* friends. They guarded *my* yard.

I didn't really feel my legs walk but I guess they did, to the other side, towards flowers and clouds, to the front side of my house. "Jesus Mary Joseph," I muttered, bobbing my head automatic on the "Jesus," out of respect. I sneaked a peek back, through the plum blossoms.

What? Were they going to snag a ribbon off my skirts, spin me out like a top?

They did not.

Anyway, I had a schedule. I loved this walk, every day after school. I clasped the picket gate back and tight. Past the end column of the front

The house on Jefferson (Watercolor: Richard Beckman; Courtesy of David Beckman)

5

porch I went, scuffing near the lilies of the valley. They nodded. I pulled evergreen tips as I passed—so slick, swing back. Soon I was down the steps to the edge of my world, the curb on the carriage walk. I turned and looked back, balanced, from a calmer place.

The dust from the cement plant gave a soft look to my rose-painted house. From out the grayed-green roof my dad's television antenna seemed to tiptoe. I was walking the wall along my yard like a trapeze artist, maybe.

I dallied away, leaning this way, the other. I should take my dance and fly it through the air on TV. I thought so.

Except, oh well, no television station in Mason City, most didn't even have TVs. But there was always Des Moines.

But no one I knew could watch—Mason City was too far from that station. The television screen in our den looked like a bucket of soap suds, even with an antenna as tall as the church steeple. What was I thinking?

Maybe someone would come through town. They'd gasp. *You, my girl, should be on TV!* And whisk me away.

Of course not.

It was Mickey who streamed up, in that way she had of walking her

Mary Beth and Don Senneff, ages seven and ten. (Photo: Gerard Publicity photo; Courtesy of Beth Obermeyer)

Mary Beth and Mickey Lannon, ages seven and almost four. (Photo: Mr. Haaheim, neighbor; Courtesy of Beth Obermeyer)

skates, her blond bob carefree. She was the only kid I knew who could skate on gravel. She was seven, handy, right across the street, my pal since she could talk. She gabbed while she keyed her clamp-on skate tight.

No, I said, no, I can't skate . . . scuffed knees for sure . . . the month of May being big "dancing-out" season. I tied her sash and my friend scraped on, down the sidewalk, away.

Time, time, time. My own steps said it now—it was time to go, from in this yard, for today. I passed my front door, slowed at the mail box. I swiped my nose through. In case something came for me? Even though it hardly ever did.

The form for the Fourth of July show could've come.

It did not.

2

Up, Up and Away

My Hopalong Cassidy bag—cool as it was—hung hot at my side. I slung open the side door and thumped on the landing. "Mom. *Momm?* I'm *home!*" I tossed out the books and sorted my music.

The sewing machine hummed, *click-click, ka-stop.*

"We're off," I yelled. I licked my lips, waited, scratched a bite on my ankle. "I've got a new step for the Fourth. Mabel's seen *nothin' like it.*"

"Honey, are you sure?" Mom's voice sailed on. "I don't know . . . what is it? Well, no matter, we'll work on it later." No kidding, me and my mom practiced every day in the rec room, fixing steps on my long wall of mirrors.

"Well, you'll just have to walk on over," she said. "Just this once—by yourself. Can you do that? Hanna had to go home early." Julie squealed and Bobby rattled his playpen. Julie and Bobby were babies, five and not even two. "Do you have your tap shoes?" Mom asked.

My mom's voice sounded hairy. Harried. "Whoa, I can do that," I shouted. The treadle on the machine started up again. One can't very well quit in the middle of a ruffle.

I grabbed my favorite cowboy hat from the hook and clutched my music. Her scissors clacked. Mom's bench rolled, scrunched, tripped on the carpet. She always worked things out, just not today.

Bump on the screen door, bang with my butt—I jumped to the walk. And short-cutted down Mrs. Starr's cinder drive. Out, out and away.

With one big breath I started my stroll, careful on those crunchy glass cinders. The babble of the Lilac Girls bubbled in the distance. They'd probably moved down the alley, into Mrs. Rosen's raspberries.

Okay, six decades later, who has cinders? No coal-fueled stoves.

On across the alley I went.

I was going to get some time—my time alone. With Mabel.

Mary Beth, age nine. (Courtesy of Beth Obermeyer)

3

The Rehearsal

Iwhirred in a circle, grabbed the air from around me. Everything looked more interesting when all by myself. I noticed more things— the overhead breeze doing its twist-the-leaves dance, they flittered like spangles. My jittery shadow danced too, twisting to nothing and back. It was a very long walk—more than three blocks—and I milked it, every step.

One had to notice the sidewalk, the finest cement, four to a square. Mason City had two cement companies on the edge of town. It was probably why bands came to our town for the band festival, I figured. Our cement rebounded like nobody's business.

Soon I was at Mabel's part of the sidewalk, and I stomped up her steps. I struggled to see my feet over the bounce of the petticoat, impatient because I wanted to look up. And Mabel, did she ever await, behind the screen door, her head pitched forward, peering bright.

I'll always remember her like that, treasured. For just a moment she stilled in the frame, like a portrait, her practical dress clinging to her chest. "So, you've got a new dance, I hear!" is what she said.

Oh, boy, my mom and that telephone.

Mabel clung to the door and checked the threshold, one foot planted, tentative. She reached for the porch swing. Swiveled. Plunked.

"Should I show you?" I asked. "In the yard?" Two steps at a time, I leaped to the grass. Mabel always wanted to see. Mabel and I had been putting dances together since I was four, for shows—Mabel on the piano, and me in my dance.

But Mabel was slow that day, settling herself. It was then or never but I took my time, too. I checked my space, the fence all around. This was my chance to pull together, under the big sky. *Get your act together.* That always circled inside me. It only could happen when I was with Mabel. I could polish it with Mom, but creating came easily with Mabel.

Maybe I'd bring down expectations just a notch. "What if my dance is not so surprising?"

"Well, I haven't seen it yet!"

"I want to zing, knock 'em out. I need something just—a bit more."

"Like what?"

I had the steps down, darn it, just not the flash, the gimmick. "I guess I haven't pictured it yet." I was wavering, shoot!

"Ho, you will," she promised. "You'll picture it. Think big. When the music comes—grab! Send it back! Let your mind fly with your feet, go figure later. *Go.*"

"Think so?"

"Yes. Go!"

My dance slid away. It turned and it kicked. I doubled the tempo. And I hoped as I hopped—I searched for that ending. *Fill the darn space.*

But, oh, criminey. At the Fourth of July—how could I forget? The finest barbershop quartet, that's four . . . Al Gerardi's Accordion Band, could be a dozen kids . . . yee, a whole rock-and-roll band could blast at that show. My eyes blurred.

And that is exactly the moment I saw it! The red, the white, the blue.

In my mind colors stretched and unfurled, battled the breeze, up under the branches. The colors whir-whir-whirled into music, the music in my head. My feet thumped on dirt, on clumps of grass. Away I went, right into the gooseberry bush, like the Ice Follies girl on the end of the line. That wasn't what I pictured, no.

But how would I do that, swirl those colors?

I raced up the steps to Mabel, sat on my heels. I rested my chin on my grass-stained knees. My body was waiting for her to speak, but my mouth blabbed. "I put a lot into it, didn't I? This'll knock 'em dead, right?"

"But what was *it?* What did you see? You know, Mary Beth, I believe you may be onto something."

I told her all about the sparks at my feet and the colors that spurled above me. "I want to leave something for forever. It *is* for the Fourth of July, after all."

And Mabel clapped! Mabel knew "it" when she saw it.

But we had so much work to do, she and me. She pitched forward from the swing to walk her short steps, inside to her piano. I scooted ahead, grabbed her water glass from the little table and offered it to her, while I puffed back to normal.

Mabel at the piano. (Photo: Mary Beth Sartor, twelve, with her Brownie camera)

While I waited I yanked off some petticoats, the under three—tired of whipping them about—and stuffed them behind the piano. I was ready to go. I stomped my thick socks good into my tap shoes.

When she pumped her elbows to the side, flipped her loose sleeves—that was her signal to start. Her little hat held her reddish-brown curls in place, the veil tight across her forehead. She'd angle those curved bumpy hands. "From the top," she'd shout.

Boom, the music, a start! I was on. The beats came through, not her fingers but her whole arms. They tapped like hammers.

I eased on in, a clatter on wood. She kept her head angled, ear to the sound, eye to the dance. She had a perpetual smile. I felt her bright eyes.

"Speed up, kid," she said, ripping the music page over. "Atta girl."

Her music was the heartbeat of my dance. Mabel could pause a tiny bit, then come back on the beat: syncopation, just right. I didn't have to think and that meant I was not in complete control either, a heady feeling. My body took over. My taps never sounded better than that day.

"Oh, my, honey, you're cooking," she'd say. I had new sounds, ones that used the air. My new step I'd worked out by the lilac bushes. Pull backs slid and walked into six-point riffs, delicate and delicious. But they might be a throw-away to an audience? Especially a crowd across a lake. This was a tap-dancers dance, hard.

I pretended my new ending, collapsing on the hardwood floor. Mabel gave me her best look, the long one. She believed.

"We got it, right?"

Mabel clasped her hands under her waist, feet planted apart, breathing as fast as me. She got up, balanced. Barely. She settled across the room, in her soft chair, closed her eyes.

I guessed she needed a break.

4

Mabel's Meredith Boy

I took that moment—like I didn't notice she was whooped—to inspect her house. My mom always said I liked to take inventory. On one wall Mabel's rose-vined wallpaper turned black and white with photos.

One I craved. Not the man with large eyes and big cheeks and a brass horn; not the dancer with eyelashes spread as her fingers. Not my first portrait, right up there, the only photo in color, and the newest. I was four years old, dancing in my white lace-up baby shoes.

"This one, again," I said. "Tell me about the guy with the piccolo." How I loved that photo. Her picture of Meredith was a boy in knee pants—not the

Mary Beth, age four. (Gerard publicity photo; Courtesy of Beth Obermeyer)

14

professional the whole town knew him to be. She came across the room to the dusty green wall and tipped her head, as though he would talk.

"This. *This* is *our* Meredith Willson," she said. Her fingers slid on the glare of the photo. The bones of her hand looked like Tinkertoys, all balls and sticks. But she stroked with care, like a palm reader.

"Now Meredith Willson was always ideas. He grew up right here in this town." Her story about him was familiar, like an easy fairytale, to me.

But that night, her words came measured, on strained energy.

"It was 1917." Her eyes were over her eyeglasses, at me. "That was almost forty years ago. I was married to a drummer, and we knew he was special." She rubbed her forehead. "I accompanied Meredith. I taught him. His rhythm found all the edges. He knew he had it. It was in him."

I lined up next to Mabel, pushed my hair back so it wouldn't tangle in her veil. She let go the table, wrapped about me. Was I already taller than Mabel? But she was stooping. "It's okay to know it's in you, you know," she said.

And that's sure not what my mother always said.

If I got to preaching, Mom'd say . . . put a lid on it!

"What'd he say—he wanted to be when he grew up?" I said, wondering. "Did he get teased?"

"Well, if you're going to listen to everyone who wants you to be just like them—especially at your age . . ." Mabel squeezed my waist, a story on the way.

"I hear Mrs. Dr. Smith told Meredith's Aunt Mae—she didn't know it was his aunt of course—that she was sure glad all *her* children were normal." Mabel humphed. "I think she was a little bit green-eyed," Mabel said. "Like Meredith always says: that level of talk can stick like pajamas made of fly paper. Or not. It's up to you."

My eyes bugged, I knew, but Mabel just smiled. It made no sense at all to me . . . well, maybe a little. I thought of the lilac girls.

"But right here," she said, "Oh, I think Meredith said he wanted to play in a boys' band. He probably had his eye on the Mason City High School Minstrel Show." Mabel turned herself, her hand pressing on my shoulder. "When he got in the boys' band—he wanted to direct. Doesn't hurt to dream. Why he got all the way to New York, played with John Philip Sousa, right off."

Meredith Willson's boyhood home, renovated. (Photo: Beth Obermeyer)

Mabel stopped to slide her window sash up, to fresh air. "He grew up just down that street a few blocks. Right now? He's reaching high. Meredith is always writing . . . books, songs . . . a musical about our town . . . for Broadway . . . New York."

She skipped words. I was in a haze of wonder, anyway. Her gold-flecked teeth usually sparkled but now they *flashed*. She forgot to hide them when she talked about her Meredith. "He comes back to see me often. I saw him just this morning."

It was a lot to absorb. I probably looked it.

She headed for her chair and lowered with her *plop*. Mabel clasped her hands to her chest, trying to keep the beat inside, that's what I suspected. "Meredith's 'organizing his rhubarb,' he says. He's struggling," she said. "But our own ideas are always easiest. That's the power. Do it your way," she said, like she was already proud of me, the way I was thinking up my dance.

Usually I couldn't get a word in edgeways because my mom was always along, and they'd get to talking. Today I had. But the afternoon ended sooner than I wanted. I would have never gone home on my own.

"Come. I want to say good-bye," she said, her arms out-stretched.

16

I grasped Mabel's forearms. I back-pedaled my legs, digging into the rug, till Mabel came to a stand, like pulling up a pillow. And, oh, what a hug.

My mother wasn't a hugger, no, not at all.

And, then Mabel gave me a book, *one Meredith wrote*, about—of all things—a girl who wanted to go to New York to sing. "Take it home," she said. "It's yours." He named his story *Whatever Happened to Fedelia*. Now his tale was mine. I stuffed it into my bag.

I hadn't given one thought about going to New York. I'd get on it.

Mabel made her way to the doorway. "You can go now, dear," she said. "I'm going to play some music. On the Victrola. I'm so tired." Her sentences came quick, on shallow breath.

"See you tomorrow at the Band Festival," I said. Mabel and I always took notes—which band was best. I even imagined a separate band made up of all the queens, all tooting their horns, convertibles six across. Now that would be something.

Mabel's eyes—all the ink in the center—seemed to shrink to a dot. She turned. Her eyes hid under lids. She wasn't opening them very well.

Mary Beth, twelve, dreaming. (Photo: Gerard Studio; Courtesy of Beth Obermeyer)

I walked out to the sunshine, waved good-bye.

I loved Mabel. When I danced with Mabel I was not a child.

I clattered on home, lulled in thoughts of New York. It wasn't too professional to walk around in tap shoes, but I so loved the *clinks*.

Sooner than I thought, I faced my yard. Behind flapping bed sheets a lilac bush popped, in and out of view, doing its job, just guarding my yard.

If only I had an Annie Oakley inflatable petticoat. I wished all the time.

5

Meredith Willson Comes Home to the Vance

On some level I think I knew, even then. Beneath the soft rhythm of our lives, Meredith moved along, ever towards stardom. We were all one, rocking our music on the Iowa ground. Mabel knew her boy well and was insistent: something was happening right under our feet. Anyone who listened to her imagined it well, especially in the spring, in the perfume of the lilacs.

And maybe he rode a train into town on this day and maybe not, but ride a train he did at some point. He did open his new musical with a scene on the rails, after all.

And here he comes.

* * *

Meredith Willson snugged next to his wife, Rolina, on a train car clicking through the night, towards home. By morning they passed patchwork fields and balanced cows, black and white spots against green and yellow.

He'd soaked up the lull in this train car—a stranger over here, a card shark right there—cigar smoke, money talk, shysters shouting, shenanigans in the corner. The wheels danced on rails—pounding, picking up, now letting go—a magnificent rhythm he could use, maybe, in his story. A jump-start. Charge ahead. Relax back.

It was already springtime, his epoch was a-flying. He rode this train because he knew one thing for certain, and it was like this: in half an hour, when he'd sit down to write, that plot would fly right out of him. Those train tracks set a rhythm on his heart, chugged over his ribs. They'd be the steam for his songs.

Because inside he knew. He was down to business, in the struggle of his life—well, he had been for years—but this was it. Two big producers had asked him to write a musical for Broadway, set in this very home town. The trick? He was trying hard to do the whole banana—the words, the music, the plot—all three. The whole kit. The kaboodle!

The train cars slowed, dinged, end to end, faster and faster, like the decks of shuffled cards that were going down all around him. A big lurch forward, he grasped Rini's shoulder. He elbowed his satchel, tight to his side. He stood and swung, over to the door.

A blast of Mason City air swung up his nose. Even as the voices from the train chanted at his head. The warm, sweet Iowa farm aroma made him smile. This beat L.A. to heck and gone, of that he was sure. He swung to the platform and landed with a thud.

Rini was a bounce fast behind. She wiggled alongside him, jabbed an elbow and a laugh. She stretched. "Now why again are we on this train, dear?"

Meredith could only shrug, sheepish at her tease. "You okay?" he wondered—all he could manage. He had to get the feel of coming into town on a train, s'all, might be, could be the key. Rini hugged his arm. He sure didn't want to put it in words and sound silly, poke the magic.

This was, after all, his favorite time of year, in Iowa—The North Iowa Band Festival, when over a hundred bands thundered through the streets. It had seemed like a hundred.

Even so, he swung back. With a hoot! To a spectacle-bar-none. He'd seen the sight often, true, just not from a train, not this early in the day. Because a torrent of marching musicians crossed the track, right ahead, over South Nineteenth Street. Lordy, it looked like a massive cattle run, all charging for a staging area. Meredith savored the reds and the greens, the royal blues, the white spat-feet shuffle. The tubas, a glint like so many suns.

Rini winced at the onslaught but she picked up his smile. Together they jumped to the street and charged, through a windmill of batons, hundreds of wind-whipping flags, endless fresh faces. The marchers straightened when they passed, like they wanted Meredith to know they *could* be in his show! Finally, out of the fray, the pair moved smoothly, along blocks of empty school buses. Emerging from the shadows, they walked to the edge of downtown and on towards Federal Street, slowing, soaking in the familiar, all they'd come for.

Blocks of this and the pavement cooked. His worn leather shoes burned from beneath. But the crossing fingers of branches—as far down the block as he could see—did contain him. Something about Mason City did it for him every time. The air, warm or cold by season, charged him, electric.

Rini, his wife of six years, hadn't grown up here, but she seemed to like his town, too. She checked her reflection in the window of Lundberg's Fashion Salon, turning in the early morning light, hands cinching her waist. "Oh, here it is, dear. The perfect dress for the Band Festival." The mannequin's dress was just like the Mason City Mohawk Marching Band uniform, but with a flittery red skirt, white pearl-edged gloves and a feathered purse with a silver clasp.

Meredith smiled. Rolina immigrated from Russia and her take on things amused him. But he hated to stop now. He circled in place, his breath keeping the pace, to him a rhythm. A song circled his head in that way that won't stop.

Ding dong ding. He could hear chapel bells ring . . .

And they did indeed, a calliope of sound. And it could go on for minutes, he knew. "I'd know where I was if my eyes were closed," he said. He sorted the hymns in his head, from all the different church bells.

Rini picked up the pace, clasping his wrist to her cheek. Her warm breath could shoot through his seersucker jacket and invade his shoulder, wrap his heart and hold it. Rini always jolted him. Perhaps, he imagined— and the thought made him happy—they were in a musical themselves, right now.

So he turned left—sharp and snappy—and straight-armed right through the wide open door of the Vance Music Company, the music store of his childhood. He held the screen and bowed. She whipped past and in.

His huge grin dried his teeth, but his big voice could boom, like it only could when he was at home. He sang away because—once again— this was the town that knew him when.

Rini marched to the back of the store, swinging her dark hair to the rhythm of the *ding* of the cash register. She wrapped her arms about her waist—to catch her breath—her taffeta skirt a-swishing.

Meredith followed, passing the wall of trombones. Imagine, all those clarinets, growing like weeds, all the way to the Steinway. This store in this town, yup, it could do it for him.

John Vance, Jr., popped up from the back, smoothing his hair, hand pumping a shake. Meredith clapped his back until John's glasses fell down his nose and his words coughed out: "Got new stuff, Meredith?"

But Meredith rarely answered right away. He liked to banter small-town stuff, like a warm-up to dialog for his show. He said to John, in his umpty-dump way with time: "How do you suppose it is, again? So many towns have marching bands around here?" Meredith's voice idled. He was teasing.

John's eyes sharpened, his voice sped—"Well, back in the forties, a slick guy from—*say a music store in Mason City*—went to every town around. Gave a music capability test to every kid." John leaned forward, fake and earnest. "Would you believe, every kid passed?"

"Well, sure, then he could sell 'em *all* band instruments." Meredith knew this tale well.

"That's the story," John said. "And you can use that in your show if you want." Because everyone in Mason City hoped to be in Meredith's show. "Anyway," John went on. "Feel at home, Meredith." He strode to the front of the store as he talked. "You've got that end of the shop pretty much to yourself. Have a go at it. It's a slow day—not much music being bought with school out, Band Festival all but over." He sat at the oak table by the register and buried his nose in the ledgers.

Meredith collapsed on the shiny piano bench. He warmed his fingers, ear to the piano. He'd work on a tricky song, move it along.

Rini sat, too, her back to Meredith's shoulder, and he felt her sway with his familiar introduction. Her opera voice was solid. The words came, insistent. There would be trouble. More trouble. In River City!

Meredith bounced his knee. His feet jumped like on tracks. He'd named the town in his musical River City, not Mason City—but it was Mason City, no doubt about it. All her life, his mama had been certain the two creeks that ran through Mason City were actually rivers.

He had to get his mama in this show. Mama's whispers came to him often, even though from another world.

On he chanted. So far Meredith had no just plain lines in his show, no dialogue. He wanted the words to be music, rhythmic, the entire musical. He called it rhythmic rhyme-less speaksong.

Half a century later we call it "rap"!

The trick? Keep meaning in his chant story, even as he stayed light. He wanted it seamless, doggone it.

His fear: he'd write infectious music with no plot. Or dialogue interrupted by songs.

Meredith would fight for this concept with producers for years. He'd spread his stubbornness, his genius over three more years of endless days, starting at 4:00 a.m. with the rooster and going till the bats circled. In a driving beat near insanity. He made that clear in an autobiography.

But a woman's voice interrupted his song. "Well, Meredith," she said, in a voice low and soft, a crash to his brain. The words chased a welcome thrill all the way to his soles.

"Mabel, my girl, I didn't see you there. How are you?" In his rush he tripped around the piano to wrap his bear-like arms about his beloved boyhood accompanist, and he knocked her hat off. The veil snagged on her glasses, and he plopped it all back, like a lid on a bottle of sloshing milk.

Mabel smelled good, like ginger cookies and coffee. Or maybe it was her reddish hair, like ginger sprinkled on white. John straightened the clarinets along the wall. He didn't have a line in this show.

Mabel balanced her hand on a shelf of harmonicas; she grasped Meredith's arm and they made their way to the piano. "So what's happening, kiddo?" she asked.

"I'm here to organize the River City Boys Band!" Meredith could fake a great face. "That could be a good line for my show. A loveable rogue, a con-man. Tricky guy he is. 'Sure as the Lord made little green apples,'" Meredith said. 'That band's in uniform!'"

Mabel smiled big but her eyebrows upped, taut. She leveled her chin. "No fooling now. I've seen plenty of band uniforms on my walk today. So how is the *musical* going?"

"Depends on when you ask, right, Rin?" Rini didn't answer. He bragged about the producers, two big ones, asking him to write it. Big stuff.

Meredith scuffed his black-and-white spectator shoes. He avoided Mabel's eyes. "There's so much for me to learn about writing a musical." He couldn't help it. He emptied his eyes at her. "I'm glad I ran into you, truly I am," he said. He led her to the piano bench.

They scooched along it. She seemed so small, like a baby robin alongside him, wrists-all-speckled. He hid his face from John and two more customers on the snoop. "The music came fast, the lyrics, you can imagine. But I might be over my head. It's the script. I have to hold them in their seats, two hours. To do that, I have to simplify the threads."

Meredith tipped his face to the ceiling. "Been at this for *four years*." His voice was sarcastic, building. "One of these days I have to—*have to*—say . . . 'I'm ready. Ready to show my story.'"

There. He'd said it. He'd spilled it in words. His stomach stormed, right behind his navel. He was in the cloud he carried with him, always.

"That's amazing, Meredith." Three timeless Mabel words. Her smile pulled tight over her teeth, too large. Her lips cracked through the lipstick. But that smile, just great anyway. She pushed his arm, a quick rough poke.

Meredith played a melody, absent-minded. Mabel leaned close. "Why don't you start from the top, try to tell me your plot? C'mon, jump right in, Glory."

The name, the blue word, startled him, but in a warm way. Glory was Meredith's mother's name for him, like the blue, so blue, morning glories that grew by their house. *The words will come*, he told himself. He'd told it over and over, to the paper boy, the laundry man, Rini, the chores girl, the paper hanger, Rini.

Meredith bowed his head to his hands, landed a two-chord overture. He welled up, started to chant, his breath hot on his hands. John Vance, Jr., tugged on his trouser knees and lowered to a chair. His role was critical. John was their audience.

Meredith imagined his characters lined up on the wall. Rini readied paper and pencil.

"*Ching ching ching.* The train pulls into River City, full of anvil salesmen. 1900." *Chord.*

"Harold Hill listens. They warn about . . . about a con man touring the area."

Mabel nodded. Meredith's eyes vibrated.

"'River City,' called the conductor. 'Ioway.'"
Chord.

"Harold Hill jumps off, plods through town. Iowa-stubborn citizens brush him off. They invite him to a barbeque. He can eat all the food he brings himself. Give Iowa a try! Those townspeople insist."

The world got as small as Mabel and Meredith. Mabel played the piano, Meredith gained speed. His cheeks huffed. "Harold Hill spots the

23

town's new pool table and warns . . . Trouble . . . He'll get them a boys' band, the instruments, the uniforms. Why it'll keep the young ones moral after school!"

Rini beamed at the new turn of story.

"But the piano teacher realizes . . . Harold can't read music. Why, he'll have to move on once he's sold the uniforms and instruments—to the entire town."

Mabel slapped the back of her hand on her forehead, in mock horror.

"He falls for the piano teacher. He tries to stop her from telling on him." The piano tinkled in joy. "But by now they both realize he has the whole town loving music. Harold learns a lesson in morals from her. He stays in town."

"So, what did she do?" said Mabel, chortling. "Someone needed to straighten out that shyster."

"Well, that's the highlight. It's a love story."

"Well, I should say. A *love* story. Oh, Meredith."

"One reader summed it up for me: 'It's just the story of a man and his Seventy-Six Trombones that captured every heart in River City.'" John applauded with wild broad claps.

Mabel pulled her spectacles, wiped her eyes. "Now, Meredith, it seems to me you should gather up some songs and dialogue and call those producers back. Let them know you're still working on it. You could take just this much and audition."

"She's right," Rini said. "Let's call Ernie and Cy tomorrow night, when we get back to L.A. They have no idea if you took their suggestion to write this or not. It doesn't have to be finished for them to get the idea."

On those words, Mabel touched Rini on the shoulder and gathered up her music. She tugged Meredith's ear.

A door squeaked and slammed at the front of the store. Confetti from the festival air drifted in, whooshed out. "And I do have to go, kid," Mabel said.

The woman was leaving. She flicked her fingers into her little white gloves and straight-armed away. She always cut off praise. Her head bobbled now, balanced on two tendons.

He breathed deep. Mabel was like vitamins, there for the moments of his life. Why, her son had been a pallbearer at his mother's funeral.

Meredith'd post a note to Mabel right now so she'd know how he felt. Meredith was a short note burster, brief with words, just stayed in touch.

And he would make that call to the producer.

The front door blew open again, this time with a siren, of horns. Mabel seemed pulled by the current of air and the music. The white polka dots in her navy skirt pulsed with each bump.

Her straight legs wobbled on ankles like baseballs. Her feet barely flexed as she walked.

Meredith's smile slacked, in a trance. Were her hands as tight as her feet? How was she still playing the piano? He hadn't noticed her hands. Meredith was transfixed till she turned to a shadow, out the door. She disappeared into a syrup of purple, royal blue, gold band uniforms. Shorter and shorter she went, until she disappeared.

He'd always assumed Mabel'd be there forever.

6

Home on Jefferson Street

I sailed on home to my mother, my dance still hatching. My perfect day, it was winding on down.

I banged through the screen door, took the linoleum in two *clunks*. A lunge to the left—the kitchen looked slippery so I whipped the other way. I skidded to a halt on the teal carpet. "Mom, I'm home!" My voice bounced around the big living room.

The monster clock in the corner *clonged*. It was 4:45, fifteen minutes to supper.

The clothespins tacked in Mom's apron pocket, announcing her every step. I squirmed quick into the big satin chair. I'd left my petticoat at Mabel's. Around the corner she came, tugging off her outdoor hair net. Her house dress seemed to whirl, green and white, roses too, of course. It was my favorite. She was a dresser.

"Did Mabel like *Alexander's Ragtime Band?*" she asked. She slid onto the piano bench to talk. We always hung on what Mabel thought.

Mother with a visiting baby. (Courtesy of Beth Obermeyer)

26

"She did." I puffed up. "It's going to work," I said, slip-sliding on my bare dress on the chair. "I got a drop-dead idea! Mabel jumped up and down she liked it that much."

My mother frowned. "What on earth did you add? Where is your petticoat?"

"I imagined a new ending, just like the movies." My words had a trifle too much cheer, I knew. I didn't want to tell my mother that I wasn't quite sure.

But not a lie though. Not like when Frank Swed told his mother: "They're trying something new this year. They're not doing report cards."

I had to watch my mouth, hang onto to myself, until I was certain. It's how ideas work and you either know that or you don't. My mother tugged the long fringe on the shawl draped over the piano bench. She was the premiere idea lady, I suppose she saw through.

And this was no light subject. She yanked thread after thread. "Mary Beth, sometimes I don't even know—will a tap dancer ever win first in a contest?" Her face even flushed.

"Mom, I know I can do it," I said, so quick. "You make me a costume that brings them to their feet. Not like anyone's seen." We were always a team, had to keep each other going.

"It's getting close, the Fourth. You really don't have time for much more imagining." She moved the sheer glass curtains, tipped her head toward the street. "No time to worry now," she said. "It's time for dinner. Look! Here comes Daddy." She was exasperated but she hid it.

We zipped around. I hung up my bag. My father hated a mess. We had time to get in order. He would inspect his car for a moment. His new car was about his favorite thing.

"Call Julie—time for supper!" Mom said. She headed for the kitchen, slinging her everyday apron onto the door knob. "She's out on the swing," she said. She opened her apron drawer and slid a pink one from the stack. She tied the starched sash into a flower-of-a-bow, on the side. Satisfied, she pushed her fingertips deep into a wayward blond wave.

I hurried to holler, out the kitchen window. Julie pumped hard and sailed up and away. I marveled at how she caught her balance, pulling clumps of grass to slow her landing, starting her run to the house in one smooth arc. It seemed like yesterday that she was my dolly, just a baby. I would just as likely now find our Julie hanging from the trees.

27

Mary Beth, ten, and Julie, three. (Photo: Mr. Haaheim, neighbor; Courtesy of Beth Obermeyer)

Julie was nice but she was such a commotion.

Mom slung baby Bobby off her hip, into his high chair. He slammed his hands on the tray like a drum roll. Supper was a big event. We were set. Mr. Fritz's farm tomatoes, green peppers and radishes spread color by the bread, butter and milk.

Now noon—the main meal—was farm big, meat, gravy and potatoes—Hanna was there to help. Supper, on the other hand, my mother was on her own. It was always fresh vegetables, maybe cold cuts and bread, nothing cooked, no mess. No sniffing good smells for supper.

The click said it, my dad, he was at the door. At the hall closet. A jingle, his suit jacket hung on the bar. I hadn't seen him for days. He was

28

Daddy's second year at the Park Hospital Clinic, 1943. Left to right, back row: G.J. Sartor, R.E. Smiley, C.O. Adams, N.C. Stam, W.N. Hanson; front row: unidentified, T.E. Davidson, F.W. Saul, L.R. Woodward. (Photo: Safford Lock; Courtesy of Beth Obermeyer)

Bobby. (Photo: Mary Beth, twelve, with her Brownie camera)

the only pediatrician in Mason City and always on call. I drifted to hang out by the dining room arch.

Through the entry he came, into the living room and he hovered before his beloved Scott Radio. My mom said it cost as much as a car and that was back right after the war. It always took a bit for him to get past that radio. He paused, too, at the clock, as though to switch from hospital to home time.

I strained to hear if he said something over the *whir*. The big mahogany fan was his favorite, too, first class, top of the line, right up there with the television set and his car. It loomed large, a Mathes fan no less, on the black marble in front of the fireplace. He greeted his home reflection in the mantel mirror, silent.

I liked how he took time to do things just right, his way. He closed his eyes and let the breeze ripple his shirt, all round his waist. He slipped his tie through his collar and lined it up on the chair. The white velvet upholstery always held it fast. He checked the playpen. Bobby kind of lived in the playpen by the French doors. Behind the dining room table, in his spare time.

29

Finally Daddy came to the kitchen door. He rested his hand on my shoulder, and I got his slow blink. He steered me back to the table. He was the only thing moving till he took his place, right across from me. But then came Julie, scrambling behind him, hands drippy and soapy, getting to her chair. My mother waited for us all to land and then took the head of the table.

Daddy straightened his knife, then his fork, then his spoon. Then his plate. He leaned back in his chair. "In the name of the Father," he said, beginning the sign of the cross. "Bless us oh Lord, and these thy gifts . . ."

His deep voice swung along through the prayer. I rocked impatient but content, my eyes on the vegetables. It was the little stuff that happened all the same all the time that made me know I could do my big stuff.

He was through with me for now, and I knew that. It'd be my mom's turn. But that always made good listening.

Julie tipped back and forth in her chair, munching a carrot with her new big teeth. Bobby lunged for a Hostess Twinkie and that got moved pronto. My mother passed the Wonder Bread. I loved the cellophane wrapper with the red, blue and yellow bubbles.

I took two slices. Cut exactly the same, every slice the same, always.

The little kitchen radio droned now, a break from the music. Even babies knew to be quiet and let Daddy listen. It was just the *clink* of silver and plates. "Shallow . . . parched . . . hog futures." I cut a slice of bread in half.

". . . Next week . . . opens . . . Mason City . . . *television station.*" My father talked at the same time as the radio. In my rush to sit up, I kicked his knees.

"Television station? Mason City? It's opening?" I rattled, I knew. "Daddy. What!"

He lifted his chin and looked right at my eyes. "One hundred thousand watts. Half million dollars. It covers the Golden Triangle, from Mason City, Iowa, to Austin to Albert Lea in Minnesota."

"Right here in Mason City?" I'd danced on Austin, Minnesota, television. I'd danced on Jimmy Valentine's show in Minneapolis. I'd had to go all the way to Des Moines for Iowa TV. Just this afternoon I'd been ready to bail to New York and now a television station would be right down the street!

I suppose I was streaming on the line of starring in my own reality show? The air held any number of ideas, after all. Everyone would get television sets soon. This was big.

"As of next week," Daddy said. "KGLO-TV." He buttered his toast to dip in his milk. I forgot to say, he always got milk toast. "Know what the GLO stands for? Think." My dad always gave me a quiz. He thought I was smart.

I shrugged, and fast as I could, I sifted sugar on my bread and butter—while I could.

"First three letters of globe, as in our *Globe Gaz-eee-ter*," his words for *Globe Gazette*, our paper. I jiggled, impatient. Our Julie bounced like she was my mirror. "Same owner, Lee Loomis. Might as well keep it all together, the paper and TV—then they'll get their story straight," Daddy said, cutting his tomatoes.

Oh, how he could talk. He was thinking out loud. Whatever I could understand would be fine.

"Bil Baird is coming with Cora for the station opening," Daddy said. Bil, a professional puppeteer, lived across the alley with his mom.

"And Father Reed will bless the station," said my mother. "And a rabbi, too, and probably some preacher." I sat back.

Because there you have it. My neighborhood was in on everything, surely me, too. (Both the rabbi and the priest lived on our block, if you counted kitty-corner: the Holy Family Church, Washington School and the Synagogue were three points, each on a corner of a block. That meant the Rosens, the Haaheims, the Lannons all lived in the shadow of each other.)

"Tee-whee," shrieked Bobby, waving like a windmill. He always thought the cream in the center of a halved Twinkie was his television set. But Mom pushed him a carrot. What did he know, last week he cracked the lid off the pink mosquito bite lotion and had to get his stomach pumped.

"How do I get on this television anyway?" I asked. The puffy vinyl seat *whooshed* beneath me with my bounces.

My dad gave me his queer look that said I was over the top. "You know, this TV thing could cut out all those little programs you dance on," he said, between bites of an oyster cracker. Oyster crackers were a new thing.

Didn't that sound like—just a warning? I tuned him out. I mulled, just mulling. Daddy's aside about the little programs blew right past me. I missed it, no, I ignored it. Nothing could stop the dancing, some things—not possible.

Because the glitter of the sugar on the table became my stage, perfect for a new dance. The salt and pepper rosebud shakers—television cameras. I pushed them around, in close and out far. A little-me spun center table, of course.

But just when I was getting to my slam-bang ending, Mabel was pumping away, my dad pulled the shakers back to center where they belonged.

I crunched my butter-sugar sandwich and swallowed hard. I licked my upper teeth, my tongue slicking butter. My parents' voices hummed. I watched them slow motion.

"Office . . . car . . . premature . . . isolette . . . on call," he said. My mother chimed in. "Dance . . . costume . . . Fourth of July . . . go."

Julie sniffed pepper and sneezed a fountain. Bobby mashed his Twinkie cream into his pink-and-white face. Now how did my mom concentrate on costumes with so many kids!

I daydreamed out the window toward Mrs. Baird's house, visions of television dancing in my head. The sing-song of children over-lapped. Long shadows striped the yard.

Fathers' cars roared and clanked into driveways in clouds of dust, like everything was normal.

Mary Beth on television when the tubes go in for repair.
(Photo: Hanna Heizelman; Courtesy of Beth Obermeyer)

7

Mrs. Sartor's Flag Costume

Bedtime came, and my mother finally got around to me. I stood by the table in my new sparkle-plenty flag costume. She knelt and tucked at the waist in fits. Her eyes glinted.

My eyes dazed in the brilliance. I flashed by the light of the chandelier. This was the prettiest thing I'd ever seen, but I couldn't help it: my shoulders sagged from the weight of pounds of rhinestones, a row of them edging each stripe. The stars on my top were loaded, too.

My mother's secret weapon, those rhinestones. My secret too. They were so heavy, once I got to turning I spun like Little Orly, of my 78-rpm record fame. He rolled down a hill, could barely stop.

She might have used limestones. They would be cheaper than rhinestones, and costumes came out of our food budget. My mother ran the food budget. But limestones were so common in our town.

Today my brother Bob says limestone is the Iowa state animal, flower, and rock all three, just for that reason. You could economize if you used our limestones. Yes, my mother had to get those rocks to sparkle but I thought sure if anyone could she could.

She was the Coco Chanel of Iowa, you could say.

And I was the costume-maker's daughter! Oh, the costumes she could wrangle.

My mom mumbled, straight pins dangling from her mouth. I shivered in the scratchy net and warm air. Finally she stood, kicking her

The flag costume my mother made, twenty-five years later, on Kristin Obermeyer, granddaughter. (Photo: Beth Obermeyer)

housedress out of the way. She unzipped the back of my costume, through the glorious red, white and blue stripes.

I stood in a base of satin-and-net fluff, probably the most beautiful military costume in all of my town. I pulled my Carter undershirt down over my Friday underpants. My spunk trailed off because my steam was wearing down.

My mother nudged me out of the costume, scooping her tape measure and sequins. She roughed my long hair, in a gentle way. But it bumped the worst thought right out of my mouth.

"Mom, we'd better pull the drapes. Kids could see. They tease. The petticoats, the costumes. I mean the Lilac Girls could be hangin' in the lilac bushes right now. They probably don't even have a bedtime."

My mom hugged the costume tight, her face soft for a moment. "Oh, for heavens sake. The ladies at St. Anne's Circle at church chide me all the time. Do I make cakes for the church bazaar? No." She shook her head, like a naughty kid. Mom cooked up fancy little-girl dresses, put the new Toni home-wave dolls in formals. "But who are the Lilac Girls?" she asked.

I told her they were really old, picked lilacs of course.

"Aren't they in the choir? Their mothers make them costumes for the operetta, I'm sure. Maybe you misunderstood."

"Oh, no. One played "Glow Worm" with cross-hands in the piano recital, remember? I danced the marigold. You can't miss them." My mom looked dubious. My daddy in the doorway jumped right in. "What—are we worried about a petticoat lynching here?"

That wasn't even funny! "Aw," my dad said, anyway. "The Lilac Ladies probably stuck peas in their ears when they were tykes and now they can't hear the music. Makes 'em punchy."

"You've had a big day," Mom said, laughing now too. "We'll get right on top of our business in the morning. Off to bed. Maybe Mr. Patten will have some ideas at your lesson."

Mr. Patten was my dance teacher, and Mabel was his accompanist too. "It's okay. It's okay," Mom always said and she was always right. How many kids got to be a team with their mother? That's what I figured. I headed for the stairs for a heavenly sleep.

Straight to tap-dancer hell but I didn't know that.

8

Good Night, My Someone

I hung on the stair rail, went one high step at a time, cutting through the evening heat, warmer each step. My bedroom awaited, spread turned down. The light on the nightstand shined a spotlight on its base, the ruffled doll, the one my dad said was a fire hazard, even though none ever burned and I was on my third. They got bigger every time. Now they were free-standing. Soon I figured one might fill the closet.

My room was so special. I could only go there at night. Once Hanna made the bed in the morning it stayed just like that. I slipped a nightgown over my head and the clothesline-smell freshened the inside of my nose, like a breeze. Baby mosquitoes leap-frogged on the outside of the screen, new hatchlings after the rain. My skin tightened. I rolled into bed. The day was finally going to wind down in Mason City.

Familiar sounds drifted from downstairs. My mother turned on the television set, *I Love Lucy.* I smiled at the music and pictured the bouncing heart on the screen.

On a normal night I'd sit on the plush davenport and write in my journal, and watch TV too, while my mother slicked green wave set on my hair. Sometimes she bobby pinned it to smooth out the curl. Maybe she'd pull my hair back for tomorrow, if it got any hotter. She never had. You never knew.

In his den below, my dad clicked charts into the accordion pleats of his hospital file, as always. His voice droned into the Dictaphone, each word sliced into pieces by the fan blades at his side, the small fan in the black wire cage. We had fans in every room, not bragging, but they hummed in the background like they were our motor. You can't have too much air in a house.

My body spun slower and slower through the purple and red of the lilacs, the clack of the piano ivory, the whip of the dance. I listened long, and soon heard a big quiet over my breath.

But my toes wiggled my tap-dance steps against the sheet. I ran my thumb on the binding of Meredith's book. It was too dark to read. Anyway my mom said, no lights after bedtime. So I hugged the book to my chest, my fingertips feeling two "L's," the two L's in "Willson."

I imagined. I could be Fedelia.

New York was my back-up.

Some kids still played somewhere, a high voice trilled: "Star light, star bright, first star I see tonight."

I slung on my side and curled up the shade, just enough to see a rabbit lurch and search my backyard. A last squadron of twirlers marched down the alley, lighted batons spiraling.

Houses waved white curtains all around, through open windows. Piano music leaked onto the air from somewhere, as from so many music boxes. The bands—asleep—but their footprints glowed.

The excitement of the day throbbed down. In no time the bass of my dad's 78-rpm records pulsed, big band music, down in his den. My house had music morning through night.

Soon he padded by my door. In no time he snored in his bed. Each of my breaths timed with his deep breathing. The *gong* on the grandfather clock swung a whisper.

Horns somewhere in the distance. Horns, train horns, the hum of horns, lots of horns.

Clack Clack Clack Clack. Whooo-ooo-ooo.

River City! I-o-way.

I had to go to sleep. It was night. The door grew tall as I faded. The toy dog in the corner bounced to the ceiling and back. My mind stopped.

Somewhere a bell rang. I was going . . . gone.

* * *

"Dr. Sartor's Residence. Yes. Yes. Ohhh. She did. Oh." He cleared his throat. "When? Must have been right after Mary Beth left."

I struggled to listen but the words rolled off my head. Where did I ever get to go, Mary Beth, and leave, alone? This was definitely not a middle-of-the-night doctor call.

His nightstand light popped a slow glow in the hallway. The bed creaked and I knew, he sat up.

My mother's voice, my father's, repeated each other, "He said, she . . . he knew, she . . ."

"Yes. That would be best. We'll check in the morning. Yes, I understand. I'm so sorry. Thank you for calling."

I wondered at the "sorry." I could not awaken. The low words sifted. My mother sighed.

The words went into dots and floated away.

* * *

They say memories stay and sear when they are emotional or sensual. To this day a phone ring jangles my head. I won't even own a cell phone.

What I do know is that this phone call came before Meredith took his swing at Broadway in New York City, and before I could try to win my Fourth of July on the floating stage at Clear Lake. So in that general frame, here it lands in my story, the call that punches my story to smithereens. No real date, in other words.

Other numbers though, they're set in concrete—and they can be puzzling compared to adult perceptions. I was three blocks to downtown and we'd take a thirty-five-cent cab. Twelve blocks from the library, eleven blocks out of my range.

I had eighty feet of backyard and 100 feet of lilacs, enough to guard the Bastille. And four tap shoes—two almost outgrown, soft, a glove fit— and two new and unusable—stiff and slidy.

My big sense of timing though, that I have nailed down. Lilacs return with their perfume every spring lifelong. Music goes through my head all of my days.

Pianos always have eighty-eight keys.

9

I pulled my eyelids up hard, just in time to see her come through the bedroom door, her duster billowing behind her. In a blink, my mom was at the window and the shades snapped up. The sash rattled too. A brightness came from the east and the scent of plum blossoms flushed through the screen, on the warm air.

On my pink brocade chaise-lounge—right where my mother always laid out what I'd wear—a white dress flounced like a flower, a lilac border around the waist and skirt. Orchid blossoms bloomed ten inches up the hem. A lavender satin ribbon bowed onto a gold barrette.

My sleepy eyes crawled down to the paper-nylon petticoat, the one that crackled when I sat in church. It flared over a white shoe, the kind with holes in the top and two straps, new stiff anklets tucked inside.

My mother busied in the closet, humming, stacking the Easter hat boxes. Maybe she was giving me a little time to wake up. I waited for her "Up you go."

It didn't come.

But I loved Saturdays. I imagined walking by my mother's side in that dress, after my dance lesson, through Madison Park.

What if I saw anyone from school?

My face burned an inch into my cheeks, to the bone.

And today was Band Festival Day. I might see someone at the parade. I'd change my clothes by then. At least Julie wouldn't go along in

Plum blossoms. (Photo: Beth Obermeyer)

The Pink Room: The chaise, the bed, the doll, and a visiting baby. (Photo: David Beckman; Courtesy of David Beckman)

her matching border print dress and shoes, pink, blue, lavender or yellow, we had all those sets.

But, oh, but how I loved that dress, and grown-ups did, too. My mother sewed up a storm. Audiences clapped hard for her costumes.

"Mom?"

Silence. My mother had stopped humming.

Finally: "Do you have a leotard?" My mother's voice sounded up her nose, like she had a cold. Or she was on her knees in the far corner of my closet?

"What do I need a leotard for?" Leotards were from *Leo's Dance Catalog.* "I always wear a dress to dance lesson." Today would be just me and my mom, Mabel and Mr. Patten in his living room studio, dances to learn, music to buy, rehearsals. And almost always a program to dance-out on at night.

I nuzzled the pillow. Most nights Daddy came home from being on call at the hospital, and drove me to programs, watched my new dances, maybe a Stunt Night at the Park.

My mother leaned her head on the dresser mirror. She sorted through the bunny dish, probably for bobby pins. I pushed my hair back.

My mother's face, yikes, it was red-eyed in the mirror, lips thin and tight. "Mary Beth, I have to talk with you," she said, her hand to her forehead. She looked like she'd rather be just about anywhere but here. She narrowed her eyes like they were stuck to the mirror and they hurt like Super Glue. She turned. I still sensed gentle and kind.

I couldn't hide. The organdy bedspread, folded back for the night, was hopelessly out of my reach. But my nightgown was soft and gathered full. I stroked the aqua folds of the ruffles around my wrists, burrowing my fingers in and out of the lace eyelet holes.

My mother's eyes drifted towards the clock. Her body floated towards me. "We have half an hour," she said. She lifted my pillow. "Let's get you dressed. We have to get out of here."

That was it?

I did not like the sound of "talk." My heart cried in fear . . . the phone last night. What was that? *Bang.* Did I dream it?

My mother waited for me to slide from bed. I dropped the nightgown to the floor. She swung—yanked—a cotton slip from a hanger in the closet and dropped it over my head. The hanger rasped back to normal on the rod while the next paper nylon slip, and finally the organdy dress—like a flower—floated over my raised arms.

I sat on my pink-ruffled dresser bench, balancing one foot under the skirt then the other while I yanked on socks. Shoes.

My mother put one hand on my head and pulled a brush down fast, hard. She stabbed like she was mad—*ouch*—but she looked like she could bawl. She threw the brush on the bed. "Maybe we should just stay home today," she said. Her face scrunched.

"Mom, no! Mabel and I practiced the Fourth of July dance last night, to show you this morning. It can only get better. I'm right on top of the big idea. We can hurry. Please, Mom."

Daddy passed the door, then walked backwards, like a silent movie. His face tipped towards us. I kept my eyes on his waist. "Downstairs, Mary Beth," he said. Scary how deep his voice was in the hallway. My insides vibrated. The bigger the trouble, the more they pronounced my name, it seemed, like I'd heard "Mary Beth" five times today, so far.

He tugged his fingers through his hair, elbows brushing the ceiling. He grimaced at my mother. "*You* tell her in the car?" He cleared his throat. "I'll get her breakfast."

They were dividing me in half: he was in charge of breakfast, my mother—what was the rest? I bent in half to scoot out of the attention. "Okay." I made my voice hopeful.

My father's deep voice carried down the stair, catching me. "She's going to be . . ." Be what? The trouble was, he was the guy who could never keep a secret. My mother always said, for a quiet man he sure had a big mouth.

I galloped, holding my white hat box at arm's length so it wouldn't bump the walls, listening to them, all the way to the linoleum stairs to my practice room. "Darn tragedy," was the last I heard.

I blinked tears through the coming wave of fluorescent lights bouncing on the long wall of mirror squares. They went as long as any stage front. Stucco walls scratched my elbows as I ran. I kicked the bottom of the curtains to find the rattle of my good-lesson tap shoes. I snatched my ballet shoes, too, and snapped the box shut. *Clatter*, back up the stairs. My stomach hurt.

"Time for breakfast," my dad said, loosening his collar. My mother hovered in the doorway.

42

I directed my eyes to my father. My mother touched my father's arm and leaned close. I sucked my knuckles. My dad drew in his cheeks. This scene was as dramatic as any I'd ever see on *Little Rascals* or *Bart's Clubhouse*.

"I have a great idea," he said, his voice louder. He wiped his lips with the back of his hand. I waited. My dad wasn't home much, so when he was, things sometimes worked. He walked through the front entry to open the front door. Early spring air rushed in. "Let's get that breakfast," was all he said.

I slid onto the kitchen stool by the island counter, stranded on a pedestal. My mother paced. Man, if this was a show, the audience would've gone home by now.

My mother's rhinestone lily-of-the-valley pin sparkled hard in the sunlight as she turned on her high heel. The back door slammed. What happened next made me sit straight. My dad sang when things went wrong, a cover, I knew. Boom came his voice.

He'd dance with the dolly with a hole in her stocking . . . knees go a-knocking, hole in her stocking . . .

This was a chipper song. What's wrong—huge! My neck tinged. On he went.

She warms so easy so dance me loose . . . dance me loose . . . dance me . . .

He always forgot the line that rhymed, even the exact words, could even switch songs. His laugh and swagger made up for it, usually.

Me, I was just happy to spend nervous energy. It was his show. My skirt puffed as I bounced the bar stool, like I was tweaking the volume up and up.

Daddy leaned on the wall, bemused. So I flopped some more. Now I was singing along.

Man I was just like Teresa Brewer.

But my father's laugh evaporated like a tag ending to his song. I knew it would. He came in close, put his hands on either side of my face. My lips stuck out from his squeeze like a baby bird's.

"Now off to the car." That's all he said. And then the horn from my mother's car.

"But Daddy, I didn't have any breakfast."

He opened a drawer, tossed me a cellophane package. "My stash," he said.

Daddy and Mary Beth, two. (Courtesy of Beth Obermeyer)

I squeaked off the stool, clutched my Twinkie to my chest, rattled to pick up my hat box. I raced like gangbusters. Me and my dad were buddies. I had almost had him to myself this morning. I'd had him until I turned seven before more kids were born.

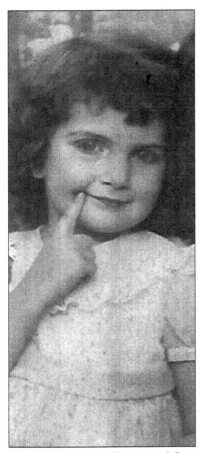

Julie, the magnet. (Courtesy of Beth Obermeyer)

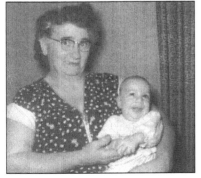

Hanna Heizelman. (Photo: Mary Beth Sartor with the Brownie camera)

And that was still a magical time that morning, just a little girl and her dad, one feeling hard to sustain through teen years. No one's fault, that's just what dads and girls are. Out I raced.

Julie was on the stairway, her feet dangling through spokes. She'd been hanging on that stair since she was two, watching me zip back and forth, going to work. Sometimes she climbed down and waltzed her own dance, my own little wind-up doll. "See ya, Doodles," I said.

She hated to be called Doodles.

"I'm stayin' home with Hanna," she said. She was bragging. "We're making cookies."

I sailed through the door, to the car. I turned at the car door to give my dad a wave. But he was gone, probably playing with Julie. She was like a magnet, that little girl.

I stuffed my skirts onto the car seat and slid in. I bounced straight on the seat, like if I was straight it'd make a difference. I wanted to keep my mother from spilling her bad news.

"We have to talk," she said anyway, lowering her voice as she went.

A hundred phones filled my humming head.

Part II

The Music Dies

10

Mabel . . . Mabel

My mother lowered her head over the steering wheel and peered at the road, as though it'd be easier to talk to the squirrel swinging in the tree than to her daughter. "Put the hat box on the floor and sit still," she said, in an insistent voice. "Listen to me."

I slid my bottom to the edge of the seat and thudded my crossed feet on the case. I banged my head on the seat on purpose.

"Something happened last night. Daddy got a call," my mother said, still staring ahead.

I scrunched my hair against my ears. I sucked the ends of my hair ribbon in my mouth, so I wouldn't breathe loud.

"It's Mabel," my mother said, slow and crisp. It was like my dad giving a shot. It just kept coming and it was sharp. "Mr. Patten called last night."

Now why would my dance teacher call? We both stared ahead in silence. The elm seeds whirred against the windshield.

"Mabel had a stroke during the night," she said.

I waited. I needed more. Stroke of midnight? Strike of lightning?

"We'll go see her as soon as she's ready." My mother inhaled deeply and her eyes checked mine. "They say she can't move her left side. She might never move it."

My mother's pretty voice was apologetic, like she was sorry to have to tell this. Mom was always strong and sure, but now her fair face was gray.

I searched the far distance, past where she could see. I pressed my forehead on the side window. My neighborhood was still there. My school had slapped its glass and doors shut, not telling anything. My nose dripped, annoying.

"Mabel," my mother said. The name came out and up with bubbles, barely past her throat. My eyes brimmed and burned. "Don't . . . Mary Beth. It isn't . . . it can't be helped." My mother's eyes were dry, so large she might have had toothpicks propping them open. They were panicked, not mean. She pressed the heels of her hands on the wheel. Like she'd for sure give me a hug if she wasn't driving.

So I talked. "I knew Mabel's eyes didn't look right. I should have said something," I said. The shrinking black dots. "She'll be so bored without music."

And. I'd have to start all over again. My sister Donna Jean left for college when I was barely seven, out the door she'd gone, with her music. Donna Jean had been my accompanist, too, on hand day and night. And I missed her but she came home for Christmas and summers. Nothing like this.

"We're going to the music store. New music will do us good. Your eyes will be red if you cry right now." My mother spoke softly but she delivered, always practical.

"What'll Mr. Patten do if Mabel isn't there?" I knew for sure, he'd be hopeless. He'd have tap rhythms, but no piano to steer.

He can't make up his dances without Mabel, Mom was sure. "It won't help Mabel if we stay home. Dance is like church—life goes on around it." I was speechless.

My life was dying.

Worse, Mabel's music was dying . . . "How can she live without her music?" I said.

"Honey, she'll live, she just won't play the piano anymore," my mother said. The sentence seemed to line up on the hood of the car, one word at a time. For both of us to check again, and again. "Honey. She. Won't. Play. Anymore."

Donna Jean, home from college, with John Roth. (Photo: Mary Beth Sartor, twelve, with the Brownie)

I lifted the armrest inches up, down, over and over, as though it was me making the car go forward. I wanted to blow those awful words off the hood, *whoosh* my bad-news mother away. A dead squirrel by the curb stared at the sky, like it also waited for better words.

Nothing went wrong on Saturdays. Words on the way to dance were always about music and performances.

My dancing days were over. "I can't dance-out without Mabel," I said, plain and simple.

Mom bit her lip. A shiny red dot of blood appeared, even over her Cherries Jubilee lipstick. She rattled her fingertips in her purse for a hanky and pressed it to her mouth, wincing at the drop of red on the linen. She scrunched the hanky in her palm and reached her hand over the center cushion towards me, but I hitched across the seat, towards the door.

"I had to make a decision this morning," she said. "Mr. Patten will lose students without Mabel. We'll just have to find something else. We want a private lesson, hard to get, so we need to move fast. And not just some lady in her basement with records, showing dances she learned at those dance conventions, either, or costumes from catalogs! We need the real thing."

It was a pivotal time in dance schools. Kids all over America were starting to dance to records and soon it was to the same records, doing the same routines, from the conventions, and in the same costumes from catalogs. Just three years before I'd been to the Chicago Dance Masters Convention and showed Mr. Patten's dance to *"Chicago,"* in my mother's hand-made costume. The idea then was to see dances and get more ideas.

But that day Mom was sure and she talked faster and faster. I leaned my hair out the car window, into the breeze. My life was blowing away. I sucked my upper lip, even though every time I did that it got red and chapped and sore. "I don't want to change teachers."

"I know," she said. "But it's a good time for change." My mom was always up, on her feet. "We'll visit Mabel, as long as she's in Mason City." Her words ran fast. "Every week we'll see her, and absolutely every Christmas Day."

"Christmas Day! We're only to spring!"

"We'll be special. No one else will think to go see her at Christmas. Her son doesn't live here and she doesn't have any other family and—we will do that. We will be her family."

The green trees blurred past. I scooted up to catch my mother's eyes in the mirror.

I'd always felt lucky on Saturdays, cocky even. This was different, going too fast. I felt like the MGM lion roared open his mouth and swallowed me.

A young Dean Diggins. (Courtesy of Dean Diggins)

11

A New Day, with Dean Diggins

I spun the window lock button, fast and faster. My mother was doing her best and I wished I could, too. Nothing like this had ever happened in my entire life. The car bumped on the curb in front of the YWCA where we could park. I didn't move. "Why are we at the Y?"

"I just want to show you something, take a look at a new teacher. Mary Beth, leave your hatbox and get out of the car." My mother's eyes darted like bowling balls off to scatter pins. Everything was hit and miss this morning. I scrambled out the car door. Geez Louise.

The purple brick building looked like a big bruise to me, with a gash of double doors and lots of steep steps. I could not bound up those stairs two at a time, not today. Mabel was not going to be waiting at the top. Anyway, Mom couldn't park that big car to save her life. My legs felt thick as the elm tree trunks by the curb.

I sat, right there on the steps, absently pulling my fingers through a clump of hair. I stuffed the fuzzy end in my mouth. My eyelids stuck halfway to open, closed out half the world.

Peggy Poppy stuck out anyway. Across the street, Peggy from sixth grade just walked along, doing nothing special, in her big black shoes and dark jeans with no plaid cuffs or anything. She and her mom lived in an apartment right about this block.

Last week, some girls went to Peggy's birthday party. I listened to the whole story in the cloakroom at school. They said they climbed a fire escape to her apartment and Peggy made all her own decorations and baked a cake, too. Her mom worked and wasn't at the party. Peggy Poppy read the cake recipe right out of a cookbook.

That's what they said. I figured Peggy Poppy turned on the oven herself and followed the directions and shook whatever food coloring she wanted into the frosting, a whole bottle, actually. That's what I figured.

"Man, that'd be the deal, wouldn't it?" I blurted, ripping the cellophane off my Twinkie. I stuffed half in my mouth at once. Chocolate crumbs tumbled over my skirt, and the center frosting felt like a mess up my nose.

Once Peggy wore *pants to school*. She colored her geography map purple and silver with shoe dye. She even cut her own hair and clipped it with every baby barrette that came in one package. I shook my head, slicking a wet finger around my lips to catch the crumbs and frosting.

Once Peggy got a bag of pink and blue and green Easter chicks, live ones, from the dime store, and Peggy emptied them on Sister's desk. Peggy'd leaned her head on her hand on the desk and crossed one leg in front of the other, and waited, plain as a pocket on a shirt, to see what Sister would say. Sister said: "Put the chickens back in the dime store window."

Nothing nice was going to happen to me ever again. I coulda been walking around playing all my life, have friends for cripes sake, instead of all these lessons. Who knew the music could just waltz away?

My mom arrived. "This is where Dean Diggins teaches," she said. "We'll set it up next week. I just want you to see. Then we'll take a walk in the park, visit the music store, just like always." She lowered the veil on her hat, as though her thoughts would come softer, slower through the netting.

I swung on the rail, one more time, my petticoat swishing the dust. Girls ran up the steps with their bags. Did anyone else have a white hat box with a pink velvet ballerina on the lid and a silver handle? Of course, not. What if the dance class saw me with it next week, me and my private lesson? I crinkled the cellophane wrapper in my hand and pitched it over the stair, grabbing one more glance of the street. What would it feel like to just wander around, doing nothing special except what I felt like? I was going to get me some of that dime store.

Inside, kids ran up the stairs and through the big open double doors of the gym. They wore sun suits, or cropped midriffs and shorts. I was glad no one looked at me in my poufy lilac-printed dress. "Dean Diggins Dance School. Second Floor," my mom said.

I could read. "Can I take gym sometime?"

"Mary Beth Sartor, this is the YMCA. Or maybe it's the YWCA. Young Women's *Christian* Association. Not for Catholics. For *Protestants*. They say protestant prayers. You can't join the Y, for heaven sakes."

"But I'm here already! I'll dance here."

"Gym's different. You'll be *visiting* the Y to dance, so don't go getting ideas."

I was getting ideas today and saying them, too, even if my mother was already pushed to use all three of my names.

I got to think anything on the day Mabel stroked.

I peeked in the studio. Dean taught in a gymnasium? With basketball hoops on each end and a stage behind each hoop. I was lost, still planted in the old. Mr. Patten taught in his living room with no carpet.

I crooked my neck to see. We'd seen Dean's recitals. His dances told stories, not just steps to music. So Dean had been kind of a dream. Sometimes Dean was in the *Globe*, he went all the way to Chicago to dance. How old was he? Old. Maybe—twenty? Like my big sister, Donna Jean. But the photo on the wall was of Dean and a partner, a girl. She looked about twelve. Once he was a kid, like me.

But Dean in that moment was oh, so real, about a half block away down the gym, at a ballet barre, with just one girl, a big girl, a teen-ager.

His linen pants hung loose under a drawstring waist. A tank top stretched over his shoulders, like it was on a coat hanger. He paced, some sliding, his hands flitting a pattern. *He was making up a dance.*

Mr. Patten with French Dolls and Soldiers. French Dolls: Anne Abel, Mary Beth Sartor, Henrietta Hebel, Mary Jean Logan. Soldiers: Mike White, Jim Frank, Larry Munn, and Michael Gaspari. The director is Lex Patten. *Christmas Carol*, the first play in the new Holy Family Church auditorium. (Photo: Sorlien; Courtesy of *Mason City Globe Gazette*)

Dean flipped around, attached to the barre. He cocked his head in many directions, like the curious birds in the window.

The high windows of the gym had steel tic-tac-toe games on them. The piano, the big space, lulled me. I wanted Mom to see, too, but I couldn't catch her eye.

Dean was coming my way! He crossed in a beam of sunlight and his eyes shone like a cat's, like glass with black lashes. His hair waved and his nose was important, and he had a way of looking over it.

He duck-walked but not to me, as it turned out. Just long steps to center floor, shepherding the girl. His hands fluttered with the count, his face alive with an opening combination. He wasn't tall and he wasn't big but when he straightened, he filled the entire gymnasium.

All the while, strains came from the piano.

He lunged and hummed. Veins traced over his forehead, like they'd blow. Power happened inside a circle, Dean's and his mother's circle, not mine. They were a team. And then he included the girl, nudging her into position. Her name was Linda Smiley. I'd seen her in shows.

I rubbed my arm muscles. I bent to scrub the backs of my legs. I could feel them coming to life. Even though Dean's words were *"Plie."* *"Battement."* *"Croise."* French.

Where was my mother? Did I have to go? Two girls my size crossed the doorway. They were in black Leotards and pink tights. One snapped the other's butt, a kaniption. "Underpants," she hissed. I whipped my eyes to the spot to see. Yes, I could see them, that girl's underpants showed, right through her tights, you could see they were under everything. A mosquito bite would show in those leotards from Leo's Theatrical!

Dean's words were in English now and I peeked back to see. The girl was grown-up, actually. "Slide forward, plow the feathery snow," he said.

"Now your cheek feels the sun." "Explode to *croise*." My last sighting of Dean that morning was this: he unfolded his arms to a front-crossed lunge and the sun seemed to burst from his chest.

The "Deep Purple" fell down those tall walls, right on me.

Oh, My God—just heartbreakingly good.

Some moments in a lifetime stay put forever. This one layered over another moment, a few years earlier. The occasion was a magical birthday party, in our all new house. Mom put a cake with pink roses and my name on it from the bakery on the lace tablecloth, on a birthday plate of a music box. For a while I wore my cowgirl hat. It was my birthday and I could do anything. But it was a gift that carried me away. Mary Ellen Swanson gave me a book, way over my head, I didn't know the pages, but I adopted it, too. It was Beaumont's *Complete Book of Ballets*, a guide to ballet through the nineteenth and twentieth centuries. Today it is the lone book on a long table in my living room, the cover now the shade of the dried roses from Mother's Day.

On that day in the gymnasium of the YWCA, in my Mason City, Iowa, Pavlova and Nureyev came to life, off the pages of that book, it seemed. Their secrets were about to be mine.

I could be in Dean's world. It was sweet on a sad day. I was lucky Mason City had Dean to make up dances.

I galloped down the steps to find my mom, a chant in my head, out every two steps. I couldn't find my breath. Music swarmed in me like marbles chiming against each other.

Mabel, ragtime. Rag-a-ma-tazz.

My piano—classical, "Claire de Lune."

My mother liked thirties' music, "Five Foot Two."

My dad liked jazz. Benny Goodman.

But it was only the purple dance I felt, behind my elbows, behind my knees, in my fingertips. Not a hop-scotch dance, not at all. It was new, rushing, pulsing inside me.

But way, way, *way* in the back of my mind I wondered: Mrs. Diggins. *Replace Mabel?*

I tail-ended my mother. She cleared her throat. But she didn't say a thing.

Mary Beth's birthday party and the ballet book. Anne Abel (a friend from school), Mary Ellen Swanson, Linda Roddy, Mary Beth Sartor, Ann Dolmage, Irene Marinos, daughters of colleagues of Daddy. (Courtesy of Beth Obermeyer)

12

Mulling It All Over in Madison Park

The sun was still warming as we crossed Madison Park—the heart of the spark of the town—past the bird-blessed statue in the middle, under the arc of lime-green elms. It was one of those spring days: if you had a summer dress out and starched, you wore it. If you got a new faille coat and hat for Easter, you wore that. I swished my skirt, my bare arms swinging. I glanced about, checking for any sixth graders who could be up and around. That's all I'd need. There were none, thank the stars.

Sandra was probably on her farm, probably chasing a chicken for Sunday dinner, comfy in rolled-up blue jeans. Jeri Martin was sleeping-in for sure, she'd had a slumber party last night, all their talk was baby doll pajamas, even though none of us had any. Frank Swed, he would be on his way to basketball practice at Holy Family playground in his short singlet.

The sidewalks crossed the town square corner to corner, with a circle where the "X" met in the middle, under the Civil War guy statue. No one walked on the sides of the block. They rolled like marbles to the middle and back out, to see who they could see. I liked that some things never changed, especially on a day like that.

At that early hour it was a park sweeper to see, shooshing his broom into the cool early air, spiffing up for the band festival. His gray trousers disappeared into a cloud as he went. A shopkeeper jangled his keys against the door of Kresge's Nickel and Dime. They languished, slow, in their precious beautiful day.

Hand-painted banners ripped and rolled flat and rippled again. They pushed the wind from every light post on the street. "North Iowa Band Festival!" they read. No bands up 'n' at 'em yet. The skirt of the breeze ruffled my hair, damp roots to tangled clumped ends.

I always loved going from sweaty dance into the flying spring air, every single Saturday morning. I nuzzled Hanna's ironed starch in my puffed sleeve, such a nice smell. That morning I was dry, hadn't danced up a storm. Actually it was kind of nice, just me and my mom with nothing special to do, if I looked at it that way.

Whether she listened to everything or not, I still wanted to walk and talk with my mother, with my dreams alongside hers, just me and my mom. The Dress, the Dance, the Day. Dean? I clicked the "D's on my tongue.

In the lull though—buried but welling in my throat—a question ached, poked and prodded, hard to ignore. Because Mabel had a stroke, poor Mabel. And now where was her music? What could possibly be worse? A ping pong ball went back and forth in my stomach. The paddle and the elastic string, in there, too.

I didn't even know how a stroke looked. I was catching crazy, half-way between losing Mabel and catching up with Dean and his piano-tinkling mother—all marching through spring in Mason City.

"Our music store doesn't open for fifteen minutes," my mom said. She said "our" because people who love music seem to feel as though they have their own personal music store. Not that I owned any music anymore. It was all at Mabel's. "Let's sit a minute," she said. She half-circled onto the iron park bench.

Here's how it went: first she swirled her full coat skirt, then she smoothed it all flat under, the same every time, almost a dance.

Me, myself, I wanted to walk and talk through the spring air. But I sat.

A blue jay skidded to a muffin wrapper. The robins scattered. I savored one more look over the back of the bench at the park and smoothed my white polished-cotton skirt under. I was settling.

I rattled my toes and heels in a cramp roll. The footwork was nervous and absent-minded, the taps sort of counting the glitter specks of the sun, a-dancing on the park surface. I waited for my mother to talk.

My mom rattled through her patent-leather purse, as though something important was there. I put my hands on the bench and raised up and down—oh, those scratchy petticoats. I tried to be friendly. "Dean's dance will be new, with lots of rules," I said.

I floated an arm across and back, leading with my chin. "It's so grown-up," I said. "Mr. Patten's ballet was like tap in ballet shoes, just slide-slide-*arabesque*." I was younger then.

"Let's not go overboard," she said. "We're lucky to have Dean, yes, but a ballet kind of dance is not going to get them off their hands at the Fourth of July." My mother always watched for hands in the middle of a dance, applause. She liked go-get 'em dances.

I slung my head over the bench back, trying to figure out how to hang onto this new kind of dance without looking boring at the Fourth. You just didn't argue with a genius.

"What would *Mabel* think of Dean and his ballet, do you think?" she asked. The name hit my jaw like a cement gum ball.

"Who will play for me when I dance out?" I demanded. "Mom, who will play for the Fourth?" No Mabel, no Fourth.

All she did was fold her arms. When the sweeper finished filling his dust pan, she stood, adjusting her hat pin. "Daddy always says . . . what doesn't kill you, doesn't hurt you," she said.

Kill Mabel? Or me.

I was kind of alive and inside kind of dead.

13

Carleton Stewart Music Emporium

Across the park was the tin sign, "CARLETON STEWART MUSIC EMPORIUM." Carleton Stewart was the leader of the band at the public high school. He spear-headed the Band Festival. Everyone in town knew who he was. He was flat-out a big deal.

Our heels clicked up the wood steps, through the screen door and along the long boards. I loved that paper-packed-together smell of shelves and trunks and stacks of music. Mrs. Knapp leaned forward on the counter. Her corsage was always the same, starched-fabric violets.

"Good morning, Mrs. Knapp."

"What's biting at you this morning? Which music today?"

"'Deep Purple,'" I said, just in case she hadn't heard the news. Such a slow thoughtful request. "Not 'Turkey in the Straw,' that's for sure."

Mrs. Knapp opened her stock book and whooshed to the "D" page, her soft dimpled arms following her hands. "Whoo-whoo, 'Deep Purple,' I want to see that dance."

"And 'The Charleston,'" my mother said, her voice quick.

I turned on my heel and wandered back into the music stands, just like every Saturday morning. I couldn't wait to see my name right by "Deep Purple" on my own music sheet. A long costume, to my ankles.

I smoothed music on the stands, slid by piano teachers. You could always tell a piano teacher. Their eyes loved the paper music as though it was alive.

And the covers were gay. The front of "Surrey with the Fringe on Top," a walk in the country, a hair-blowing bare-foot walk. A gazebo and horns on "Alexander's Ragtime Band."

The sun blared through the dusty window. Mom lolled by the trumpets, talking to Mrs. Knapp. She always talked while I looked at music, but today I knew the big news was about Mabel. All of Mason City could know something in minutes, it was true.

Sometimes my mom went in a booth and listened to a record, but not today. Today she just collected our new music at the counter—and talked.

After the right amount of time I loped to the front of the store, pulling a white sock up out of my shoe on two hops. They zipped their lips like they were talking about nothing. I sided to my mother, next to her crackly bag of music, and we followed the sidewalk through the park to the hospital. We'd meet up with my dad and go home to get ready for the band festival.

I hid beneath sounds.

My mother's heels sounded like nails on concrete. My own leather soles rasped on the grit, muffled by padded socks. My mother was the solo and I was the percussion. Our *click* and *chug* changed as we hit the marble

Mrs. Maye Mettler, a nurse for the children. (Courtesy of Beth Obermeyer)

floor of the hospital. Now typewriters in the lobby set the pace.

But my dad's office was empty and quiet, and we sat on the big dark chairs by his desk. His nurse, Mrs. Mettler, passed the door, stretching her legs as far as the starched white uniform allowed, red sucker in hand. I could use some sugar but a screaming kid wailed in the next room. At least I didn't have to get a shot.

My mother pulled the new music out of the bag, slow, careful, respectful. She looked

Mother and Father, 1933. (Courtesy of Beth Obermeyer)

long at each cover. "I had lots of music as a girl. Covers from that time were so beautiful."

I slowed my breathing. Sheet music meant Mabel. My chest expanded, maybe to catch the quick moisture that readied to roll from my eyes. The last day had spun out quickly and I could lose control, even though I never ever cried.

I pushed my fingers into the rhinestones scattered about her coat, one to the next. Cashmere was the softest. I held still to hear more. I liked slow time, my mother talking, playing. I liked knowing my green eyes looked elfishly like my father's as I nuzzled her coat. She liked his eyes.

"The music covers—oh, twenty years ago—were like posters," my mom was saying. "I worked at Uncle Chuck's theater when Daddy was in medical school in Chicago. I couldn't teach anymore. Women couldn't teach after they married."

My mother draped an arm about me. "I loved the film posters, too," she said. "I got to see the musicals over and over. And over. I memorized the costumes and the tap dances, between taking tickets and cleaning the theater." I knew this story. She knew tap dancing from way back when, the good stuff. Somehow I knew she was making a case. That's how she worked.

"And you and me, we go to movie matinees together, every Sunday afternoon," I said.

"You and *I*," she said. "You and I still pick the good music." She stroked my hair. "And now . . . you get the costumes and the dance lessons and piano lessons. You're going to be fine."

I pressed my face on the coat. The spring day danced through the slits in the blinds. "You are a lucky girl," she said. Maybe you'll even dance on our new television station, if the costumes are good enough. *If you do* dances the audiences can relate to." Boy did she know my buttons.

But I wasn't sure about this luck thing. I worked hard. I knew the right stuff when I saw it. Why was my mom so sure, what dance? I never saw *her* dance or anything. "Did you get piano lessons?"

"Oh, no, no one did. But every farmhouse had a piano and if you wanted to, you learned, taught yourself to play. There wasn't even radio then, the piano was the background of our lives. We'd sit around at night and play cards and bingo and dance to the piano music.

"Did you dance?"

"Oh, yes, Aunt Leone and I taught the Methodist boys to dance. In the Depression, Daddy, in medical school, no one had any money. I had to live with my parents, but they were wonderful about it. I was back home at the farm. They didn't have money either, but they had food. We grew all our own food, and we were fine." She pulled her hatpin and smoothed the felt.

"I stayed on the farm for ten years with baby Donna Jean, until Daddy was through with his education. He came home summers. I wasn't making any money. And did I ever get an idea."

"What was your idea?"

"I took men's suits and made them into women's suits on Grandma Nang's treadle machine! The trousers became skirts. I cut off the worn hems and cuffs. I re-cut the jackets. I sold over one hundred of those suits for $3.00 each and that was our spending money. I even sent money to your father. He joked that all the little towns all around must have been filled with housewives in my suits."

My mother was a go-getter. She could figure anything out of the worst trouble. I must have inherited it.

"This is simple for you. You're not worrying about food for a baby and a bed at night. You have to do your best, and Mabel will be so happy, proud of you. Just do your best for Mabel."

She had no idea. How did she know I wouldn't die without Mabel. Mabel was all but dead for all I knew. If I could latch on to Dean and "Deep Purple," just try that, why couldn't she?

My dad slapped a paper file into the pocket on the door. He unbuttoned his white doctor coat. I knew he'd been listening. He didn't like arguing. He didn't even like opinions. "How was your morning?" He checked our faces.

We answered fast, saying way opposite things. She got the last sentence in.

"Need to put on a good show," she said. "Coffee grinders!"

I hate coffee grinders. That old leg swinging step where you dropped to the ground and jumped over a circling leg with the other foot. Like a helicopter gaining speed to fly.

But I didn't open my big mouth. I didn't want to concern my dad with all that. He'd make a decision all right, fast. Instead I got demure. "Is Mabel here?" I asked. "The hospital?"

He smoothed his coat on the wall hook. "Mabel's resting now," he said, too matter of fact, like he was arranging words for a child. He pulled the screens in and slammed the sash. "How about we go home now and you can take a nice long nap? You've had quite a weekend so far." The scent of cotton balls soaked in alcohol took over the room, trapped in by the shut windows.

"Daddy, can I please see Mabel?"

"You're too young for visiting hours." And "She's not ready," he said, again. "It takes more than a day to stabilize from a stroke. Mother and I will sit by her side." He pushed the lines on his forehead. "But her son gave me something for you." He put an envelope on his desktop. "This came for her today."

Meredith! The return address was his. A beautiful "M" to start "Mabel," was scrolled in ink. I could hardly take a breath. "It must be important," I said, fast. "Mabel told me all about him." Meredith Willson himself—this letter was from *him*."

"Put it in the bag with our music," my mother said.

"No, no, I'll carry it. I'll go see her and read it to her . . . When she's ready," I added.

"Good plan," my father said, leaning back in his chair. "But she'll need a little time." Boy he was being patient. Something else was up. I think I knew it then.

We walked to the car, two and one, me bounding ahead and back. If given a choice I was usually happy. I slapped the hanging oak branches with the Meredith letters, then jumped and clapped the tail of a Band Festival banner. I'd rather think about all that.

Because in a while me and my mom would find a tree, right there, unfold our striped canvas chairs, wait for the Band Festival.

Because last year thunders of hundreds of trombones led the big parade. Giant shiny-gold paper clips. Bands from all over Iowa played concerts at the parks, at the foot-bridge, the library, the museum.

Surely Mabel would hear them in her hospital room. Did just one ear fail with a stroke?

The car door opened. I climbed in, kicking the petticoat into the car. I clutched the letters to my chest. My bands came along.

The Crystal sugar fairy on the plant wall. Since the 1970s, a loading dock has trapped the pixie against the boards (on the right). (Courtesy of Beth Obermeyer)

14

Mabel's Letter from Meredith

I jiggled my hat box against the seat back, trying to stand it up straight. The tap shoes rattled, in the case: *ka rattle, ka bob: ka boom boom boom.* It was just me in a bubble in the backseat. I pressed the envelope to my face and sniffed the stamp.

Meredith licked this stamp.

My dad took the long way home. I liked to ride past the sugar plant and see the big pink fairy, painted on the wall. When I was little I pretended she flew over town, sprinkling sugar. That's why we sparkled, it made us give music. Or we breathed better air? I was going for a moment of light-hearted there in the back seat, looking back to a better time.

I slunk down where I could still admire the fairy but dwell in my letters. I eased the envelope flap with a bobby pin. *A letter from Meredith Willson.* I could feel my eyeballs jiggle. I unfolded it extra careful.

Pencil scribbles—from a really dull #2 pencil—went top to bottom of the page, half a dozen lines. I traced the sloppy script, mouthing the words, his words. Meredith probably thought faster than he could write. He wasn't a slob, not Mr. Meredith Willson, so I hunkered down into his words.

"Dear Mabel." So far, easy to read. "Bug news! I'm sending my shoe to a producer! Two of them, Cy and Ernie. Sent the telegram today. Bugger News—I'll call! Love, from your favorite piccolo player. Meredith."

Meredith Willson's "M." (Courtesy of Beth Obermeyer)

Big news. *Show.* "My Gosh." I bounded forward, my head between my parents, interrupted their whispers. "I can't believe it! Meredith has a producer. At least he mailed the show to one! And there's more!"

"Good for him," Daddy said.

"Wonderful," said my mother. They went back to what they were saying. I stayed put.

"He's divorced, you know," said my mother, like it was just an aside.

"Oh, my gosh, I'm not going to marry him," I said. *Do not argue, do not.* That would have been smart. My Mom knew what she knew. She wouldn't even watch the *Jackie Gleason Show.* Gleason was divorced. We'd watch the June Taylor dancers at the top of the show and she'd snap off the set.

Mom and Dad were wrecking everything. This letter was exciting.

Soon the car lurched and stopped in front of our house. My dad's arm slung past my mom and he placed it on the seat back. I shrank. He raised tall, a big frown for wrinkles.

"Now you listen to your mother," he said, his voice steady on just one note. "Don't go getting fancy ideas with your dances. She knows what our crowds like." His voice was staccato, the kind where I just knew there was something more, not his regular mood.

I hadn't been listening to them, the talk in the front seat. I'd dropped the ball. My mother must've filled his ear with stuff about our morning. I froze.

"Furthermore," he said. "You can just stay home from the Fourth if you can't listen."

He loved to go traveling, his new car! "Whaaat?" I wailed. "I have the *best* dance this year. Mom'd said: we'd find a way. Like she did making suits." What was Daddy doing anyway, throwing in his two cents worth? But he pounded his flat hand down on the seat back, only once, but it scared me.

"I'm sorry. I know it's important to you," he said. "I just want to be clear. Now that we don't have Mabel, it's a good time to be clear. With the polio scare it's just not smart—crowds, no reason to go in them now."

It was polio he was really worried about. He was being a doctor first. Mabel was just his excuse to shut down the dancing in crowds. "Noooo," I said, soft. "Mom, the costume." But she just looked ahead. I knew the feeling. She'd painted herself into a corner.

But I kept on a-going. "Frank Swed had polio back in first grade but he's fine now." Daddy worried about going to fairs, the crowds, the polio. But why now? He was being cranky.

"Don't we have a vaccine?" I asked Daddy. When I was nine the big *Life* magazine had landed on our coffee table, with the little girl on the cover, a shot as big as a gun pointed into her arm. Her mouth was open as big as a horse's, her blond braids stapled tight to her head, who could forget that image.

"You don't know what you're talking about," Daddy said. He did that long blink between sentences and sure enough, there was more. "It's a risk we don't need to take, those crowds."

He got out of the car. *Slammed the door.* He turned away from me, that flat-footed pivot that he did when in a hurry. Up the walk he went, under the big evergreen and away in the shadow.

Deep inside I knew. When my father had to say something that hurt, when he had to say it, he got gruff, abrupt, blunt. And that only made it sound worse.

I flipped on the seat, hair frizzing over my eyes. The Mason City air went to black.

15

LuLu Baird
Saves the Day

The front screen door slammed behind my parents, and I waited for my my head to cool. I sure wasn't hungry even if Hanna and Julie went and made their own noodles. There would be no tears but the lump in my throat froze and grew. I slunk, through my front yard to the back, ducking past the kitchen windows—fat chance. Hanna missed nothing. I nearly fell in the cinders taking that horseshoe drive, lunging between sobs. Now that would have been tragic, Daddy tweezing rocks out of my knees, even if it was just me a tap dancer with nowhere to go!

A marching band came down the alley. I waited for that *din* and *boom* to pass. I ducked and scrambled across. And now—it was sprinkling.

LuLu Baird's house danced past, fast, on my left. I batted a big sugary gumdrop of a bee, buzzing my hair, out of my hair. He was just looking for a nest too, probably.

One window was open. I could stop to see Mrs. Baird, tell my Mother I took a round-about way home. Mrs. Baird, she loved a kid with ideas. Her son was a professional puppeteer. Daddy said she got to be unusual. She mothered Bil Baird, and he was a genius. I was with Daddy on that one. Yes, I'd stop, talk it up.

I stepped in the twigs and scratched through the bushes. I jumped tulips to the window and peered through the screen—one eye, then the other—through the gauze curtain.

The old woman sat, her back achingly twined, like the wheels of her chair. But her white hair swept up to a velvet ribbon and her long skirt moved so pretty, in the breeze. "Mrs. Baird!" I scraped fingers on the screen. "Mrs. Baird. Can I come in? This is just an awful day."

"Oh." The woman unfolded, sat up. She jerked her chair towards the window. Her eyes shuttered aqua in a haze. They vibrated straight ahead. Wide open, they talked to beat the band. I loved those crystal eyes—no looking away—because she couldn't see if I stared or not.

This woman could not see my full dresses and long curly hair. She was pretty much blind. Mrs. Baird knew people only by words. I didn't ever have to say: "My mother made my dress. Yes, those are forget-me-nots above the hem." I pressed my face on the screen. "Did I sneak up on you?"

"Hon, you're not much of a secret. You've got your tap shoes on!" And, oh, I did. I'd put them on in the car thinking I'd go to my mirror room to dance.

Mrs. Baird reached out her arm, all white and blue, her fingers all ways all at once. Those were piano fingers: she graduated from college, a pianist. Daddy said to be proud of her. Women didn't often go to college, more than half a century ago.

Her head tipped. "I hear voices behind you," she said. Her voice was a rasp. She could be dramatic. But I did spin my head. And for crying out loud, there they were, the Lilac Girls, climbing out of the stairwell from the church. I squatted. My heart pounded like I'd seen the flying monkeys in the *Wizard of Oz*.

I edged up to the screen. "Mrs. Baird." My voice came out in a hiss. "Those are the . . . *Li-lac Girls*." A slow sprinkle of rain now tapped on the house. The girls crossed the alley and clattered up my back walk. "Those girls pop up ev-er-y-where," I said. It seemed so that day.

"Oh, oh." Mrs. Baird closed her eyes. "Honey-bunny, you'll get along, don't you worry. Do children tease?" I pushed my chin onto the window sill.

It was like I was talking over the fence. I kept an eye on my yard. "Well. Some are nice. Some are—just plain mean." This was hard to figure out. Did I sound like a baby? She *asked*. I was in a foul mood, probably exaggerating. Everything was fine in school. It was *out*, and that didn't happen often.

71

"Come round to the door. A cloud's breaking open. I have something to show you. I've waited for you to come by." Her fingers wrapped about something. I'd never miss that.

I jumped along the house. I shook off the water, dragging feet on rag rugs. A race now, I dropped to her chair, placed my hands on her knees. Mrs. Baird laughed. "What a commotion," she said.

Who, me? I stroked her hand, hoping it would open. What did she have? For me?

Amazing, how her hand could be soft as a baby and hard as a rock, yet cool on a hot day. Her thumb stroked the treasure, such a tease, revealing a tiny bit of old wood. I gently pried her hand open, impatient. "Is it?" I kneeled closer, peeking. "A puppet?" Oh, it was. The handful, it was . . . "Who is it?"

Bil Baird's puppets were on the *Ed Sullivan Show.* "Is it Snarky Parker or Mirabel? O'Toolova the ballet dancer? No?" I bounced on my heels, trying not to roll her chair.

"He didn't name all of his puppets. I don't believe this one has a name. You name him."

"My gosh," I managed. Mrs. Baird slipped the bar into my hands and a tall lanky puppet unfurled. His feet tapped like checkers. Old paint cracked on knee joints and elbow hinges, flaking down to the wood. His big head, higher than my knees, dangled like a baby's. Its large features caught the light. A warmth came up that wooden munchkin, until the dizziness made me shake my head.

Mrs. Baird smoothed my hand flat, between her palms—to straighten the strings—except her old fingers curled. "He went to a puppet show at the high school. He came home to our attic, made one puppet after another. I don't know what came into his mind when he made one like this. It's carved from lilac wood out of our back yard, except the face. That's balsa."

The woman leaned back on the wicker and jiggled her tea cup in the saucer, a cinnamon stick clattering in the cider. She tapped the spice and sucked the rough surface. Her nostrils pulsed. "I haven't heard a puppet on the wood floor in a good many years." Mrs. Baird could make you forget the world outside her doors.

Scott Joplin must have been a boy in a room like this, playing his ragtime on an old piano, the velvet fringed shawl. The Bible pages goldened beneath a leather cover thin as paper. The swags of heavy fabric framed woodwork, coarse as a tree branch. Nothing minded being old here. The open cracks seemed made to store dust. The sudden shower mixed green with the closed air. I'd forgotten to shut the door but it wasn't cold.

"I thought of giving this puppet to you," Mrs. Baird continued, "because Bil's dad gave *him* a puppet when he was a boy. He kept it his entire life." She squeezed my arm. "It seemed to give him ideas. And, the puppet can keep you company." I breathed deep, appreciative.

Bil's puppets sat across the fireplace mantle, eyes a-sparkle. I had seen them a million times and thought they were funny. My eyes slowed.

On the end, there was Hi Behind. He had a huge curving tail that hung a tassel right over his cat head, his bulging eyes actually in his mouth! The next one was only a curved bean-like head with crutches for arms, no legs. Crutchhead. All over the mantle, scraggly clown hair and gangly legs and big feet dangled. Today they looked spooky but not scary, exciting, not silly.

"Did he name that end guy Hi Behind because his behind shows with his tail up? Or because his tail flops over his head and says 'Hi?'"

"I think so," Mrs. Baird said. She smiled. "All I know is after he made the puppets, and they clacked a rhythm, Bil said their words and brought them to life." Her fingers flitted on the chair like puppet legs. Her blank eyes were worn down, but so alive.

I waltzed my puppet around the fern stand. The slanting floor made the planter wobble. I swayed left and right. And then I blurted what was inside me out. I told her about Mabel and the stroke and polio in crowds and now I couldn't do my dance in the flag costume at the Fourth of July. That about summed it up.

"Well, you aren't having a good day, are you?" she said. "But it won't help Mabel if you fuss all day. You have to work hard so you have something. Surprise her when she's ready."

"I don't even know what kind of dance to do anymore."

She looked at me like I was in need. I wasn't used to that look. The rain splashed along on the sill. Mrs. Baird's lady was going to have to mop up those gray circles on the floor. Who cared.

"Mary Beth, it's not like you can cure polio or strokes. Let's focus on the *idea*. It's easy in *this* town to make music and dance and art," she said. "It's in the air. You're a lucky girl to live in Mason City," she said, her voice low and delicious.

I perked up. "Maybe polio isn't in *our* air?" I'd run *that* past my dad, good and dramatic, fat chance. "I could tell Daddy about my fairy sugar-drop theory?"

Mrs. Baird's hands found my face, either side. She could sort of see through those fingertips I thought. Why else would she touch? "Bil's dad moved us here so he could work at the Crystal Sugar plant on the edge of town," she began. "And you are right, that is a fine fairy, painted on the plant wall." She straightened her back and continued, plain and clear.

She gripped my hands now to hold me still but I kept a-going. "We're the biggest town around," I said. "We're so big that all the little towns bring their bands to our Band Festival, every year in the spring. Hundreds of bands."

"No, oh no." Mrs. Baird shook her head fast. "Mason City is not a big town." She delivered the news carefully. "We lived in Detroit before we lived here. Now *that* was a big town. Downtown went on for miles, not three blocks. The biggest difference is this: in Detroit, they make cars." She beamed. "But we make magic in Mason City."

"Music? Or magic?" What *was* she saying?

"Everyone makes magic in this town." Her mouth sped up. "Whistlers. Tap dancers. Harmonica. Accordion, guitar, ham bones. Hand slapping, ventriloquism." She threw her hands up. "Puppets. Every kind of

Cement workers Christmas Party, 1947. Cement, Lime, and Gypsum Workers. Fred Bosnack, master of ceremonies. Left to right: Judy Ready (tap dancer), Ralph Geer (magician), Clarence Best, Mary Beth Sartor, Joan Thornbury, Beverly Adams (tap dancers), Al Jolson (impersonator), Alf Sunde (accordion). (*Globe Gazette* photo: Courtesy of *Mason City Globe Gazette*)

music, music, music. Music!" She caught a breath, and I could tell she wondered if I was listening. I could be a scatter brain.

"I've seen all that when I dance out. Yes, oh, yes." I wrapped my arms around my puppet boy.

"Oh, dear," she said. She arranged her shawl. "When you dance, you'll dance for yourself. Bil says music will become electronic, anyway. Live accompaniment will be a thing of the past. Records are cheaper and easier." Mrs. Baird was so practical. Could I? Dance without Mabel. Didn't she know the music had died?

Mrs. Baird reached for a book and slammed it on the table. I startled. "Use your head! Look at this. Just last year Bil wrote *Whistling Wizard,* an elf who has a magic flute. A flower makes him dizzy. A witch steals his flute and when she plays it, he turns into a bird in a cage. Now that's imagination. He could still sing!" She smoothed the cover. "Come back some day, read it to me. You'll see."

I chuckled, mostly out of nervousness. I hadn't thought of that. If someone took your flute, did the music die, necessarily? She frowned. "Did you laugh? I've lived a long time and I'm wise, little girl." Mrs. Baird pulsed her fingers over my lips. I clamped my mouth tight.

"My mouth was just open because I'm surprised." Mrs. Baird didn't want to be laughed at because she wasn't being funny. I did like the way Mrs. Baird let me hatch my ideas. But my head almost ached, so filled with talk of magic and fairies, of polio. And now no Mabel. "Can Mabel still think music?" I just couldn't figure this stroke. My imagination could find a way to bring music back? I needed to get my hand on that whistling wizard book. And I didn't even know how to whistle . . .

A circle on the kitchen wall ticked the air and the house seemed to come back to regular, normal. The clock! I jolted.

"No. Oh, no! Look. She waits for me, my mother's at the window. I know it!" I tripped on my skirt getting up and lunged towards the door. I grabbed at the planter for balance and ran, strings flying. "Oh, I *have* to get home. So, oh, thank you. I love my puppet! I know I'll have lots of ideas now that I have him. I'll figure this out. He's my friend."

"Now. Don't tell anyone about the power of the puppet. They'll think I'm loony." Her cheeks tinted just a hair.

"Oh, no, Mrs. Baird. I mean my mother doesn't think you're loony either, I'm sure." I folded the puppet in half over my arm, wanting to linger

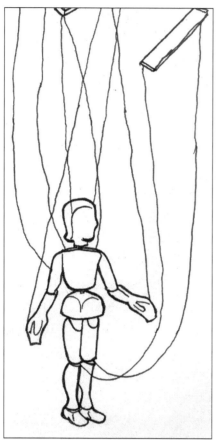

A real puppet and its parts, 1954 sketch. (Courtesy of Beth Obermeyer)

but couldn't. I ran my finger over his foot, bumping, pulsing over the carving, underneath the blue toes.

So she'd know I didn't just tear out of the place, I took a little time. I asked: "Is it Bil's signature, carved on the bottom of the puppet toe? Why is Bil spelled with only one 'L'?"

Her posture lit up, her son after all.

"Oh, does he? Oh, yes. Well. People don't pronounce the second 'L' anyway, now do they."

Good, good, good. Bil Baird was way too unique to have a one-bell, two-L-name.

Bil, much better.

Photo of an original Bil Baird drawing of a puppet in the home of Anne Abel. (Photo: Beth Obermeyer; Courtesy of Anne Abel)

16

The Flying Ribbon Dance

I sailed along, and the puppet toes clattered. The drips came only from the trees now, good for the Band Festival, which I probably was missing. Both cars were gone now. Probably my parents sat by Mabel at the hospital. I couldn't find the cheer to go anyway, not without Mabel.

I crossed my yard, cupping hands on my puppet. His head, his bottom. I turned my circle. No one hung round anymore, I didn't think. I was alone, one with my boy.

I'd be his world and he could be mine. You couldn't get polio from a puppet.

Picking up steam, I breathed a puff. I was in a musical? But I took too big a breath, inhaling the lilacs, my feet caught in strings.

But I waltzed away anyway, my eyes glued, to his. His lids dropped half, a clack 'n' back.

He wanted to approve, looked so wise.

"Clackhead," I said.

His name clicked, the breeze. I listened for music. Pinocchio? Not pine. "Lilacchio?" Did his eyes sparkle?

Faster I turned, the more the circles, a cyclone. The lilac perfume turned to nubbles of petals, somehow stuck in the corners of my eyes.

You'll never know till you try, said the Mabel in my head.

I imagined the stage at the Fourth of July.

"What if," Mrs. Baird had said. Her what-ifs pulsed, my every turn. My scared energy turned to something new.

I slowed my turns, let the strings whip. The wooden feet rattled. The swirling strings looked like ribbons, making air clean

What about ribbons? To swirl the dance? My fingers squeezed.

His cracking mouth, it made a smile. He liked his sailing strings, too. Claps came from behind me for a moment and then Mrs. Baird's lady must have cracked the window shut.

Later, yes, gymnasts would make ribbons an art form. Maybe they already had ribbons in the Olympics? Not in Mason City.

I raced along the walk. I bounced past the bridal wreath bushes. Petals flew like snow. Across the back porch I went, high off the ground, skipping my steps, just like on my stage on the lake. Far away from the audience.

Far from my audience . . .

That was it!

I'd be far away from the crowd on that stage on Clear Lake, me and my ribbons.

I ran for the house, practically just delirious. And ribbons! I had to try my new idea.

First I had a bit of housekeeping to do. I sidetracked to the grandfather clock, bundling the puppet as I went. And I stuffed him in the base, next to my Meredith book.

It's where I stashed stuff important. Next to my cap gun. I was thinking of a new use for caps. I didn't want a bunch of questioning until I got my ideas hatched. I sure didn't want Julie waltzing away with Lilachio. Or Bobby, he stood and plopped on stuff. Squeak toys were Bobby's speed.

And that's when I saw it. I was squatting, in the corner, shoving the Fedelia book in, when out slipped—a glossy photo. It was cracked across the bottom, hanging out of the book a bit. I didn't know it was there. It was of just the head of Meredith Willson! Mabel gave me my own picture! It was like a senior high school official picture except he was old, like my dad, likely forty-something. His eyes sparkled and his teeth were shiny, his nose just right.

I looked over my stash. These were likely my most valuable possessions. A puppet, a book, a photo, ammunition.

Ideas and dance, that was all I could do.

Part III

Finding the Way

MONDAY

Meredith Willson portrait. (Publicity photo; Courtesy of Meredith Willson)

17

Meredith Auditions His Show: Cy and Ernie

Ten states away, on the edge of the continent, Meredith carried Mabel's wish—his too, of course.

He'd make Mabel proud. He had to let go of his baby, his musical, let it fly through the air, get it to a producer. Time was a-wasting.

At the telegraph office the rack-tack-tack of the machines played in Meredith's head. He leaned on the counter and waited for the clerk. "Let's see, lemme see," Meredith said, impatient, although he could see the clerk couldn't take the paper out of the machine until it said so. A cigarette wobbled around more Meredith words. This was the telegram Meredith had waited years to send, to Ernie and Cy, the producers. When Mabel's right, she's right. It was time.

The Western Union clerk pulled strips of paper from the stomping machine. He chopped them in fragments and glued them to the telegram, his green visor shading the print. Meredith steamed his glasses, straining to see his words on that yellow paper. Finally, it floated to him, still wet.

Meredith stroked a brown-stained thumbnail across the raised strip of type, clicking off the end onto the paper. He spread his large hands on either end. Every word counted on a telegram.

"Have Combination Essay, dialogue and song," he read, with a satisfied sigh. "Time to show my stuff," Meredith said, nodding to the man. "Johnny, I might not be completely ready, but I've been writing this musical for forever."

"This gram's goin' to New York City. Who are these guys anyway?" Johnny peered at Meredith through his visor.

Meredith tapped a rhythm on the silver bell. "They're big producers, just opened *Can Can* on Broadway. In September they open *The Boy Friend* and *Silk Stockings* for Christmas."

"Misters Cy Fuer and Ernie Martin, producers," read Johnny.

"Care of *Can Can* STOP Shubert Theatre STOP New York City," said Meredith, like a state fair barker. "I'll head home and wait for an answer. Thanks, Johnny."

Meredith strolled the L.A. side street to his car, past a fragrant Hawaiian flower cart. He edged around large-breasted dancers draped in fuchsia blooms. A boy pulled a toy dog onto Meredith's foot.

Meredith sashayed in the rhythm of the women's long hair and high-stepped out of the toy leash. He was oblivious to where he was.

They had—Cy and Ernie—*asked* him to write this musical, after all. And that was fine, but a musical wasn't a song or a book. He felt like a guy who hadn't played baseball, just bounced a ball. Considering that, his was a Herculean effort.

He slid his fingers along the large silver wing of his Buick. He opened the door, cranked down the windows and got in. Head home and wait, was all he could do. He relaxed his right piano arm on the armrest. He hummed in the sunshine about a Wells Fargo wagon coming down the street. He wondered how he wondered. What could be?

Meredith cruised his Westwood neighborhood. He hummed all his verses, happy to have made a move. He crowed and crooned into his driveway: "Maybe . . . well, just maybe . . . Cy'll have something? . . . just for me?" He scatted the end and went back to his den, to write.

Three hours went by. He rubbed his pink eraser wheel on the typing paper. But oh, well, dang it. That first draft had come hard. The next years he'd torn it apart. And now, here he was, ready to audition. And his play was, oh, three hours and forty minutes long now, howdya do. How'd that happen? He ignored the doorbell. He flipped the wheel to the brush side to clear away the shavings.

"Western Union," sang a young male voice, through his den window. The young man startled Meredith, popping his head through the frame that way. Meredith jingled into his pants pocket for change, and leaned to the window. He tipped the boy, a dime, and ripped the envelope open with his teeth.

"BRING IT TO NEW YORK IMMEDIATELY."

Meredith howled.

He spun his big feet out from under the desk. Piccolo the puppy gave up keeping four little paws out of the way and climbed his leg. But of course the producers were interested, Meredith assured himself, scooping the puppy under his sleeve. "They asked me to write this. I'm ready," he assured the soft fur in his arms. He raced to the phone to get airplane tickets.

* * *

The next morning he stood in his entry, set for New York. He hitched his trademark plaid sport coat onto his shoulders and curled his toes in black and white spectators. His suitcase and satchel leaned by the door.

Rini—beautiful wife, Rini—was ready to go. His Rini was always ready to stand by him and that filled him with confidence and love. She was part of him and God knew he could not do it without her. In New York, she would stand by his piano and sing his songs at the audition while he did the dialogue. They were a team, always, all ways.

Usually, every morning about now, he went for a walk around their Los Angeles neighborhood. If he came home with even a skeleton of a song, Rini was ready to get it on a score, just in case.

Now he looked at his Rini, black dress, black hat and veil, black high heels, white gloves. He smiled at those pretty legs. She showed him an ivory smile better than any keyboard. Rini filled him. Right now she was stringing him together.

He jerked his watch from under his cuff: "Two hours to flight time, seven hours to New York."

He scooped his score and slammed it in his briefcase. He pulled his bow tie. "Ready as I'll be."

"Dear, you're who you are. Don't worry." Rini clicked her purse shut.

He was who he was, of course she was right. He was Meredith Willson from Mason City, Iowa, and he always made sure everyone knew that. If you weren't who you were, then who were you, anyway? If he could just get this musical on paper right, the whole world would know him and his town.

"Well. I'm not Morton Gould from the East or Ray Charles from the South. And I'm sure not going to change until no one knows where I'm from." He shook his head. "Not when you're from a place like Mason City, Iowa, *no, sir*. Worked for me so far." He swung his briefcase into the cab.

Rini flashed her eyes. "You're absolutely right, dear. You're absolutely right."

The sure rhythm of her words calmed him, all the way to the pads of his fingers.

The phone rang, inside the house. "Honey, we forgot to shut the window, the little high one by the front door," he said.

"But it never rains in southern California," Rini said. And the sun would shine down on the Willsons for one more day.

In New York City, the couple headed to the taxi stand. Meredith kept an arm out for Rini to grasp, in case those little high heels twisted in the jostling. He raised his other elbow as though to salute. In fact, he was running his John Deere combine of a hand through his graying field of hair. He was making the jump of his life, from a dying radio career, right past television, all the way to Broadway.

People, all sorts of kinds of people, clipped along the sidewalk. A model with her hat box slung by on tiny heels in a hot-pink slinky dress, scarf aflutter. He caught a phrase of the model's words: "Pandora sweater, pettipants, under the Pendleton, matching the skirt," she said.

Meredith had no clue what that meant, but he heard the rhythm of "P" words. People whizzed both directions: Spanish, Dutch, brown, white whirled his head. His town was pretty much white. He watched his face in the rear view mirror. "Rin, they'll like it, don't you think?"

"I know they'll prance on it the minute they hear it." Rini was Russian and sometimes she scrambled her words. Meredith smiled and relaxed. Her sentences came in a quirky order, but at the same time made inspired sense. Her hand was smooth on his cheek now, that worked, too.

The cab driver wove between lanes to avoid a shoe-shine guy, standing between lanes, at a red street light. "Shine, mister, shine?"

Meredith saw the fist rap on the back seat window. In a way, he wanted to adjust to the frantic pace because he knew what was coming next: Ernie Martin and Cy Feuer. They talked in snippets so rapid they slowed even Meredith's spray of words. He'd listen tonight to what the guys with money had to say.

They climbed the stairs of the brownstone, confident they had something, not sure how far from a musical. But he still thought Mabel was right. Get what he had out. *If she could see him now.* He'd thought of practicing at home with cotton in his teeth and gums so he'd be used to being all dry mouthed—that thing that happens, can't explain it, can't avoid it—when you go to show your stuff.

Meredith wrote about this evening in his autobiography, *But He Doesn't Know the Territory*. His humor stays in my mind as I write. The scene unfolds.

Ernie ushered them in. His smile seemed to have no reason to be there, or not to be there either. Meredith braced. This was not Iowa here, where a smile meant something clear.

Ernie's smile was automatic, separate from his thoughts. To boot, the smile was up high: Ernie was tall. You ended up looking at Ernie's jacket and Ernie was an awful dresser. The jacket was olive green, smelled smoky, and he must have gone fishing in a drawer for a sock that couldn't find a mate in a pickle jar.

Cy pinged to Ernie's pong, up and down, a pug with a butch haircut. He also turned on his face randomly, teeth in a row now, gone now, like he was in a View-Master.

Meredith got the uncomfortable feeling he needed to get some of that, too: slam-bang, some grins. He felt his shoulders tighten, his chin lock down. He was losing his sense of being himself and *that* shaved on his confidence.

One thing he knew since he could remember: don't be afraid of big wigs and don't fear getting embarrassed. Mind over matter.

One other person came to the door and she was a boost. Cy's wife, Posy, and just the name felt great, didn't look like a pushover—even her perfume was spicy. Meredith felt good about her right away.

"Meredith Willson, I've listened to your radio show for years." She squeezed his arm and grasped Rini's hand, fast. Meredith held tight so he couldn't slip away down Cy and Ernie's slope of words. She flitted about in her navy faille dress with the big circle skirt. Faille had a way of rasping against itself with an efficient sound, he always noticed, like a Porsche engine. She moved from marble-topped table to paper-thin vase to satin sofa like the layers of richness could change tomorrow—sit, drink, whiz past like you were over at Camp Gaywood, please, her actions said.

Her eyes came often to Meredith's in a way that made him feel special, good as a warm Iowa welcome, but her way. The talk before between Cy and Ern must'a been good, he surmised.

"Gotta sit down," Ernie said.

"Get Cy his chili," said Posy to the woman in a white apron.

"Ern only eats canned spaghetti. Sarsaparilla," Cy said in a spurt.

Posy laughed. "We don't have canned spaghetti."

"Ernie has his own."

"Just get him a big cigar then," Posy said with a shrug to the maid. "And heat up his spaghetti." This reputation would follow Ernie his entire life. Hard to forget.

Words went around the group, but Meredith didn't sink in. He wasn't even sure: who said what? He moved through the showroom of furniture, a touch to an elbow, a nod to a word, to the far side of the room to his piano. Don't distract me, his body said. Rini cut through right behind him, easy in his large wake.

He caressed and rapped the keys, like the piano's sounds mattered most, warming his fingers and his energy as he couldn't in-talk. The big piano loved him back, tones warm and strong, one octave perfect with the next. He wanted to hug this Rolex of a piano.

The small crowd gathered into the chairs like on cue. "We'll knock them down for a loop," Rini whispered in his ear. Her words were just right.

Rini and Meredith eased into patter and song. He planned to stall the producers' words with a two-hours-too-long—four hours total—audition.

Rini glittered her beautiful voice. Cy, then Ernie, smiled. She was the perfect foil for Meredith's droll humor, as perfectly timed as his songs.

The food got passed to the right people and the clatter of dishes slowed as the smoke thickened.

Rini sang about home again—Lida Rose . . . the sun in the sky.

Posy moved from chair to chair over the hours, always in Meredith's view. He heard the rustle of petticoats and saw the blur of her poppy-colored fabric corsage. He saw her brighten every time Rini took the lead with a song and he tried to relax and bounce his energy into the piano in chords. He socked it, exaggerated the rhythm tempo.

In between, he focused on the rose leaves on the beige carpet. He couldn't afford to be rattled by Ernie's face: *that* was a whole . . . 'nother . . . thing. He was grateful for the smiles, but he still didn't sense what caused them, a disconcerting thing. If he tried to figure that out, he'd lose any opinion at all about what he was playing. Instead, he spread Posy's look like frosting about the room. He even licked a few solos, adlibbed away.

The smell of spaghetti and chili hung in the smoke. Meredith and Rini inhaled the food on the drag of cigarettes, a habit they couldn't break right now.

Rini sailed on, her operatic soprano voice clear. The couple talked to each other by touch. Over the hours, Rini moved from standing, hands on his shoulders, to sitting, her back to his side of the bench. She bounced her voice off the curved glass on the china hutch, the thick green-edged glass of the wall dividers, the larger-than-life glassed art as she circled the twelve-foot grand, sometimes leaning to bounce her high notes off its sound board. Rini appeared to caress the piano with love lyrics.

She sang, "Good Night my Someone . . . sweet dreams."

Her voice drifted, with just the right tremble. Meredith saw the end in sight, stumbled over a last ad lib riff. Having Rini next to him was just like having Mabel alongside, back when he was seventeen.

Mabel was just there. He knew what she thought of him and it was good.

At last, Rini sat, quiet. Now it was Meredith who trembled. He turned to face his important audience, hands clasped. He leaned over spread knees. Rini took water for both from Posy and leaned her back into Meredith's elbow. She clinked ice in her glass, as though unable to be totally quiet after all the song.

The response from the group came like bowling balls down a lane, smooth, then chopped. "All you got to do is shift around the plot and the subplot. And prune it down."

"Of course we gotta change the title of the show." Cy walked away two paces. "*The Silver Triangle?* C'mon. Have a Broadway title."

"I know a Broadway title when I hear it." Ernie pivoted fast. "And that ain't it."

He thrust his hands and leaned, like a Vaudevillian. "Silver Triangle, nah, doesn't got it, not t'all. Sounds like a mid-forties' grey-haired woman having a fling with a married man." Meredith chuckled in spite of himself.

"Gotta watch that spastic boy, Mere. He'll steal every scene." Feuer and Martin bantered like cannons, like each knew the other's mind.

If Meredith let his mind get trampled, he was nothing. That spastic boy was central to his plot, been there from the beginning, and he loved that character like his own child.

"Josh Logan to direct. Perfect." Josh Logan, now there was a director. It was dizzying to get so much feedback.

"Go home, Mere, we'll call soon." The handshakes were promises. But such fast promises. "And don't change a thing 'til we get to you. Not now. Do not touch the manuscript without us." Faces locked, straight-lipped, stern.

"We gotta finish *Silk Stockings*. December."

"Ya gotta have a love story. Shift the attention to a love story. Remember."

In his autobiography, Meredith goes on for pages with advice from the word-busters. Really, Meredith would do nothing. Who could absorb them?

The trouble listening to these two was, the faster they talked, the more they said, the louder they said it. Even with the ceiling fan going, their voices could be heard if a marching band tromped by and they'd get in the rhythm to boot. Not arguing, not at all, even though they said different things. Meredith could have written their overlap, their speed, their acceleration. He could set a metronome by it. Let it tick, turn it up.

He had to drop out a moment, find himself, hug Meredith. Did these guys practice this reaction all night? They couldn't have. They'd just done this a lot, that's all. Meredith knew there was some truth in what they were saying. He massaged his tired hands. Rini stroked her throat, chin up, eyes closed.

Meredith and Rini went back to the hotel on angel treads. He'd heard a lot of things to fix but the producers would help. Not now, but in December they'd help. Their chins bobbed, grins slipped over teeth only there was no Vaseline on their teeth, none at all.

He called Mabel but she didn't answer. He was certain of good news. Nothing could go wrong, they didn't think, except he couldn't sleep, if one counted sleep.

By morning, they counted Mabel.

The phone call caught up with them. It was from her son.

"Mr. Willson, I have bad news," Jim Kelso said. It so took the edge off of what should have been a perfect day.

Meredith and Rini came down, hard. Meredith was glad he had seen Mabel just a day ago. As was his way, he began to hatch a plan, in the midst of chaos. He knew the perfect thing for Mabel.

He would surprise the life out of her. Or into her.

And he would be back to see her, soon. He told Jim about his producers. He would make Mabel proud, that was all he could do right now. But he was sad.

* * *

Two weeks and Cy and Ernie were in LA to see the Willsons. They gave Meredith ten minutes warning by phone before their car roared up the drive.

Meredith leaned his forehead on the leaded glass. They piled out of the car like firemen, he thought, to put out a fire. Like the military, to knock on his door, tell him his son died, that's all he could think. Only he didn't have a son.

He had a play. Meredith opened the door. He took big strides to the car. He glanced back for Rini, too late to call her. He wanted her by his side.

Ernie didn't even shut his door properly. "Josh Logan . . . interested . . . tied up for a year though. Has to finish *Picnic. Bus Stop.*"

Meredith tasted breakfast oatmeal in his throat. No director. No, they had no plans to sit a spell. Cy spieled, Ernie spurted. It came out like dialog in a play Meredith didn't want to watch.

"*The Music Man,*" short Cy said to Meredith's shirt pocket.

Ernie: "How do you like it? That's your title?" His words blasted down on Meredith's graying wave.

Meredith opened his mouth to say just fine. The words didn't come until the next breath. He knew a great title when he heard one but right now his brain was faster than his lips.

No director. But he had a title. Cy slapped the trunk of the car as if he'd had a fine dinner and was leaving. Meredith felt as though he'd eaten ten courses in a gulp. The gentlemen jumped back in their car, did a backwards "V" in the drive and were gone. Mere ran into Rini in the doorway.

"What happened?" she asked.

He slumped to a bench and stared at his bare feet. "Well, Tweety," he said. "We've got a title. Look at it this way. They like *The Music Man.*"

"It's wonderful, a wonderful title, dear, wonderful. Don't you think? Where did they go?

She whirled. "Did you invite them in?"

18

The Floating Stage on Clear Lake

July 4th, 1954

Alow sun was setting in Clear Lake and Daddy's long white car eased alongside the road and crunched onto the sand. He rocked the steering wheel and swung his eyes left to right, edging the tires through the family throng crowding its way to the waterfront for the big show.

It had been a month since Mabel had her stroke and Daddy said she still wasn't ready to be visited. I did answer Meredith's letter for her. But he didn't write back. He was probably as sad about Mabel as I was.

So with all that energy I worked that dance for the Fourth like she thought I would. I guess I thought if I won the contest Mabel would be so happy it would cure her stroke. I hadn't seen what a stroke looked like yet. What did I know? I could not accept that music could die, so I charged on with what I *could* do. I had to win this contest.

So far part of my brainstorming worked: I got to the Fourth! Like this: the stage for the Fourth was way out on a lake. No crowd: no polio!

The day I heard Daddy clack the chalk on my blackboard by the back door was music to my feet. "July Fourth audition, Thursday next," he'd written, in his flourished script. That blackboard held my schedule.

I was good to go! I was home free just that once.

And—I made the top fifty of 125 acts! Then the top twenty-five! The cut to ten was brutal. The music?

For just this once, this could work, Daddy said. He'd made a record on his record maker of Mabel playing at a practice at our house. His hobby was electronics, not fishing, like most dads. Not the same as having Mabel play. We were doing our best.

First place: seventy-five-dollar prize!

I would buy a train ticket to New York! Mabel would be so happy.

Mom leaned back from the front seat and crossed her hands behind her head. Daddy turned towards me, pushed his hand into the back seat. "We're getting close. Pass card please."

I slapped the parking card on his palm and plopped back, fluffing my flag costume around me so it wouldn't wrinkle. He licked the card and shoved it into the corner of his windshield. I cherished every detail of that gig, my dream coming true.

I was so ready.

"On the sunny side of the street," Daddy sang, true to form. He often started at the end of songs and fought his way back. He reached below the dash for his beer and raced the brew down his throat between phrases— without swallowing, that I could see. He sang his ditty.

I jiggled to the merry-go-round music and scanned the crowd on either side, to see who could see me. You had to be a finalist in the Fourth of July show to drive your car right up to the dock. I was like a float in a parade. My eyes tickled. In fact, I *was* flat-out tickled.

The car slowed as it neared the water, and heat swelled through the windows. The lake glittered in fast-moving slivers. The sun liked it best when it shined on water. My mother scouted for the best drive-in approach. "There it is. Right there. See the parking posts?"

The last of the jovial crowd bumped past. A kid lit a firecracker. Daddy traced its path over his cigarette wiggle, shook his shoulders at the bang. On such a day he was at ease.

Me and my mom? Chock full of energy.

Daddy swiveled out of the car and opened my door, stomping the sand from his shoelaces. My mother snagged my epaulet. She called to Daddy. "Just carry her to the dock? Sand clogs her taps."

My dad scooped me up over the sand. He stood me on the dock like I was five. I balanced over the water. "Give 'em hell," he said, with a smile.

I began the walk, my mother behind me. The wavy-tippy dock went out about a block, heel-toe, heel-toe. Liquid light from the Ferris wheel rolled on the waves, right up under us, dizzying. I kept my eyes not on the water, but on my feet. And they jutted just fine from beneath the flame-red net. I pressed my hand on my royal-blue chest top to feel the stone stars. I breathed deeply, hanging on to happy, and a tiny bit seasick.

A pair of contestants walked twenty feet ahead, so the dock wouldn't whiplash. Water lapped the edges and seeped up between cracks. The plank stage loomed close.

But this was old hat. I couldn't wait to see who was there. I just couldn't wait, period.

The fish smell faded. Shouts from land sounded like the school playground at noon hour. A calliope warbled. I cleared the space between the dock and the stage with a leap. The stage didn't move as much as the dock.

I hurried 'round the piano. Mabel should be sitting on that bench, but no. I tugged my hat elastic and pushed the pill box back. Everything scratched when it was that hot. My hands sweat. My fingers had red and blue dye from the crepe streamers in my tambourine.

My dad was afar, lifting the record player out of his trunk and onto a dolly. The bleachers looked filled with confetti from this distance. Soon all I'd see would be the circle of floor inside my spotlight—and the footlights—scary. A blinding line before—water.

Bob Cavanaugh hunched over the microphone—big as his face—and recited names from a handful of papers, one eye on us. His hair shined black over the glow of his suit. He was slick, the microphone like greased silver.

Every word he said bounced in a circle, from the stage to the bleachers, a big endless echo. He came close, dragging the mike. "Listen *only* to the words in your head, not the sounds that come back." I snapped the elastic on my bloomer. I'd probably sing "You're a Grand Old Flag" all the way to "wave" before the record let me pause. Taps'd sound like such mush.

I jiggled my knees, about my Fourth of July, the water, the crowd, my tap shoes. Having to dance was like having to pee.

I missed carrying my music. I missed everything about my Mabel.

Bob tapped the mike for attention. Ten-year-old Joleen peeked around her mother. She dragged her red satin pointe shoe over and over like a colt, her hands on the waist of her tutu. The shellac of Revlon's Satin Net hair spray held her hair to a bun. She looked exactly like the child toe dancer at the end of the movie *White Christmas* in her red-velvet costume. Maybe the judges would think she was, not fair.

I tried a double pull back. And a-one and-a two.

Might as well throw *that* away. And Dean's clean ballet line, never read that from shore. If the judges were band directors, would they even like a tap-dance? I rotated my chin in a circle. This contest was *so* hard.

But I had seen worse floors. I squeezed the sweat from the corners of my eyes. How hard could this be? Once at Kensett Corn Days I'd danced on the slant of two flat-bed trucks, pushed back-to-back. And the apron of the movie theatre stage in Albert Lea slanted down, back to front, like the stages in England. No footlights, of course. Those were the days. I'd learned to monkey up.

A clown sweat down the edges of her wig, over the sealed edge of her make-up. Al Gerardi's son wheezed his accordion. The big skirt singers, skirts with flocked dots.

Larry Heinz licked his harmonica and it flashed. I knew all these acts. Jerry Jackson with his sister—The Whistlers. Tommy Hufstetler, the Yodeling Cowboy. He warmed up his voice, made me a little jealous. He had more fun than anyone and I knew why. The yodel from his head met the voice from his chest. More air came in, a dizzy joy.

And maybe all that I remember was not all on that Fourth. Maybe those acts came from all different years, in one grand show in my head. I was in six different Fourth contests, after all.

What I do know—and it seared my head—was how I hoped and how this one ended.

Clarence Best, another kid, was the Singing Engineer, in bibs. Boy could he project.

"What grade you in?" I asked.

"Seventh," he said. He looked about fifth. That was going to be a problem. I was tall and the judges would think he was good for being so young.

"What kind of taps?" I asked back. He put his foot on his knee and hit the round single tap. Clarence seemed nice so I showed him mine. But I didn't show him my secret, the caps I'd glued to the toes for fireworks. Even though he'd never tell. Not Clarence.

The tricky thing was sometimes we bragged a little and we knew if we lied. But, oddly, we all believed each other.

My dad twisted a wrapper off a mint. "Sugar. Energy." Clarence took the candy and gave my dad his chair.

I told my dad I was just the right amount of nervous. I shivered in the heat. My bites felt like electricity. The wait was getting long. I shifted my shoulders and watched the moon with my dad.

The police band horns glinted in the distance. The drums pounded. They marched onto the dock in my memory. Or some tribe crowded the stage, every year in time for the start. The wood walkway swayed with rhythm, the arc growing with every measure. "One of these years," my dad said, as he did every year, "the momentum's going to pitch them right into the lake." I stood to see this better but the band swarmed past me. I covered my ears. Bob waved his flag. My mother scooted for her chair by the record player.

The lights from shore flew onto us, a million candle power. We were on! The spotlight zoned down to just Bob and slammed big for the first act.

Soon it was act number two, the whistlers. They ran off stage in that way entertainers have—run and lurch, a sudden stop out of sight. And then Bob announced: "Mar-y---Beth---Sar---tor." My name echoed in ripples. I readied. Mom dropped the needle.

I ran for the mike. Anyone could hear the gasps as my costume hit the light. My song and dance, my life, began. I was determined to fill the planet.

The words of my song did come back to me from shore but I concentrated hard. Bob had laid the mike on a pillow. I stayed close with my taps. Spot turns were harder with a spotlight in blackness, especially with twenty feet of water under the stage. A smile never showed all the way to this crowd so I worked extra hard on the sounds and the turns. Moves had to be crisp.

Only trouble, and it was huge. I couldn't speed up and up with the crowd response because my music was on a record, like it was in a can.

The end came near. My crepe paper glowed against the sky. I glowed, too: I got three hands in the middle. The sparks flew from my toe taps. I let the crepe paper go in the wind at the end. The red and blue strips floated over the waves, got caught in the waves, and galloped toward shore. *I should get extra points for that effort. Effect.*

Two and one-half minutes. Then it was over. I ran behind the piano, the applause went down, and I raced back for a curtsy, a bow. The applause started again. I got two more bows. I spun off, my striped skirt like a piece of Christmas candy beneath me.

Except, the spotlight jerked off me and I spun into dark. Faster and faster, the weight of those rhinestones. Limestones?

Oh, that moment of air and a slap of cold water, a wrench of my arm.

I swung like a pendulum, leg slicing through the lake. My dad hung above me, grasping the post of the stage and me by the elbow. For all the world he looked like Gene Kelly in *Singing in the Rain,* swinging on that post.

My arm all but ripped off but I scrambled to the dock. I sat down on my chair, struggling to get to the top of a breath. The other acts circled murmuring. I sure hadn't noticed the Accordion Queens up against me. And Sylvia Ann Downs, a powerhouse nine-year-old singer from Wesley. They were top notch.

The final line-up came. I dried in the heat, in no time. We stood across the stage. I felt small. Bob's papers crackled over the silence. My ears pounded like I had plugs.

"Round and round they go, where they stop, nobody knows." Bob crowed just like Ted Mack. Up and down behind us, he walked. The spotlight banged past, over and over. The audience clapped. This contest was so big no one could load the audience.

Suddenly, the big-skirt girls squished forward in their tiny high heels. Bob must have said "Third Place." The girls were happy with third place, but not enough to grin their heads off.

"Oh," I heard the audience say. Bob squeezed my shoulders and the light warmed.

I stepped forward, rocked on my heels. *Second.* My applause quieted fast, so they could hear who was first. I turned my tambourine, a quarter turn at a time. I grinned, my eyes wide, even if the light wanted them to close. You couldn't jump up and down when they said second.

Mrs. Sartor's flag costume (the first one), twenty-five years later on Kristin Obermeyer, granddaughter. (Courtesy of Beth Obermeyer)

Better than the eight acts who went home with nothing. Everyone said that to me, every year. One of the dumbest things I'd ever heard.

Bob moved on down the line and the light went with him. All I could hear was quiet, and an occasional slap of a wave on the stage edge. And out of the line-up stepped a girl and boy, pale-blue costumes a glitter. The whistlers? Or did they dance. It didn't matter. The girl adjusted her tiara each time she convulsed. She wasn't a jumper, more a gasper. The boy swung his arms to front clasp and back, checking his shoes in between. You couldn't even tell they were a pair, not any more. But they were first, the real winners, two of them. What would I do if I won first?

The performers thronged the winners. The gnats swarmed the footlights. The Police Band marched down the dock, horns swaying. They peeled like synchronized swimmers, head first in a splash. No, they didn't. I was too tired and I played with my mind.

I'd seen it all before: the sky rained fire on the water, all around. Clusters of sparks grasshoppered on stage. My dad said the stage could go up in flames. But it didn't.

But how many kids got to stand in the middle of a stage in fireworks every year?

The mayor squeezed past Mom at the side of the stage. "Nice job." "Great show." "Oh, thank you" filled my night air.

I gasped smoke into my throat, my ears, the backs of my eyes. A man squeezed my shoulder, clapped the singing cowboy on the back. Bob Cavanaugh shook hands with the judges. I eased up close. "I liked the little girl with the flag dance," the first judge said. "But you know, you know— it just never would fit in a television studio."

First place only, invited to be on *television?*

"Heavens, the lariat . . . hit overhead lights." And . . . "knick the piano," said the music teacher judge.

Bob's white teeth cut my every breath off . . . "And you need dark for the sparks, her tap shoes to show. A great little dance outdoors at night, just not for TV."

Not now ya little chowderhead. They might well have said it right to me, get to the point. Tallulah Bankhead spouted that once to a photographer. Meredith heard it, right up his alley

The tops of the whites of my eyes—the part you never see—tasted salt. I never cried. I walked the dock towards shore, after my mother.

I crossed the sand and gritted and ground. Second place wasn't so important that I'd take care of my taps. My dad leaned on the trunk, between the car fins, hands on his hips, his face to the breeze. Good job's what he said. He put my head under his arm and rubbed his knuckles on my soft spot, as if I was a baby. "You made music. You're the best tap dancer I ever heard."

I pulled away. I was attracting a crowd, boys my age. "Whew, whew, whatta figure. Two more legs, you'd look like Trigger!" I didn't know them.

My mother pressed her hanky under her bangs. "I have to say, your idea looked great. The boys ran away. Let's get out of here, beat the crowd." She said all that over one big sigh. I really wanted to ride the Ferris wheel.

I crawled in the car and faced backwards, leaning into the window shelf, my chin on my hands. The fireworks stayed big and the crowd got small as the car drove away from my floating stage and Clear Lake. The Ferris wheel churned. It rolled over the enchantment without me.

I couldn't have done any better. No one told me. I knew. My parents' voices hummed. I won fifty dollars, well a savings bond. I'd bought my own swing set, a croquet set, my bike with my winnings other years.

I settled down on the plush seat and sand tracked on the carpet. What had I thought was so important? Doing a good job? Right.

I'd wanted to win. I coulda been on TV. I sucked my hat elastic. My hair stuck to my forehead, even in the breeze. Telephone poles clicked by. They throbbed Mabel's measures, her music always in my head.

"Contests," I muttered. "Just someone's idea of who's best. And do you know what? You can't even compare dance to song to band."

My mom leaned back. "You were just one little girl on a big stage. I don't think it mattered what you did, too hard to win first."

Too big for Bob Cavanaugh's TV show? And too small for my mom? My heart thunked but my mom went on.

"Well, you just can't beat a good pair by yourself." My mom's voice sounded so darn stupid sure. And what could I do to fix all of that? Dance with my puppet? My mother stared at the ceiling light. The front seat was silent.

I punched my tap shoes on the seat front of me. Now half-moons dented the new upholstery. I was hot inside and out. My tongue was thick, stirring up juice and meanness.

"I coulda just *won*. That dumb-stupid simple." My voice blurted. It didn't even sound like me. I was almost scared what I'd shout next. What

97

really made me sad was I'd gotten just this one reprieve when the music died. I had Mabel's flag dance rehearsal on a record. What would I do when I needed the next dance? Would I ever dance again without her music?

What would I tell Mabel?

My dad checked my face in his mirror. "Here's what Grandpa Sartor always says. 'Stop your mutzin!'" is what he said, his voice loud over the highway. "Don't talk that way."

Boy, that was a low hit. "Drop it, right now, that's what I say," he said. "Not worth jumping in the creek."

I slammed my head back, face to the ceiling, just like my mom. I suppose they could say next that I was a bad loser but that's not it, not it at all.

What was really wrong—*I'll be the judge of me.* What I was really bad at was being judged. It was my song, my dance, my call.

Heck, it had been my one chance. I bristled.

"Well," I said. "Here's what *I* always say." I said it not to myself at all, way loud enough to be heard. I closed my eyes tight, let it go. "Well . . . doesn't that just *frost your tits!*"

"Heavens sake," my mother said, like if she shouted her words would backlap over mine. "She said, 'Teeth,'" she said to Daddy. A blue silence fell over the car. The telephone poles flashed by faster, speeding the beat.

"That's what Ba said, on the farm!" Daddy finally said. My mom grew up on a farm.

Mom spoke under the wind: "Nooo, not the farm! It's that Meredith Willson and all of his books. *Eggs I Have Laid*—now there's a title." They were talking like I wasn't even there, like I was a weather front coming in.

Mother turned to me. "You do not say frost your *anything.*"

But yes sir, that's what I said.

Bang.

19

Half of Mabel

Finally. I would get to see Mabel. "It's a nursing home," my dad said, easing his collar with one hand, gripping the wheel with the other. "Just so you know what to expect," he said.

I expected I'd wet my pants right in the back seat of the car, I was that nervous.

My father's eyes filled the rear view car mirror, right at me. I forced a cool face. I sure didn't know what a stroke looked like on Mabel. It must be pretty bad. It had been a month since it happened and she was only just then up to visitors.

"A stroke is when a blood vessel explodes and short circuits the body," he said, like I'd asked. "One side of Mabel's body doesn't move." His voice forced a monotone. Maybe it was the heat. He clicked to my mom like . . . *how'm I doing?* I leaned into the breeze, closed my eyes, trying oh-so-hard not to just bawl my head off.

"She's twelve," Mom said, her voice low as the motor of the car. Barely, I wanted to say. "Sometimes ten. Sometimes an old lady," my mother said. Mom's lips were the first thing she'd moved since she climbed in the car. "You sound like Mabel's body is a science experiment," she said, to Daddy.

My dad was just being careful, I knew. He always said I was growing, so maybe he wasn't sure: how old was my mind? Sometimes he'd forget his doctor booklets on the shelf in the den—like *Menstruation, The Female Body*. I caught that one. I had a quick look at it and the whole thing was disgusting, all the body talk. Strokes, puberty. Unnecessary.

"Her face, an arm, a leg—paralysis," he said. "But she'll be glad to see you."

Well, I was scared to see her, especially her piano hands. I felt dumb about that, but there it was.

My father swung the car along the curb and pulled his comb from the visor. He took his sweet time, struggling through his waves, front to back. He patted my mom's hand, in the way to say—she's my wife. One long limb at a time, he stepped out the car, so I scrambled, too.

He led us down the walk, over the grassy cracks, up the stairs of the old folks home. What kind of a place is called Old Folks Home? Old? Sick? Dying? What?

Fans blew across the porch. They wheezed from the front hall, and out of their windows. Soggy smells whooshed thick. Tired women in cotton print dresses perched everywhere.

My parents had been here before, so I did what they did: I smiled and said hello to every single person I passed. Two talked, two didn't look, another slept, her head back, mouth open. In a perfect circle her lips went . . . breathing . . . sleep. Most watched me pass, withdrawn in a daze, like I was on television, not likely to ever talk back.

So I touched the one most frozen, so still, with a squeeze. Her hand was cold on this hot day, but her eyes tipped up, warmed, focused. Expectant. Her mouth opened, and that meant something. I scanned the porch, one more time. Did anyone watch? On I went. This was no audience I'd ever seen.

If it was a home, it didn't look like that, either. Every room was a living room and bedroom in one. Beds on wheels had sides. Some beds bent in the middle. People all sat, lots of them to a room.

"Emma, time to walk now." "Harriet, time to change you." "Inez, finished your pudding?" Helpers talked every word loud, like they were on a long distance wire.

I checked each person off my list. Not Mabel. Not Mabel. Not Mabel.

But my dad stopped by a bed and leaned, with a kiss for a woman. My mother slowed, covered her chin, her eyes growing large. The pale woman nodded her head left to right, hair tufted and pink.

It was Mabel. My heart started a rhythm. To myself. "Mabel, Mabel, on the bed, dressed in hankies . . ." I didn't finish. My rhyme stilted and I was not jumping hopscotch. Could I hug Mabel? Mabel hadn't seen me yet. I backed towards the door to watch, only until I got my balance.

My father cranked the bed, propped a pillow. He massaged a corner of Mabel's mouth, to match the other. He lifted her hand, the piano hand. It fluttered. "Ah. That feelth—good," she said.

I counted seconds between Mabel's blinks. Five—ten—jeepers. Mabel's eyes stuck, shut.

I lined the door frame, grasped its edges. Hot burned my face, ice stiffed my feet. My pillow hands. In between my hands and feet, I was empty. Nothing in my stomach could push a breath.

Mabel plain looked like a ghost. I didn't want that, but there she was: white.

Dr. Sartor—not my father but being Dr. Sartor—pulled a chair to the bed. A second chair. My mother sat. He nodded to me. "Pull up a chair."

He pulled over a third seat. I sat. My dad was acting like a television show host. I was glad because I sure didn't know what to do. The matter with me was my brain.

I asked the little Scottie dogs, printed velvet all over my skirt, one at a time: "Where did Mabel go?" My fingers pushed the black puppies, scattered them. The dogs swam, down the gathers.

My neck itched enough to cut my head off. I unbuttoned my collar, popping six little buttons. So much concentration, like that's what I came to do. Anyway, I needed the collar, to blot in case I cried.

I wasn't going to, of course. No one else was. I closed my eyes to keep that thought in.

Mabel's lips moved, but the sounds made no sense. Her tongue and lower lip pushed her top teeth. She swallowed like to choke and tried again.

I needed to pull myself together. What was wrong with me? A twelve-year-old dumbo?

Her shoulder slumped. Her hand looked like a fish. Not that that mattered. But how could Mabel's piano hand not move? Mabel was here but the music was not.

Where was my own tongue? Usually I practiced what I was going to do, did it, and enjoyed the scenery as well. I didn't know this mood.

My dad nodded. Say something, his face said.

"Mabel?" I said.

Mabel answered. She raised her chin.

What now? Not about the Fourth! "I'm learning a new dance from Dean, 'Deep Purple,'" I said. "It has a story. I'll do it next time. It . . ."

Mother cleared her throat like a typewriter zinging a new line. "Mary Beth did the flag dance on the Fourth, on the stage over Clear Lake."

"Oh? How did—go?"

I was on, I knew. My turn to talk. I crossed my feet beneath the chair, scooted to the edge. "I—really put a lot into it!" I wanted Mabel to know that, first. She pushed her head into the pillow. "The echo went round and round on the song. Bob put the mike on the floor for the taps. I didn't trip on the cracks. I let the ribbons go in the wind, what an end!"

Before Mabel could even be proud, my mother dumped it out: "She was second. Third year."

Mabel slid in the direction of her eye and her mouth drooped. But she stayed with my face. Dr. Sartor popped her up, a doctor with a puppet. "Mabel, you played! . . . the record I made . . . great!" he said.

Mabel stared, like she might say something. We all stared till our eyes dried. Out the window, at the flowers, into the diamonds on the wallpaper. I glanced about, but the other old people zoned out.

My mother rattled her hand in her purse, filling the silence. She found her paper. "Let me read."

"Um," said Mabel. Maybe she listened. She smiled at names. She'd played for them, too. She thumped her hand, not the old piano roll, but more like a faucet on drip, on its way to on.

Mabel's eyes bubbled until they boiled over: "Forget the Fourth of July." Words on just that one big breath had surprising force. And she wasn't finished: "Doesn't matter. It's over."

We startled. How loud she was. Her next deep breath, a warning— more on its way: "Just get your dance ready, something will come along. Get yourself over to *Varieties*, to a whole orche-shtra. Get the kid lead!" Mabel went silent, probably from shock.

And my pal was right, right when she should've been in the dumps. I shouldn't even need Mabel to tell me. *How could I have moped in here so sad?* The Fourth was over, that moment—gone. No need to be play dead. A new crush was waiting, right around the corner.

Daddy took over. He didn't seem surprised at her spunk. He probably wasn't even listening. Because he started his feel-good talk, giving Mabel a chance to get more wind.

"Cement plant's blowing a lot these days. Good time to be inside," he said.

My mother took her turn. "We went to a musical, Fred Astaire in *Fascinatin' Rhythm.*"

I skipped my turn. Best not mention more dances. My dad wouldn't like the idea of crowds because of the polio epidemic.

My next thought: the old Mabel is in there. Why she spoke right up. I clenched my chair and bounced closer alongside.

"The last movie . . . I saw, James Dean in . . ." Mabel said. Her eyes moved forward like a lens, so focused. She tried again. "Not many musicals . . . anymore . . . terrible . . . vio-lench . . . Good days over, I'm a-fraid."

My father clasped his hands between his high knees. "The world's changing, that's sure," he said. "Civil Rights flare up, down in the South. About negroes riding on the front of a bus, sitting at a lunch counter. Or going to public school."

Whaaat. What are we talking about in front of Mabel? My mind, it stuck, on *Darktown Varieties*, Father Reed directed, it involved the whole town.

Sort of like the music man.

So I jumped right in. "There might not be any colored people in *Darktown Varieties* this year. You know, the row of chairs in front of the curtain? Before the show. Silly jokes and good rhythms on their tambourines and ham bones . . ." I bobbed my head, clowning: "'Ham bone, ham bone, them . . .'"

"Mary Beth!" His voice could have awakened the dead around us. I waited for him to go on, to see what my next line would be. "Those are not really colored people," he said. "It's make-up!" He enunciated every word like I was eleven.

"Oh, she knows that," my mother said. "It's make-up because there aren't any colored people in Mason City." My mother just didn't get around so I wasn't sure she was right that time.

I almost stopped. Common sense said stop. But I rushed on. "Oh, yes, there are, Lucille's colored and she was one of the children in the show. And there's Jungle Jim. Just those two, I don't know if there are others."

My father slammed his chair back, his eyes sharp, as though to erase my last words. "Mary Beth. His name can't possibly be Jungle Jim. It must be James. He probably brings the children into the office to see me. What makes you say something like that?" My father clamped his fingers tight on the chair arms. I got defensive.

"We made it up. We got a new Jungle Jim on the playground . . . and we put two and two together!" It didn't seem quite so clever, all of a sudden.

"He's Mr. Jones or Smith or whatever . . . to you," he said, his voice still full of glass shards.

My dad said he took care of all colors of kids at the office. He was prejudiced because he said they were all the same, but I knew everyone could see they looked different. They *were* different! And what was important, anyway.

I stepped in deeper. "Even if colored people can't ride at the front of the bus, they can still dance."

My dad regrouped. What he did when I went off topic. "Ever hear of Raven Wilkenson?" His voice challenged. This was the biggest conversation I'd had ever had with him. Who'd thought it would be in front of Mabel after her stroke? What was Mabel thinking anyway? She definitely was thinking, her dark eyes darting from face to face, like she was at a tennis match.

"No," I said. "Who's Raven Wilkenson?"

"Probably never will hear of her," Daddy said. "Her dance company just sent her home from a tour in the south. She's black. The Ku Klux Klan

came to a concert, marched right up on stage. 'Where's the nigger?' they shouted."

"Then what happened?" my mother asked.

"Not a dancer moved. It was a face-off," he said. "The Klan left the stage and went home. The concert went on."

"Is Raven a good dancer?" I asked.

"'The best,' is what the choreographer said. 'Could have been the next premiere dancer.'"

I loved to hang on the jungle gym. (*Globe Gazette* photo; Courtesy of *Mason City Globe Gazette*)

No one would see but my eyes got shiny. My shoes got my attention. Raven, a dancer, could tell a beautiful story to people with her dance, and they wouldn't let her? Not an old dancer, a just-starting one. Not fair at all. Dancers dance because they can. No peace inside unless a person does what they can do. What if I got a lead in *Varieties* and couldn't do it? Well, polio, no crowds, there was a reason, huge.

But Raven couldn't dance for such a dumb reason. "I don't see why Raven can't dance just because she's Negro," I said. "Ruby Keeler is a famous tap-dancer and she *married* Al Jolson, and he's black. She must think it's fine."

"Mary Beth, I give up!" Now he was livid. "Al Jolson is in black-face. *It's make-up.* No real person looks like that, big white eyes and mouth." My father threw his body back on his chair like a huge limp doll. Oh was he frustrated. My mother was laughing. She knew better.

"I don't even care," I said, hiding my face in my hands. "I wasn't thinking hard. I probably even knew that." *What a dumb-stupid thing anyway, to talk about first with Mabel.* But I didn't want to risk ranging into the polio epidemic and worry Mabel about that, either. I looked to my mother. Maybe she had something else in her purse, like fold-her-hanky-to-make-twins-in-a-cradle.

But it was Mabel who rallied. She stretched her piano hand, fingertips funneling through tufts on the spread. "Land, you better open your ears, America." She speeded like a stutterer, a bunch of words every gasp. "Black music is some of the finest. It's our own music, jazz. Tap dance has

The Last Jitterbug, 1950. (Courtesy of Beth Obermeyer)

105

African roots. Anyone can hear that, if they care to listen." Mabel waved her good hand towards the night stand, closing the subject, just like the old Mabel.

Get-to-the-point, no-complaining, Mabel. She batted some papers. I was glad. I was getting mixed up. I'd jitterbugged in *Darktown Varieties* when I was nine. "Darktown Strutters Ball," with black face paint and black hose and a turban over black yarn pigtails, but the make-up was plain black, no white smears around the mouth and eyes. I thought I was just playing a kid, a role, on a stage full of kids, all kinds, doing jacks and jump rope, a jitterbug with a girl. The trickiest—messiest—part was the logistics, getting the grease paint off in time to don a white satin formal.

One could say—what were we thinking? It all sounds unreal now.

I know what we were thinking—that blackface was *normal*, that can't be explained.

What I will remember and cherish is the music that came to us back stage, from the minstrel line in front of the curtain. The banjos, the tambourines, the bones in rhythm. I loved my jitterbug dance. I am proud to have been there when the grease paint and the mannerisms faded. I carried the dance and music forward. And I was fortunate to have followed town leaders ahead, out of the minstrel line.

⁂ ⁂ ⁂

I was daydreaming. I eased a letter from under Mabel's water glass. It's where she was pointing. I jolted at the handwriting. "Should I read Meredith's new letter?" Now good talk would get going.

I showed it around, to the one-two-three of them. It was not printed stationery, like Daddy's. It was creamy, looked like it had been wetted with water spots, pretty by design. "Here we go," I said, in my most important voice, like a ringmaster. "Dear Pal, I'll audition for TV game show host, Meredith"

What the heck did that mean? TV host schmost. The pause was embarrassing.

The old Mabel might have cheered straight up in the air, had the meaning been clear. But she did not.

"I'm proud of Meredith. He'll find a way," was all she said. I could see three more letters and I wanted to snoop. That sure came out of the blue to me, television host?

"I remember the night of the Tennessee Waltz," lyrics. Donnie (Don) Senneff and Mary Beth Sartor danced, along with Mary Jayne Craig with Vince Paton and Henriette Hebel with Eugene Lotts. A white satin scene in the 1950 "Darktown Varieties." (Photo, Elwin Musser; Courtesy of *Mason City Globe Gazette*)

Kitchen dishes clinked. A knob-headed man shouted. A young woman circled a peach crate, playing chess with herself, her piccolo lining alongside the board.

Mabel's lids lowered, like a curtain.

My parents took to talking to each other.

Mabel's head snapped back. The back of my own head shivered. "Did Mabel die?" I hissed to Daddy. She wasn't moving.

"No, no. Mabel will probably live a very long time," he said. "Don't worry about that." He put his hands on his knees to stand, so slowly. "We should go," he said.

"We don't want to wear her out," my mother said. We'll be back often, shorter visits."

The 1953 cast of Darktown Varieties. (Photo, Gibbs; Courtesy of *Mason City Globe Gazette*)

The three of us walked the sidewalk to the car. My insides jerked back to my walk across Mabel's porch on the old folks home.

I would think up a new name for this home. A breeze inched moisture across my cheek. *Man, sometimes you just gotta cry.*

I slowed for awhile, behind my parents. My dad tipped his face to the trees overhead. My mother folded my collar into her purse, watching the clasp so it clicked just right. Light bothered my mom's pale eyes—that was it. She sure wasn't going to cry. My mom never cried.

The music was dead. Mabel couldn't make music anymore.

And now I had prejudice on my list of problems!

"Surrey with the Fringe on Top." Mary Beth, ten, with Marlene and Virginia Becker, vocalists. (Photo, Gibbs; Courtesy of the *Mason City Globe Gazette*)

20

Scrubbed in the New York Times

One sunny day, I biked to see Mabel. Mom saw to it I got there, a lot. I leaned my pink Schwinn on her porch trellis and raced in to see her. She'd been waiting, I could tell. Her letter from Meredith was on the nightstand by her side. I ripped it open, but carefully.

Dear Mabel: Flubbed the TV show audition. I'm touring. What else? John Philip Sousa toured so I can too. I'll be back rich and running, wait n see. XXOO Meredith

I didn't get it.

"He's bluffing," said Mabel.

"Why would he want to go on a tour now?" I asked.

She pulled her hand along the bed sheets and up, to support her head, to see me better. "He has to do what he has to do, for money. That's what I think."

We talked it over, ten ways each way. "Maybe he . . . he could of . . . he probably . . ."

Just when I was thinking of scooting, Genevieve dropped a *New York Times* on the bed, a bomb it turned out. Meredith subscribed so Mabel could read about New York music. I paged through. New York, after all. I crackled a big page over, and it only took me a second.

"Oh, no! Look at this!" I said. Mabel's eyes flew open. I helped her hold the paper, and I pointed to a column. She scanned through her bi-focals and sank, deep into her pillow: "Get me the phone from the hall," she said.

I snagged the phone from the telephone bench, shook the coil behind me, and raced back to the bed. Mabel mouthed Meredith's number to the operator, one syllable at a time. She hung her head over the phone, her entire mouth turned down. I put my ear next to Mabel's.

Rini answered. Mabel talked.

"Mere, honey," Rini said, interrupting the music in the background, something she probably never did. "They've put Mabel on the phone."

Meredith clicked onto the phone. "Ya, kid," he said, "You okay?" I leaned on the pillow.

"Oh, Meredith," Mabel said. Her tone of voice gave it away. "Have you read *The New York Times?*" Mabel said. "Oh, honey." Honey was getting to be a name I didn't want to hear.

"What's it say?" he asked. "About me?" He sounded incredulous.

"It's in a column, Flash . . . you know it?" Mabel rattled her newspaper. "It's about you."

Meredith's voice muffled. "Rin, get the *New York Times,* quick. Flash." After an eternity the newspaper cracked and snapped. "Blockbuster producers . . . Cy Martin and Ernie Feuer have tabled . . . Meredith Willson's *The Music Man* . . . concentrate . . . on other projects . . ." Meredith read in gusts and bursts.

"Ah, well," he said. "Thanks, Mabel, for calling. No, we hadn't seen it yet." He sounded like he wanted to bawl.

Like a little boy, he got brave. "There's other producers out there," he said. "Hon, my heart's beating faster than my opening train."

"It only takes one," Mabel said. "You only need one producer."

He could not quit, she said, not yet, maybe never. He could do this musical like no one else could.

He was an original. It just took time for someone, just one, to see.

"Hang in there, guy," said Mabel. "Soldier on." Nothing more to say, Mabel hung up.

She swallowed. "Meredith told me months ago, that Ernie was in LA and went home. He'd come to Mere to help. He stayed for months. Maybe things went south," she said.

Mabel paused. "He was excited—then deflated—when the CBS deal for *The Music Man* came and went." She eased her forehead with the back of her hand. "But he still hoped."

"And, I know what's happening now," Mabel said. "Meredith's rolling Rini in his arms, smashed the paper between them. 'Oh, honey,' he'll say."

I didn't think either Meredith or I seemed to be getting where we were going.

New York sounded tougher than I'd imagined.

21

The Friendlies

FALL

Everyone had those lilacs, from cottage to lake home to store to funeral home, on country roads and in doorways. It made us equal. But I'd soon learn: we needed more.

I went back to school, to wait it out until *Varieties* began—even though I knew I fit in like nothing. Part of the trouble was I danced all the time. Classmates were having parties in each others' basements, while I tap danced in mine. I had no practice and I'd soon be a teen-ager.

One day, it got to me.

I loped along the narrow sidewalk by the church. I shaded my eyes, squinting towards the school. It was a maple syrup kind of back-to-school day. And that was the thing about Mason City. It had four seasons and you got a fresh start every time. That helped. It was fall, so fall was my favorite. Each tree lined the path ahead, each atop its own color carpet. Parents waited until they had a moment and raked piles as tall as the house for us to jump in.

It was decades before leaf blowers would howl.

Sometimes we had a bonfire of leaves and got to stay up late, the fall version of sitting on the lawn after *Our Miss Brooks* on the radio, watching the moon, the fireflies, feeling the breeze we couldn't capture in the house.

At school they'd stack leaves as high as the building and we'd all come to roast marshmallows. The boys practiced basketball and the girls their cheerleading. Kids raced and dazed, roasted and cooled, like in a snow globe but fire.

For sure the colors stayed crunchy for us until the last leaf fell. No one vacuumed yards. It gave a sense of season and time.

I was so content in that world that I made a risky plan.

Anyone on the steps of the school? Oh, yes. That would be interesting. I scuffed the leaves, trying to look casual, hanging onto my mood.

But my head hung. Not that my outfit wasn't beautiful. My mom laid it out for me to wear. Just not for that *of all days*.

But what? Could I wait till everything was in order to make my move? My mom had no way of knowing that day was going to be different.

As it turned out, neither did I.

I'd end up—in the toilet.

* * *

I tried a long breath. My corduroy vest—black and white zebra—*God help me*—wrapped tight. A hot pink skirt billowed—longer than last spring— more zebra was added, a border. The whole thing spun like a top in the sunlight. I'd never seen anything like it.

Neither had Steve or Patty, I was sure of that. It sure wasn't Grace Kelly. But my mother was an amazing designer so maybe she saw Audrey Hepburn in something similar, at a Sunday matinee movie. But on a kid? But I did like the brightness, loved the soft of the corduroy, the swing of the skirt, bright pink, black, and white.

In fact, Barbi the doll would be born, in just two more years, in just such a suit. But how'd we know that? My mom. *Way* ahead.

The pennies in my loafers flashed in the sun, each step. The shoes I definitely liked. I saw them on a seventh grader, Mary Ellen. I pressed my petticoat flat, to see the shoes, but the white net frothed, like whipped cream bound in pink satin. And the school came closer with each zebra step.

"Escape from a zoo?" Roland's voice crashed in before I could even do my "hi." He grinned from the top of the steps. His crew cut, Monday-short, stuck in clusters.

But already? This was the day everything was going to go right. Roland wasn't even a mean kid. Maybe he meant the joke for only Susie and Peggy to hear, didn't mean to hurt my feelings.

"That's so funny!" I tried agreeing. If I just laughed along—it wouldn't be so funny if I didn't look hurt. It hurt. I galloped up two steps at a time, to get out of the wind. I stood by the wall alongside the door, just like everyone else.

Sharon and Mary Magdalene laughed. They pulled their skirts around their legs, probably so the fabric wouldn't blow up their legs. Or maybe to show off how sleek the dark skirts and narrow hems were. My skirt was full, my hem a fur border. Their dresses came straight from Sear's catalog, where rows and rows of dresses looked just right.

Just right to wear to school.

Mary Magdalene had only two of these dresses, both short-sleeved. Her elbows showed and they looked like she leaned on rough wood. The inside of her collar was darker white than the rest. She ran the dirt road to home every night. Probably left the dress on till bedtime.

I'd wear a dress like that to school every day too, if I had one. I clutched my books to my chest, to hide the zebra vest. Why it all mattered on just that one day I don't know, but it did.

I caught all of my blowing hair that I could with one hand, while holding tight on the building. I inhaled, like I could suck that hair close, but no way.

Sharon's hair was braided tight to her head, down either side. Her hair didn't move. Mary Magdalene's hair didn't fly either and it was straight, too, held in place with a black headband. It went with either of her dresses.

That moment on the steps seemed to last until Christmas, and I decided right then and there. I'd never put myself through that again. It was an experiment and if I wore zebra tomorrow, so be it. Because this was pain, full of needless pain.

Finally the school bell rang down and the doors burst open. Sister Mary Ritella stepped out. Sharon and Mary Magdalene and I grabbed the top steps—one-two-three. We faced the building.

Roland was the leader of the boys. We were the oldest to go in this door and so we tried to look bored. Sister said we always got in place first and were quiet before all the other grades. But that was because we were too old to play on the jungle gym and swings so we clustered on the steps. Our double line stretched to the sidewalk.

Children screamed across the playground now and lined up on the part of the sidewalk for their grade. From the top steps it looked as though someone closed a book and all the letters fell into the binding. Then the invisible book opened and left boys on one edge of the sidewalk, girls on the other.

And surely someone turned a knob on the sound. Two *click-clicks* from Sister's fingertips—her little metal clicker—and we started in, five hundred children, a block long.

In the dark cloakroom, I listened, walked slow, squeezed past the kids, one by one. They loomed in silhouette. More than one grade. A single-paned window at the far end would have illuminated the other side of the faces, if I had only managed to make it to the far side. "Rudd comes today," I heard. "That little town probably barely has enough boys for a basketball team." It was the first game of the school year. I'd never been to it. We didn't play football so basketball was important.

"Gonna stay after school for the game?" Barbara asked. It was a new year after all. Dance practice could wait. That was my plan.

"Sure," I said.

I'd never said "sure" before. I hadn't asked my mother if I could stay for the game. I was going to that morning, but I just hadn't. I had not.

"So, do you have three pennies for milk? You go to the lunchroom at 3:00 if we're staying after school," she said. A dozen flat cotton dresses moved around and past me like a pinwheel.

"I'll get some money at noon when I go home for lunch," I said.

"Do you have any pants? We can wear pants to the game, Sister says." Three girls were talking, all at a time.

"Sure. I'll get them at noon. That's what I was planning."

"Your dad's rich. You have a television," Martha said, out of nowhere. The pinwheel went fast and faster. I felt the last words like a poke. Maybe I shouldn't have come to school early to talk by the door. I wouldn't have cared if I stayed after school.

But no way, not now. I fired. "That's his hobby. He likes tape recorders and big radios, and we just got the television."

Eww, that sounded like bragging?

The voices multiplied and seemed to come from the walls, every direction. Soon sweaters landed on the wire hooks. My white Eisenhower jacket toughed it out on the end hook where I'd abandoned it yesterday. I always hung my jacket on the end so I could just listen, stay out of the fray. If only I'd got to the end hook today. *Who gives a fig!* I was wearing down.

"So, sometime I could come to your house and you could curl my hair, and I'll do yours in a pony tail?" Barbara twisted hers over her hand.

"Sure." Was she being friendly? "Tuesday's good. My mom plays bridge at the . . . she plays bridge on Tuesdays. Hanna might let us go up to my room."

The bridge club, "The Bridge Kids," at the Hanford Hotel, their Christmas card photo. My mother is sitting in the front row, second from the right. (Courtesy of Beth Obermeyer)

"*You can't go up to your room?*" Sharon squished an ant with her saddle shoe. Her face closed in. "How do you wash your hair anyway. It's so long." She leaned on the wall beside me. "I bet her mom washes her hair," someone said, like I couldn't hear.

My mom did wash my hair every Saturday night. Right then I might have bailed, gone home. But Mom would be gone, to play with "the bridge kids," as Julie called them. She had her group. This was mine.

"Have you ever set your own hair?" My hair felt like cotton candy.

Esther licked her lips. "I saw your picture in the studio downtown, a costume with ruffles. Your little sister in a pink fluffy one. So you dance together?" That last sentence was sarcastic. So far it had been more curious.

Like . . . what does the dancer in the petticoats do in her down time? Esther moved between me and the door. She was older.

Oh, I was never going to fit. I wished it was yesterday.

The silence meant I should say something. "It's for a show," I said. "It's a part." The words plugged my ears. My own voice stayed inside. I swallowed to clear my head.

Esther had a straight skirt, and she kicked the back pleat right open. I jerked my elbow to get out of the way, but hit Esther instead.

Thank the dear Lord, Sister jumped in the door right then, like a bat. She slammed her papers on the counter. "Whatever is going on in here?" she said. "Please take your seats!" I felt the wind from Sister's claps half a cloakroom away.

The girls whirred out. The cloakroom cleared. I wiped my hot face on my zebra hem. Sister disapproved and disappeared, *click, click*.

I slid down the wall to the floor and sat, chin on my knees.

I'd go get my jeans at home, at noon.

Everything would go better in jeans.

Friendlier.

Jesus Mary Joseph.

* * *

A few hours later I was in the gym doorway in the best Audrey Hepburn pony tail I could muster, my first. Half the people I didn't even know. Rudd boys clambered over bleachers and sat cool, their shiny hair in duck tails. Boys in tight shorts dribbled balls, warming up. Others sat on the sidelines, in case. Children ran back and forth in front of our bleachers, hands full of licorice. If they stopped, the big girls on the bleachers pushed them along.

I smelled toothpicks dipped in cinnamon. They were against the rules during the day. Once Anne Abel brought them to class, in folded wax paper. She always gave me one. I didn't see her now.

I moved on in. Mary Margaret scrunched close to Doris, so I kept walking. *Please God, open a spot.* I was like on a gangplank. I didn't want to have to turn around and walk back, so I stood on the very end, bunched up with the cheerleaders, which I wasn't.

"Want to go to the bathroom?" Sue Anne's voice trailed. She didn't have a spot either. Her mother was divorced but that was okay with me.

I ran after her, flat-footing the floor like everyone else, following Sue Anne's pony tail.

In the daytime kids lined up and went into this bathroom two at a time. After, school—new rules. I bumped in that door with the crowd and banged my hip on the sink. The girls in the bathroom looked like popping corn. A big girl stood in front of the mirror. She pushed a bright pink lipstick in a gold case across her mouth, twirling the bottom so it went up and down. A small girl darted. I had to look hard to even know who was who, what to do.

A fourth grader dropped her jacks across the tile floor. A bag of marbles let fly. They clattered and shoes tipped off balance on the sprawling toys. A rotten apple stunk. What was I to do? A stall door swung open.

Cassie swung like a monkey from the overhead bar and she kicked the stall door with a twist, every swing. Jane Ann jumped from a radiator and swung-slammed into the next stall. Doors went every way if you kicked hard enough.

I could swing higher than Cassie. One bar was left. It felt like a jump rope was turning and I should jump in.

I ran under the transom windows, into a stall. I stepped up on the toilet rim, a swell pivot. I flexed my knees into a grande plié squat. I sprang, launching towards the gray metal bar, an audience of girls of every size beneath. I swung on my pipe. I was on stage.

"Yeow," I shrieked, a perfect primal basketball bathroom-stall swinging pagan scream. I knew I could. I twisted on my jungle-gym, calloused hands, gaining.

I was in jeans, after all. No petticoats nor free-swinging frizz. My underpants didn't show. A girl dangled in every stall opening now. They hung like clothespins on a rope. I grabbed a stall just in time or I would have been left out. My pony tail smacked my neck on the swings back, like go-go-go.

I angled sideways and changed direction. I threw my head back. I sang. "She *flies* through the *air* with the *greatest* of ease." I barely heard my own voice in the din.

My knees soared to my chest, my red Keds passing my head. Pump once and back, pump twice and back, big pump three. I pumped my last pump and sailed, body straight.

Pump five wasn't what I planned. My feet touched the glass window, just a little hit.

117

My head swiveled to see beneath. I tried to stay cool, but the pipe was wet. I slowed fast as I could, dropped my legs on down. My hands released. But the toilet was beneath.

It was kind of like trying to stay inbounds in basketball. One knee crashed on the lid, then into the toilet. It was like I was planted.

"Outta here," a girl shouted. I rolled gingerly onto the floor, against the wall, hugged my knees to my chest. Blood gushed.

"OW. Ow, ow, ow." I didn't hear one other sound but me. Girls flushed out the door, tiptoed on those sneakers. Wild eyes tossed snickers, at me.

I was solo again, just not quite how I'd planned. After school— way crazier than I thought.

* * *

At home, I said I'd fallen on a stick on the playground. I got a tetanus shot for my trouble. Probably germs on a toilet seat, anyway.

All the while Daddy grilled. Did someone push me?

He preached. But kids were kids, he finally said, with a shrug. I hadn't been attacked, no one even touched me. He told Mom it would leave a scar on my knee. It's still there.

But he'd made his point: one thing kids did was notice the one who was different. They picked the scab.

"No logic; it's what kids do," he said.

But inside I knew—the point was moot.

Maybe I brought this on myself.

I was a mini-*Glee*, sixty years early.

But we knew of no such thing in 1954. If I spent all my time in costumes and dancing, so be it.

Dancing was what mattered, my job.

But I was toast on the friend front.

22

Calling All Kids
to the Church Basement

H oly Family School in the daytime was much more nailed down. Sixty kids would do that every time, when they were all in one classroom. School desks, ten each row, lined up like six trains on wooden tracks, going nowhere.

I laid my head on my desk and my finger tapped the fountain pen, plopping ink into the well. Heat drifted on sunshine onto my back, through the row of half-open windows. *Varieties* rehearsals could start any day.

Sister Leontine sat at her desk at the front of the room. She clapped her hands and started her song. We picked up the melody,

Classroom of sixty. (School photo: Courtesy of Beth Obermeyer)

119

humming as we wrote. Nothing moved but our pen tips, but I have to say I never looked sideways to check.

The ink circles on the top line of my paper coiled out in rhythm, like a slinky. Every eight measures I'd start a new line.

The kids from two rows on my right were at the blackboard, clacking sums, our percussion. And in the cloakroom, children in the other two rows planned the afternoon play.

Sister just might have the best act in town, the way she got our class in a whirl.

Fifty years later I would be surprised. At our high school reunion, I found many did not love this nun as I did. I mentioned a different nun, one I had found difficult. And they loved that teacher.

It was what it was. Fifth and sixth grades—when we had Sister Leontine—that was the time of my life. Smooth.

That particular day I was antsy. Today Father Reed would choose his cast for *Varieties*. He was in choir practice that morning, bending to hear each voice.

My head on my desk with hands folded for meditation—I peeked. The shape of a nun hovered on the pebbled glass of the door! Our Sister Mary Leontine was swift. Holding her long rosary quiet by her side, she went to the door, slipped through the crack and out.

Our leather soles grated, under the desks. They could be talking about *Varieties*, those nuns.

Sister returned. "Sister Mary Franzeline has an announcement," she said.

"Father Reed has selected girls from each grade, for important roles in this year's *Varieties* show," Sister Franzeline announced. "They'll rehearse in the church basement, half a day, every day, for a month or more. Boys will be chosen tomorrow."

Our Sister Mary Leontine shot back, "They must color in their Marian books," she said. It was the year of Mary, Mother of God. Sister Leontine was new in town. My feet might as well have been plugged into an outlet.

"A message will come to your room," said the music nun. "Which children and when."

The two nuns connected their white buckram head frames, to talk more to each other.

"Not only that," I heard. I listened up! "Children and parents from public schools . . . practice all night . . . in our classrooms . . . After dark!"

"Lutherans!" said the other. "Adults—singing and dancing ones!" The white headgear lit their faces and their eyes crackled. "Perhaps God has blessed this town with music, Sister Mary Leontine. I believe we should be supportive." And with that Sister Mary Franzeline exited, back to her music room in the attic of the school.

We waited, so patient. Soon a gentler rattle came at the door. Germaine slid from her seat, head of the first row of desks. She opened the door a crack, grabbed a paper. She closed the door with a practiced *ca-lick-clack*. This seemed to take hours.

Sister Mary Leontine's face looked important, like when she asked one or two of us to stay after school to clean the blackboard. She unfolded the paper. "If you hear your name, you can proceed to my desk and directly to the door."

Yow, my name! And more. Names.

I squeaked off my seat, closed the slab on its hinge—shhh. I eased it against the desk back. My insides thrummed, but I walked to her desk to check out, with the others. *I was in the show!*

My knee burned when it flexed, all the way to her desk. Daddy couldn't put stitches on a knee, it would just have to heal and scar. He hadn't thought to warn—don't swing on the bar over the toilet. Not a lot was left to my judgment.

"I'll send work home with you," Sister said. "Use your time wisely. And be thankful for the talents God has given," she whispered, to each of us, like a litany.

Go, is what she meant.

My eyes held in a war whoop. We slipped through the door, a chosen bunch, slow as possible. Like firecrackers we were, lit and tossed to the hallway, sizzling to get outside before we popped.

We lined to the center of the hall. We had permission but we minded our feet, staying clear of hall doors, no silhouettes on the glass. At the granite stairs we escaped in a clatter of a gallop and slammed open the front doors of the school, into the light.

I was so in, in this group.

But I had to glance back. As I distanced, the school's window glass only reflected trees, like nobody was inside. But in one window on the first floor, the window was open, and two big high school girls sharpened their pencils.

23

The Whole Banana

Down the church stairs we zipped, past the telephone room, *shazam*, skidding into the bright light of the basement. We had to act big.

Father Reed, himself in person, leaned on the stage at the opposite end, handing out scripts. I warmed to see him again, his dark wavy hair, his swimming brown eyes. More big people drifted in the side doors. Father darted forward and tied to each one with a hand or a word or a smile. They landed in chairs, set up in rows, probably fifty already. I paced down the auditorium, past rows and rows, picked a chair on the end. I could swing my feet. We were the only kids so far.

Father rested his hands on the stage behind him, rattling his fingers on the wood in a rhythm. He winked at me, I was sure, a wink for a kid. The papers in his audience stopped crackling, a bit at a time. "We're all here, of course, because we're going to put on a show," Father Reed said.

I twisted to see the rows behind me. Where were the other grades? They must have stopped in the phone room to dial their mothers, to tell them. Being in the show was a bigger deal than making the basketball team. We thought so.

"Today we're going to read parts," Father said. "It's called . . . *Wishing World*." Mr. Harry Ross turned and passed back scripts. He and I had done lots of numbers together.

Father John Reed. My father's hat is on the piano. (Courtesy of Beth Obermeyer)

One day I would see Adrien Brody in *The Pianist*. Mr. Ross looked just like him.

Hushed giggles, chairs scraped. "C'mon, Father," I mumbled. If he were a tap dancer he'd have to start faster than this. People were going to start talking about hot dishes and furnaces if he didn't do his thing.

"The plot . . ." he said, his voice like church, only English. "Back-yard . . . wash blowing in the breeze . . . Irish . . . Jack sings "I'm a Yankee Doodle Dandy" . . . chocolate chip cookies . . . soft worn cotton dresses . . . singing policeman . . . old house." Five-hundred eyes sifted up to down, paper to stage. I counted.

(None of them had polio.)

"Second scene, sky, clouds, fog, rays of sun. No, look up . . . angels fly . . . Dorothy, you die!" Father pointed his eyes at Dorothy. The sun angled in from high windows in shafts. Even the dust spun.

I peeked behind. Who did Father pick? Henriette's blond page boy was shining under a navy ribbon. Margie was all over her script, so wise.

123

Seventh and eighth grade. Michaela wiggled in her chair, feet straight out, the baby of the group, only first grade, a round face in her Dutch bob. She was already my friend. But I was around these kids at school all the time, just not out of class.

Father waved his script and walked down the aisle. Paul MacCauley's hopeful eyes followed. Jim O'Reilly—a real-life policeman, was an eight-kids dad. He didn't bring them, of course. "If your part sings or dances, don't think about that," Father said. "Take the script home. Imagine tonight." I sniffed fresh purple ink, rolled from the mimeograph drum.

"Music and dance is synonomous with existing. That's why we are here." Well, that was vague. But it was crisp as the collar on his cossack.

"The show is in six weeks, public high school auditorium. I've picked *you* for parts, based on the past. If you know someone who would like to sing or dance or act or play, send them over." Sometimes he made up new roles.

"Remember, this is not a Holy Family show. This is a Mason City show . . . a story about wishes and worlds, heaven and earth. Every synagogue, church, school, family, person can do this. Weeks of nights and matinees, so get your calendar. You'll find dates, last page. Now, let's turn to page twenty-one, the cast."

My fingers jumbled. What would my dad say about all these people? He did not like crowds. I'd looked them over. They looked healthy to me.

Oh, my gosh, it was in my lap all the time, whatever my part was to be. There it was, the purple words. "Mary Beth—next column—character name: Debbie." I fumbled through to find what Debbie did.

Like Debbie Reynolds?

Oh, Jack Johnson would be my brother, Lanny! He could sing up a storm and learn the dances too. He did last year. And now he was in eighth grade. Mr. Ross would be my father. I loved that. Right below Mr. Ross's name was "Lance" from cross town: he'd be my uncle. Except his father was a chiropractor.

Father Reed closed on us kids now; he sat. "*You*, my ladies." Every one of us giggled like we were burping pop. "You are going to be spirits in the heaven scene. Henriette, your face will be painted blue and yellow. Others will be green, yellow, red, and purple." Our squirmy rows came to a standstill.

"Mary Beth," he said.

I braced, tucking my shoes behind the cross bar of the chair. "You will dance in a white nightgown." I bounced shoulders with girls on either side. "The scene is a dream."

Father moved on, across the aisle, to talk to the barbershop quartet.

Did I have a solo?

Father stood, faced us all. "Mabel is not able to be here this year." I flattened my script on my skirt, as though if I leveled the page Mabel's name could get back on the list.

"Sister Mary Franzeline sent two pianists to take her place. We'll see how that goes." His eyes promised: "It will go well. Shorty on drums. Ralph Height, Jr., piano."

He bowed his head. "But let us take a moment to think about our friend, Mabel Kelso, our town's music woman."

"Although her body no longer is able to make music, her spirit is with us." His eyes raised, searched the audience. "Perhaps you can visit her at the home and show her your song or your dance. Mabel has always been here for us, and we can't forget."

Would they? Visit Mabel? Would it help? Could we replace her music for her, the music she used to make?

"We'll break into groups," he said. If you have lines, stay here to read. Girls, to the stairs. Kay the choreographer will be here soon."

A clatter started. Where should I go? Lines or Kay and the girls? Father continued. "River City Quartet over here." A hushed hum developed in concentric circles, all about.

Father came back. He stopped at me: "Start memorizing lines, tonight," he said. "You and Jack have the leads, plus many song and dance numbers."

I'd never had a speaking part! Jack had, Mr. Ross had, but I always came onstage to dance and sing and leave. *This was the whole banana.*

And then—a Lilac Girl plopped next to me. And her red lips relaxed. She clicked drumsticks in rhythms on the chair in front of us. Couldn't help it—I kept time. She pushed at me, laughing!

Danny hitched his pants and plowed his shoulder into me, rough-housing too with the boy, other side. The glorious sing and dance and have friends days of *Varieties*. We had begun.

Elves in rehearsal: Mickey Lannon, Beverly Frank, Henriette Hebel, Margie Hubbard, Mary Winger, Kathleen Skram, and Virginia Courchane. (Courtesy of the *Mason City Globe Gazette*)

24

Rehearsals

Eight girls for the Heaven scene raced about the auditorium, like their heads were cut off, waiting for Kay the choreographer.

And Kay—in she *whooshed*. She was barely taller than I was. Her black hair was rolled under, her bangs too. I knew a secret. Her suitcase was in Donna Jean's bedroom at my house, and that's where she'd stay through the month of rehearsals, and a bit into the run. It was only a secret because if I said it, it sounded like bragging.

Lucille's mother dusted chairs, watching. How proud she must be to be the mother of a girl in Kay's heaven scene. Somehow, that day Lucille looked more beautiful than ever, with her long neck and rounded forehead.

Kay whipped out her ribbons, one for every hand. "You are elves. Close your eyes and think 'elf.' What does an elf think about? How does an elf run, walk, sleep. What do they eat? What is your elf's favorite color? Create your elf, inside yourself."

"The elf in my *self*," said Mickey, her eyes saying she was the best elf.

We cavorted about. The ribbons snaked and whipped and dragged and flew. When Kay clapped, we dropped the ribbons right where we were. We followed their pattern, jumping to another ribbon when a strip ended. Like playing kick the can, zigging, zagging, only with music.

Mr. Ross held his music sheet far out, an Irish song. "H-A-double-R-I . . . G-A-N." He spelled "Harrigan" as he sang. Probably ten Lilac Girls kept drums in rhythm.

The most beautiful dance I had ever seen continued. No one even had a lesson. Free dancing was so different from learning a pattern. It was different every time we did it. It had the joy of hop scotch. No one dancer was best. They bounced, escaped, quite perfect. Truly contagious, the joy of this dance, soft and wild.

Finished, we sat in a circle. Henriette asked Kay about the colored faces, just checking, she said.

"The colors don't matter," said Kay.

I didn't get what Father meant with all those colors of faces that year, not until decades later. He ended the minstrelsy. It didn't go easy, minstrels were common in towns around, too. I danced in Garner's "Bigtop Varieities" for years. The "Mary Beth Sartor in minstrel show," headline jars me now.

That year the *Globe* only said "Varieties." The program cover, however, a beautiful art stairway to heaven, still said *Darktown Varieties*. Whoever put new dates on just didn't notice.

The next year the theme had Uncle Tom's cabin except it was hilarious, a gas station on a highway. "Unlike the average minstrel show, this builds up to Mardi Gras," said the *Globe*. "Comedy and vaudeville." Mabel had played for silent movies, after all. I'd tap-danced on the apron of a moving picture stage, common before film fare in her day. We were dancing on the cusp.

But all I "got" that year, 1954, was that in heaven we would be all different colors. Father Reed didn't tell us. He showed us.

Varieties, music, the dance.

And I loved I had friends.

Music changes everything.

Program cover. (Central Show Printing; Coutesy of Beth Obermeyer)

25

Can I?

I screamed into my house, waving my script. My knee was shrieking. I tried to hide the hobble. Mom! Daddy!"

"Where have you been?" My mother was waiting. "It was time to practice dance two hours ago," she said. Her box of polished limestones sat along the window sill behind her, all sparkled up with nowhere to go.

"I've got a script!" I slung myself on the barstool. My fingers stuttered through the papers to the cast page. "Even the biggest Lilac Girl and her friends are in it." Mom pulled a few sheets at a time to her apron, careful so her wet hands didn't make the purple run. She sat, spent a few seconds each miraculous page.

Daddy ambled into the kitchen and placed his doctor bag on the counter. He straightened the combs and bobby pins like they were tongue blades and cotton swabs.

But he couldn't miss Mom's eyes. They shined, the first time in a long time. "Oh, the costumes I could make," she said, to him.

"The dances *I* can make!" I said to her.

"Why do you two talk so fast?" Daddy said. He swung his head, did his goofy look. "I have a *great* . . . Why don't you *both* get all the ideas!"

"Let's see," said Julie, hiking herself on her elbows onto the counter, another country heard from. She slung a leg across the island, straddled it.

But it was my moment and I blurted it out: "Surely. I can go. The rehearsals are in a church basement. That makes it all right? Right?"

I had a good point? It was *in the church.* Just school kids in day practices. Well, some theatre folk.

Surely polio wasn't in a church. He'd okayed the stage on the lake after all.

Daddy arranged the handles of his bag, up, then back. I almost turned thirteen, waiting.

"We'll see . . . we'll see. We'll see." Begging seldom worked but away I went.

"Can't I just do the rehearsals and we'll decide later?" But he put out his gauze, his cotton balls, the alcohol. He lined my leg on the counter. Hanna was not in sight, thank the stars.

That was her pie-crust rolling spot. He went to work, spiffing up my knee.

I closed my eyes, dropped out of the world. Daddy always said as long as the counter got wiped clean with Phisohex, we were good.

My leg vibrated in spite of myself but this was better than the mercurochrome they used at school, like sliding down a razor blade into a pool of alcohol.

I kept on with my better thoughts. Julie grabbed her moment. She sang her "Davy Crockett" for Mom. By verse three, Mom and Daddy were talking. I listened up this time.

"I think music is good for the brain." It's what Daddy said!

That was a yes? I slung my leg back, he was done, and grabbed a crayon and the script. I started through, underlining my part. The script was mine?

"Mason City's secret weapon on those Iowa Basic Skill Tests," Daddy said. "Because Iowa kids are on record, among the smartest kids in the country. And Iowa has more marching bands than Missouri." Education was up there with his car and the fan and the clock.

So music improved education. But did education trump health was what I was wondering? Or church was the key? I did not know.

Mom and I held our breath. Julie eased onto my lap and I let her color the page, just a little. Bobby pulled the back page off the clip and got Mom to fold it into a fan.

It was our triumph, Mom's and mine, and the end of a perfect day.

26

The Last Darktown Varieties

The weeks of rehearsals flew like feathers in a chicken coop, keeping Mason City in a buzz. Finally it was dress rehearsal and Father Reed stood in the dark orchestra pit, stripped to his undershirt and dark trousers. He leaned on the stage at the public high school.

His glowing white collar hung over his chest. Stage grime and stubble darkened his chin. Dust flew like gnats over the footlights. "That's it, house lights up," he said. Lighting cables popped and crackled, sliding on the balcony floor.

On stage, our cast of hundreds, rumbled words, in a pulse. It was emergency dress rehearsal number three. Heads hung low, so low the sound fell to the floor and rolled around our feet. We were supposed to be ready to go and we were not.

Officer Riley ripped open the buttons on his jacket and blew air through his mouth. He didn't look like a policeman. Baby Face the Crook stood at the back of the stage. He stroked the layered paint on the scrim and it billowed in a gentle wave, like thunder.

"Light cues were in the wrong time zone," Father said, his mouth a wry slant. "I don't care if you have to pull the rope all the way to the mens' bathroom. The curtain has to open all the way. I never even saw the alto section."

"Maybe they *were* in the men's room," a voice joked.

"I'm going to be tarred and feathered if this show comes off like it just did. A lot of people have spent a great deal of money to get us this far. Opening night is three hours away."

My chest went into a figure eight, inside. I'd never seen Father this angry. Not in all the years of *Varieties*. Connie had got her skirt caught in the revolving stage and it pulled her in circles. One set couldn't roll up, and the next one didn't drop all the way so the stage was half alley and half heaven. Paul got sick right on the stage, and we danced around it.

Father Reed leaped up and over the apron of the stage. He pulled me to an "X" on the floor. I'd ended three feet off. He read a page, another page, pages of notes, right over my head, spittle flying. "That was no show," he said, ending in a shout. He dropped the sheaf of papers to the floor. He dropped to one knee and clutched his head. "Folks. Brethren. You may be seated." He closed his eyes until every sound stopped.

"You tried hard. I know you did." Father Reed, with his dimples and pursed lips, looked like Eddie Fisher but on a very bad day. "You know the lines, the songs, the dances. Don't worry about that any more. Paint the picture in your head, the way you'll look on this stage in a few hours. Close your eyes. Now." He pulled to his feet, plunged hands in his pockets. He dragged his feet, nodded as he paced.

"You have to believe in yourself. Don't act. *Be* the person." My eyes burned from the dust. The piano tinkled, a little rehearsal over there as well. Father's eyes searched, face to face, forcing us to look at him. "Before you go on stage, close your eyes. Use the think method. Think. How should it look?" The words floated away and came back. Father tapped his script and accented the first word of every sentence.

I wished fresh air from the painted sky would spill over us. Father was talking to just plain people here, did he forget? To this day I wonder: is *The Music Man* really fiction? I was just like Mrs. Paroo . . . standing in a gym waiting for the townspeople to suddenly know how to sing and dance when they did not especially one month ago.

If Meredith were here, he'd name this man in Meredith speak, a bang beat, bell-ringer of a fellow, of that I was sure. Father Reed was indeed Meredith's every time a bellringer type.

Soon Father's voice was staccato, like a pep talk. Voices behind me chugged and voices from above whispered. Everyone was either starting to stand or standing. I propped myself beside Mr. Ross.

"Debbie and Lanny." Father called us by our show names and pulled us together by the shoulders. "Work to do on the 'I'll Take Manhattan' number. Nothing wrong, need to add some moves and lines for Debbie. Some reactions for Lanny. Stay after and we'll start with you, just the one song." Then barbers, then angels.

People moved to small groups, like rain drops on a car window. They talked low, some drifting towards the wings. Was Father catching all the stray threads? If they fixed all this, would our story come through? "The rest back here, costume and full make-up, 7:00 p.m. before curtain. We'll finish the loose ends. You can do it."

My Angel Child costume stuck to my wet arms and the organdy scratched my neck. If only I was taller, stuff probably wouldn't smell. But at five-foot-two, my nose was halfway between sweaty feet and stale make-up and right in the middle of wool suits. Everyone was gone from the stage but me and Jack. Ralph Height, Jr., leaned over the piano in the pit, and Father Reed leaned over him. Horns left upright in chairs waited for new direction. Ralph, then Father Reed, then Ralph, scribbled and slapped the music. We had the best. I scratched my hairline at the make-up edge.

It was great to have friends in the show, but when it was time to go on, we'd be on our own, sink or swim. My mother wouldn't like that Father changed my dialogue at the last minute.

After my rehearsal, Mom and I walked through backstage. "Mom, it's okay. It's the finale. I won't be the only thing moving on the stage." We hurried to Room 213.

We were learning to give and get something back. Collaborate. Musicians, costumers, designers, and sound and lighting technicians, ticket takers, ushers. We mixed with other kids, public school ones.

Sometimes a scene got cut that made the show too long. We had to read the cast notes before each rehearsal to know what had changed.

I had to trust the pulley when I flew over the stage in my nightgown in the heaven scene. I had to rehearse a solo over and over so the cast got their parts with me, and me with them, even when I had mine down. I spent nights learning the group dance in the heaven scene. Everyone gave to make the whole show. And gave and gave, tired, sick, busy. Boy did they believe Father Reed. Anybody could learn this, sing, dance, anything, that's what he said.

Two hours later, the classroom filled, with rows of people getting made up. Mrs. Camiotti leaned close and dotted little red spots to the inner corner of my eyes, to make them appear larger. She drew extra black

The 1954 Varieties. "This year's show is a trend toward musical comedy and away from the old-style minstrel show used in the past," *Mason City Globe Gazette*. Leads: Mother, Dorothy Gettman; Father, Harry Ross; Sons, Jack Johnson, James Grell; Daughter, Mary Beth Sartor; other lead roles, Dorothy Wilson, Tom Pattee, Carlos Melendez, Gary Nolterieke, Helmer Kapplinger, Ann Good, Tommy Huffstetler, Kay McGuire. Front row Cherubs: Loralette Austin, Janis Budzius, Linda Meinecke, Michaela Lannon, and Mary Kay Wiltgen. (Photo, Elwin Musser; Courtesy of *Mason City Globe Gazette*)

eyelashes on the outer corners. Lipstick on a brush curved up the corners of my upper lip. Powder puffs flew.

Mrs. Melendez leaned from the next table, frowning over her palette of make-up. "Debbie, don't you sneeze. Your eyes will smear." I was Debbie now, a product of many people.

So it was Debbie, not me, who walked down the tiled hallway to Room 203 to change into her Act I costume.

Father said my dress had to look like I was playing in a backyard. Mom had a hard time with "not fancy." My skirt was pink and white pin-striped, the top a pink vest laced over a dotted swiss blouse, no petticoat. She had to give in, and it was good Father didn't get as far as the shoes. Mom didn't know shoes could be anything but white . . . no leeway there.

Daniel walked ahead of me, keeping that rhythm, shaking the white bones in his hand. "Darktown" may be leaving just *Varieties*, but Father left just Daniel and his bones in the heaven scene.

Daniel could jerk his arm straight and immediately set those spoons to "sprattling like a shinny stick on a picket fence," as Meredith said in his book. He couldn't just quit, no sir. I wasn't sure which guy Daniel was out of black face. Was he really white under the make-up or was he very dark?

27

Sparkle Time

Fifteen minutes to curtain. Father Reed poked his head in Room 203. He started to sing as though he had just thought of the show. His voice boomed: "Another Openin', Another Show." Whatever Father Reed did, we grabbed like a lifeline. A Pied Piper he was.

And when the man danced—well, there was only one Father Reed. Another half minute and we grouped backstage left, quiet. The only light spilt under the curtain, from the auditorium.

Each song in the orchestra's overture belonged to someone; each melody lit different faces. The audience crackled programs and coughed, their last chance before they fell into the story. The curtain moved as a few took their place. Hot cones of dust whirled over footlights. I slid my fingers over a hanging rope by the curtain and let the slivers prick, so I'd know I was real.

No one peeked through the curtain at the audience, not professional. Each of us stood like a painted statue and looked at different things: the corner of the piano, the mop bucket, the canvas back of the stage, our "think system." The cast was so large it filled backstage and the hallways of the second floor of the high school. It was surprising there was anyone left in town to be the audience.

A little town of people ran about over our heads, too, on boards with ropes and headphones. Okay, I peeked out the curtain to see the control booth, faces frozen in place, their jaws hanging, waiting.

The chorus marched up and down in front of the curtain. From our side they were shoes under the curtain, dents in the velvet. That year they sang, the "No Business." The crowd screamed, already.

Our eyes darted in a countdown to curtain. We just hoped: no surprises. I wiggled my toes in my shoes. I had to pee. No, I didn't.

I touched my toes, legs straight, humming my song. I was full of every move and song and line. I couldn't wait to get out there, like nobody's business.

Whoosh. Like night with a bright sun, I was on. The lines started. Wait for the laugh.

Act One.

Eight counts and I was on Lanny's knee, singing. Father Reed, from the orchestra pit, pushed his palms towards each other. That meant get closer to the mike. We did.

The light level changed. I could only see the first two rows of the audience. They clapped and turned, bumped noses and back.

Father raised one finger, telling the orchestra to take the first ending and repeat the strain they were playing, to stretch over the applause. He closed his fist for the orchestra to stop.

I rushed off the stage, behind a cotton net bush, to change from tap shoes. The bush wasn't real but it seemed normal.

Another song and Act I curtains closed like a wind. I turned and ran. The backyard painting rolled up, right on time.

Costume change behind the Act II horse. Button up, hair brush, drink water. Never saw this person before. Maybe because it was too dark backstage? My organdy nightgown, light as a petal. I pulled on the harness to fly across stage. I tested my bounce. A man held my rope.

Act Two.

Stars sparkled in the sky. My friends with colored grease-paint faces, the elves. I crawled back onstage through a crack in the curtain, to a fog, a choking fog, for my "Angel Child" song and dance, following the ribbons with elves for awhile, flying through the air, into Mr. Ross's arms.

We dipped behind the curtain and I twisted to help the men get me out of the straps. Swoop. Back onstage. Mr. Ross picked me up high, held me inches from his face and sang. I stared into his red lipstick, shiny tonsils wavered in his throat. He'd eaten spaghetti for supper. Whiskers dotted through his pink make-up. Sweat dripped past the red eye dots.

"Angel child, I'm just wild about you . . ." Mr. Ross sang the words against the inside of his cheeks, and they blasted four inches, into my face. Why do singers come so close together? It looked right from the audience, I knew. To make a tight picture. He gripped me so hard I felt a pinch on my sides, between my ribs. It must be hard to hold me high in the air and sing at the same time.

Mary Beth Sartor, eleven, Jack Johnson, thirteen, doing "I'm a Yankee Doodle Dandy." (Photo: Elwin Musser; Courtesy of the *Mason City Globe Gazette*)

Backstage: Elves in Heaven with all-color faces. Left to right: standing: Kathleen Skram, Beverly Frank, Henriette Hebel, Mary Beth Sartor, Margie Hubbard, Mary Winger, and Virginia Courchane; seated: Mickey Lannon. (Courtesy of Beth Obermeyer)

Whoosh, I was off, dancing, turning. I pushed my dress into turns, slow at first, the hem of skirt ruffles heavy. I picked up speed.

But my skirt caught the curtain, slowed. I wished I could turn inside of the costume.

No more vocal. I no longer touched the hug of the man with the song. No rattling sounds from tap shoes, either.

Horns from the orchestra to one ear, violins to the other. I bent with the strings. The perfume of dance caught the strains from the orchestra. I was alone, in black and light.

The wind from my turns threw dust and hot light in my nose. A brush to soar through air to fly, not grab and land. Air came on music like bird wings.

My forehead pulsed the rhythm of Shorty Bickford's drums. The head Lilac Girl bounced alongside him, up and down on her stool, drumming, grinning.

More floor came up to meet. More marbles under the skin brought me down to land, not shatter. Hands clapped the music bubbles away. Light and dark found my body, spun my head.

Dance. Better than food. I was not a kid when I danced to this music. I could never be at peace unless I could do what I could do.

Everything in life led to a dance, first for myself, hold tight; then let fly to an audience.

But the sound of clapping made me know, I was here, not a spirit. The back and forth of the

Backstage: Harry Ross and Mary Beth. (Courtesy of Beth Obermeyer)

dance with the audience, the joy. I thanked Father Reed every day for the day he said yes.

Lights. Black.

Down in fog, I sat in organdy, wood slivering. No more effort. My insides pounded. My breathing went up and down. The curtain rumbled over my dress; whoops. I'd missed my mark, the taped "X" on the floor. The curtain billowed, open, closed, the claps loud, soft. Lights blared behind the curtain. The invisible voice boomed: "Fifteen minutes. Intermission." The audience headed in a noise from the auditorium.

The nightgown went up and over and gone. My pink-and-white cotton dress and dotted-swiss blouse slipped over my head, from Agnes the dresser.

Act III.

I sang with Jack, our voices braiding, my taps accenting. Now I had to think about Father's changes. I maintained eye contact with Jack and we did it.

A breather offstage. The show wrapped up. An armful of roses, so soft and red. I bowed, ecstatic. I'd never been this happy in my entire life.

In the balcony Daddy sat over his his reel to reel recorder, getting it all for Mabel.

I so wanted to plug the music back into her.

140

28

The Curtain Comes Down

All the fun making music, getting the show just right. Everyone was in such great moods. The Lilac Girls got along. The kids had fun, me too. But now. I had all the time in the world. I splatted my hand on the water in the tub, watched the rings form and disappear.

Everyone in *Varieties* was back to jobs in stores and factories and farms, school, back to friends, away to their own churches. Kids were back to being kids.

The night before my mother had unfolded the *Globe Gazette* in the living room. "Oh," she'd said, with a quick intake of air. "Listen to this! The 'Bouquet of the Week' goes to Mary Beth Sartor and Jack Johnson." She turned the paper to Daddy and tapped the square at the bottom corner of the editorial page, the one with roses. She glowed triumphant, from her eyebrows to her chin.

"The youth . . ." She pushed her glasses better. "Oh, listen to this." She spread on her back on the velvet sofa, paper overhead. The paper rippled. Her toes pointed in glee.

"'The youth carried the show on their backs, two children shining like stars, covering themselves and the entire cast of *Varieties* with glory. They sang and danced themselves into the hearts of Mason Citizans.'" The photo of me poised on Jack's knee was right there in the paper.

"Really," my dad said. "But really, this is for *everyone* in the show, because it would be just as true if the bouquet had gone to Harry Ross. Or to Father Reed for directing and writing the script. And it's about the entire town, not just Holy Family."

True. But it said—me! And I was hanging on to those roses.

But who cared anyway, all I could think. The shows in town were drying up, just as Daddy said. Everyone was home with their TVs. I soaked, withered in my Saturday night tub, the washcloth soothing my eyes.

And then there was the polio epidemic—I couldn't go in crowds. I could not think of one other place to dance that had fresh air like Clear Lake did on that floating stage. Clear Lake did have the market on fresh air. Well, there was that string of cottages, dozens, connected by one long back porch that followed the shoreline. I was five, one of my first programs to dance-out. It was the Outing Club. I could tap away and enjoy the scenery, too, that lake behind the audience. I blubbered through the washcloth, feeling tight for fresh air, the more I thought about it.

Who cares. Nothing nice will ever happen again.

Here's what I knew, and I'd learned it well: I had friends from school *in Varieties,* long as we made music together. I didn't have any friends *at* school.

Dancing was easy. Being a kid was not.

The bathroom window panes blurred with moisture.

I wanted to scream but no one at my house ever did.

Bil Baird: Babes in Toyland on the Television

FEBRUARY 1955

I leaned on my closet door. What to wear. I rubbed cold toes on the back of the other leg, indecisive. With all my growing that winter, my shadow looked a bit like Redi Kilowat—the jagged lightning bolt cartoon fellow on the electric company sign. To boot, I even looked a bit like a stork in a costume.

Redi Kilowatt statuette. (Courtesy of Beth Obermeyer)

But that was going to be the night Bil Baird's puppets were on national television. Bil had made it, through the wars. His mother was coming to watch our television set: Daddy said. Wow, I had to say it: "Wow." Bil Baird, a professional puppeteer, grew up right across the alley.

What to wear? What I was really thinking: TV. *Fly on TV.* I was thinking more . . . *me.*

The red-quilted skirt seemed to jump out of the closet. I fingered down its length onto the black loopy appliquéd dog. He had an embroidered leash. He looked like a puppet on a string. I would take Mrs. Baird's hand, trace her finger over the threads.

I stepped into the waist of the skirt and snapped it over my blouse. I snapped the vest and tugged the points, twirling the skirt for the mirror. I swear I'd grown an inch a month since *Varieties.* But in the starched white of the shirt, the black corduroy of the vest and the red circle quilt of the skirt, I felt just right.

The clock in the entry chimed five. I headed down the hall, my loafers quiet on the carpet. I pulled into the kitchen, the last to supper. I slid into the chair. I squeezed my half slice of Wonder Bread to balls, the quicker to eat.

Soon Daddy wiped the corners of his mouth with his bib. "Mary Beth," he said, "help me tune the television. What's the name of Bil's show?"

I slid past my mother and scooted to the den to kneel in front of the TV. My dad leaned behind the set, turning the antenna dial. His TV was even more precious to him now than his Scott radio, it seemed. I hoped he didn't move on from me to a newer model! Sometimes he said to me, "How tall are you?" He'd answer himself, "That's tall enough."

Julie rattled the door of the den and peeked through the panes. My mother clinked dishes in the sink.

My job, he said, was to watch the screen and tell him when it went from soapsuds to fuzzy shapes. When I recognized the Revlon spray-net can on a commercial, he was elated. I felt smart. Satisfied with his TV picture, he headed out to get Mrs. Baird.

Soon the back gate squeaked. Daddy and Mrs. Baird glided up the walk, almost as though ice skating, stepping right, then left, together. Mrs. Baird tipped her face up to the remaining light, eyes closed, as though she could see the air through a circle of lips. Daddy knew just how to support her.

A tall chair waited for her in the den, and Mom positioned it just in time. I stood behind it while she unbuttoned her coat. Hanging onto the shoulders of the coat, I lowered it softly so as not to startle her. My mom frowned. "Oh my, Julie, we should have had you in bed."

Right. Mrs. Baird was *my* friend, after all. I was the one who slipped over to her house to visit. LuLu Baird and I were best friends. My dad called her LuLu. I didn't, not out loud. Rarely he called my mother LuLu because her name was Luella. So it sounded okay at our house.

"Tonight it's *Babes in Toyland*," Mrs. Baird said. "You have to tell me what you see. Don't skip anything. Julie will like it, too." She patted Julie's sweater and smiled.

Julie wedged herself between Daddy's chair and ottoman and the television, casually hanging her arm over his legs. She tangled his shoelaces.

Her round face sure didn't look sleepy. Kids at school said that face looked like Darla on *The Little Rascals,* the curly hair. She was a doll. Mrs. Baird couldn't see that.

"We have at least ten minutes before it starts," I said. This had to be one of the biggest moments in Mrs. Baird's life. My dad was thrilled to please her, I could see.

A commercial started and Mrs. Baird leaned forward. "Horse Clown is my favorite. You watch and tell me what he does." Julie spun to the center of the floor to see.

I moved closer to Mrs. Baird. I wished I could be alone with her. Maybe my parents would take Julie to bed, or go in the kitchen. But they all stayed put.

Horse Clown turned out to be a wooly horse with a skirt and wooden bulging eyes, so alive. Mrs. Baird said the horse was red and somehow I did picture him in color. On his back was a clown with a pointy nose. His clown shoes were plenty enough feet.

Julie wiggled on the floor, the pennies in her taps jingling. "Julie," Daddy said, in a whisper. "You'll bump Mrs. Baird." He hoisted himself on his long legs and stretched his monkey arms. "Beer break," he said.

"Popcorn," my mother said, with a bound.

"Not a beer drinker myself," Mrs. Baird said. My mother didn't approve of alcohol except for beer. And she did like her beer. Mom and Daddy left for the kitchen but not before Mom sent Julie upstairs to put on her pajamas.

I put my hand on Mrs. Baird's knee, so she'd know I was still there. "I can't believe," I said, "that Bil's on television. In New York."

She reached out a hand to find my shoulder. Her eyes closed, as they did sometimes, when she had to brag. "My Bil has a show on television, every week, *Whistling Wizard.* He loves doing television." She arranged her shawl. "I want to tell you something while we're alone. Life takes some strange turns sometimes. I'll miss you, but I'm moving to New York to be with Bil."

I could not believe my ears, not what I expected. I shuddered. "Do you want to go?"

"Bil has a new project, far down the line. A film is going to be made about an Austrian family. The seven Von Trapp children do a scene and he'll create large puppets and a playhouse. It's set in the Alps. The music is "The Lonely Goatherd." It sounds like a lot of music to me, this show."

All exciting, and I wanted to say something nice. But I couldn't. "Now even you are up and leaving. Everything's happening at once. Dean's going to Chicago. He'll tap dance on *Ed Sullivan's!* Father Reed—transferred." I still was not over that! And Mabel, poor Mabel. "You all just fly away away, and stroke."

"Well don't you sound like a frumpy little lady."

I flopped my head back and threw my legs out straight. I clunked my feet so she'd hear, banged so hard the TV picture jiggled.

"Mary Beth. I can't tell you what you're supposed to do. But this lull, if you grab it, is an opportunity. Keep dancing. You'll get better and better. And you know, there's something more you could do while you wait for the next great solo."

"What."

"What do you expect? Oh, I know. Everyone left you for bigger places. But you're sitting right here with everything they gave you. Now what do you think could happen next. You're a smart girl."

Dean Diggins heads for Chicago and New York with The Mattison Trio. (Courtesy of Dean Diggins)

"I have no idea what you're talking about." My voice sounded rude but I was exasperated. "Not sugar, sprinkled from fairies."

"We grow as things change. *Varieties* even changes and goes. But some things stay and look different, but they stay. What do you think stays?"

"The puppet."

It was a good thing Mrs. Baird couldn't see my face. Mrs. Baird's mouth pressed tight, like she might give up on me.

"Music. Music stays *in* you. Dance stays."

I sat and mutzed and I knew it but I didn't know how to turn things around gracefully. But I *was* thinking about what Mrs. Baird was saying. "Is the music still in Mabel?" I asked?

Before she could answer, if there was an answer, Julie was back and buzzing about. So far she was only into her Carter jammie tops and underpants, still in tap shoes.

Soon she was on her feet and her noisy tap rhythms clicked on the plastic carpet protector by Daddy's chair. Her curls bobbed as she hung onto the chair arms, the better to do her riffs. The sounds clicked, five from one foot, one from the other, clear as could be. Julie was good.

"Mrs. Baird. Did Bil have a brother?" I couldn't help but sigh over the clatter.

"Oh, yes, yes."

"What does he do now?"

"Right now he is in New York with Bil, helping him with his puppet theatre."

"Does Bil like that?"

"Oh, yes, he is a great help. He likes to do everything Bil does."

I closed my eyes. Mrs. Baird couldn't see anyway. The air got even tighter around me when Julie closed in with her *tap-tap-tap*.

30

Julie Lands in My Lap

Mom and Daddy and Mrs. Baird laughed and talked their talk. The rest of the show flew. Julie climbed on Daddy's lap and emptied his shirt pocket of tongue blades and flashlight. She shined it in my eyes and then put it all back, something she'd done since she was two. Daddy leaned back, smiled, content.

"Bil's going to be in a big movie and do a puppet scene," I told them all. I wanted to show off to my parents that I knew Mrs. Baird better than they did.

"So we could go to the State Theater and see him in a movie?" my mother said. "What's it about?"

"A nun who leaves the convent and falls in love with a captain who has seven children."

I nearly fell over. Mrs. Baird was protestant. She had no idea what it was to say such a thing.

Right on the downbeat, my mother said: "Oh, then we won't go to this movie. Nuns do not marry."

"Stranger things happen in real life, I'm afraid. It's a true story," Mrs. Baird said.

"Does everybody go and get divorced?" I asked. My mother didn't like Meredith Willson, Jackie Gleason, Frank Lloyd Wright. That was a lot of not liking. My mother even worried why Dean didn't get married! "Is Bil divorced, Mrs. Baird?"

"Well, yes, as a matter of fact he is."

"Divorce is a mortal sin," said my mother. Daddy leaned his head back on his chair.

"Mrs. Baird, have you ever tried dandelion wine?" Daddy asked.

"Do you have some, Dr. Sartor?"

He pulled to his feet. "I ate dandelions in salad when I was a kid," he said.

"Dandelion *wine*," said Mrs. Baird. "Why, when I was a girl, I would put my sunbonnet on early in the spring, for shade and to keep my ears warm. Before the plants blossom, you pick the leaves," she said, like my mom might take notes. "Take the roots too, so they stay fresh. Add watercress for a peppery taste. I made my own dressing. Oh, my, four quarts of blossoms or so will make you wine. Add a lemon and two oranges. And four handfuls of dandelions plus lemon and sugar make you syrup. Doctors use it for get up and go." She laughed and Daddy did too. My mom had no opinion.

Okay, the night was winding down, or so I thought.

A commercial came on. I paid it no attention. I was down to worrying about whether Mrs. Baird would send a Christmas card with Bil's drawing on it or forget us. All of a sudden, my mother threw her legs out and planted them, apart. "Look. At. That!" She was on her feet.

The man on TV talked on, his mouth clapping like Charlie McCarthy. "A big talent contest . . . coming to the fairs in the area . . ."

I slapped my hands over my face. "What dance would I do? Mom? 'Deep Purple?'" I opened my arms wide, a done deal. "Deep Purple."

A Bil Baird family Christmas card. (Photo courtesy of Anne Abel)

149

Grown-up, "Deep Purple," thirteen. (Courtesy of Beth Obermeyer)

But—even so—it's hard to get a standing ovation—but those that could stand did!

The applause, more applause than I could get alone, I knew, and the dance *was* snappy.

Julie looked a bit taller to me than she had. Our mother, our father, Mrs. Baird, their faces "beamed like a quarter to three." Those were Meredith words, Mason City talk.

Maybe if I cleaned up the dance, it could be fun.

Maybe Julie was a gift from heaven?

But it wouldn't be like Bil's brother helping with Bil's idea. I would have to do Julie's dance with her. Not new or exciting territory for me, not at all. But . . .

"Now that's an act," said Mrs. Baird. "And I'm going to make a prediction: Someday I'll come watch your television set, Dr. Sartor, the *Ted Mack Original Amateur Hour.* Mr. Ted Mack will spin his wheel of fortune and say . . . 'From Mason City, Iowa! Round and round they go; where they stop, nobody knows!'"

I could not believe my ears. Mrs. Baird thought a sister act was special. That meant something. And my mother's eyes stilled, large and blue, like Julie's. "Ted Mack does his show in Radio City Music Hall," she said. "That's huge."

New York!

"Maybe I just need a bigger TV studio," I said, clapping a bit now. And then I got carried away. "Maybe we *could both twirl lariats.*"

I sat down by Mrs. Baird and wrapped my arms around myself, my eyes on my own taps. My mother was thinking the Lennon Sisters, minus two, I knew.

Julie plopped on my skirt. I couldn't get away from her now if I wanted to. And I didn't want to. But I'd had so much fun, making my own dances just right.

"You could all come visit me in New York," said Mrs. Baird, onto something new . . . and then she told my mother about the move.

Daddy was done. He inched out the big Scott radio from the wall and squeezed behind the back to look at its insides. Bobby, awakened by the noise, had climbed out of his crib and crawled behind with Daddy. Bobby loved to take things apart. It was something they had in common, something they did together.

Dancing at twelve. (Courtesy of Beth Obermeyer)

My mother marched to the kitchen and came back, a beer and a silver opener, flashing like a sword. She meant business. "Did you hear that?" she said. If you win, you go to New York for the *Ted Mack Amateur Hour.* Could it be bigger? Maybe we're not ready this year, but they'll do it again and again, I'm sure."

New York, my dream! "I could . . . 'Deep Purple' for sure. I could . . . well . . ." I waited.

"It might be hard to win by yourself," she said. What she didn't say was that I wasn't a cute four-year-old dancing in baby shoes. I wasn't even the compact eleven-year-old I'd been a year and a month ago. I was thirteen. Now when I danced I'd have to compete with every woman up to twenty years of age, because of my height.

"I was thinking, if . . ." Mom started. Julie stood by me, jingling her taps.

"Little kids aren't on network television," I said to Julie, just to be clear. But my mother, she just smiled.

Mrs. Baird leaned to massage my shoulder. "I've never heard you tap, Mary Beth. Why don't you dance for us? And I'll have another glass of that wine, Dr. Sartor."

Now Julie's tap shoes seemed to jingle all by themselves. "If not this year, there's always next," my mom said. Again. She was sure.

I shivered. I'd never say no to Mrs. Baird, even if I was in a horrible mood. Julie scrambled to the front entry and plopped by the archway. *To watch.*

Daddy pulled out the four-by-eight-foot masonite boards and lined them up. The last time I danced in the entry was when Mabel played the piano in the living room.

Well, where was my steam? I pulled my skirts and moved it. I flexed my tap shoes on the boards. "I'll be the music." That was obvious, I had no music. No Mabel. But I did love hearing the high clear rhythms of taps alone.

Mary Beth dances for Mrs. Baird. (Courtesy of Beth Obermeyer)

I turned as I danced, and in the big mirror over the fireplace at the opposite end of the living room—my body fattened and thinned. I fooled with sounds and slides and syncopation. Riffs and pull-backs, even frontward ones, like Paul Draper had shown Dean. Three sounds to the bar against a four-four structure, how was that? I imagined Larry Adler playing his harmonica like he did for Paul Draper.

"I especially like tap-dancing," said Mrs. Baird. My dance r a close. "And that was the most beautiful dance I've ever heard," sh

"I'm thinking about how it would look on television," mother. She had a point. Crowds loved the tap.

"Now Julie," Mrs. Baird said. "You try." *Mrs. Baird was nice to Julie, how nice.* But her last two words carried weight. "Yo said to Julie. I dropped, cross-legged. Julie scrambled to her checked for the freckle on her right hand so she'd know to st right foot, that side. The little kid tapped clear, simple. She finisl to nice applause. And sat down. I was so proud of Julie.

I scrambled to her and whispered in her ear. "Do m pushing her back to her feet. "Put some hard stuff in," I sai bugged eyes. "Show Mrs. Baird." Julie was a rattle-snap of a ta

Julie pushed her legs straight and bounced on her hee dimpled knee look. "That's the way I learned the dance," she hi on my waist. Soon I was up and at 'em, doing steps, challenging J

The little girl did it back. The heels and toes I tossed a lot harder.

But the kid did it again, right back. Not even a pause, it back.

Maybe I should trip her up just a bit. I clicked it faster

Now the little girl bobbed her head, her hands on extra heel in my dance snuck past her, but our crowd did crowd now included Walter the shell-shocked veteran fro lawn-mowing snow-shovel-up-a-storm man, and Hanna come back to be part of the evening. She did that sometin

I repeated the last steps. Julie picked it up this t nose in the air. She answered every step! Spurts of ap around us. Their hands blurred—clapping in the middle,

The two of us were going to bring down the hous house, but still. Mom was on her feet, her play shoes toe

I put an explosive tag-ending on and offered a h shook it, in a hurry. Short arms shake fast. We repeate together.

In a way, the together-end part grated on m sounds she was slipping underneath. Faking, a little. B her long. Still, it was like if I moved I had a shadow.

It was set in con-
crete. I would dance with
Julie. That night, I walked
Julie past the grandfather
clock. I showed her my
puppet. I let her take him to
bed. Julie was a racket,
letting the puppet feet bang
on the slats up the stairs.

Did I ever have a
bedtime story for Doodles.

And for Mabel.

I was settling in on
New York.

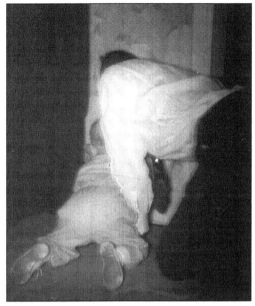

Daddy and Bobby take the radio apart. (Courtesy of
Beth Obermeyer)

155

31

Dancing on Ice

Months ago my Mason City Iowa had seared through the fall, hot-golden reds. Before that summer had lushed over in ripe blossoms and greens. Spring: fresh lime and sticks. I'd grown, one with the changing colors.

But winter came, monochromatic, the snow harsh and soft at once. And how it stayed, in a no man's time, that just past Valentine's Day when nothing was on the horizon, no time soon. I'd eased off that red-and-green Christmas feeling long ago. Oh, the days when I could wear my red-velvet flats with the holly on the toe to candle-lighting at church. All that— jingled out of sight. I was upon the days of galoshes and wool over-pants.

I swear it was not even snowing when I made up my mind. A hole stretched inside me and maybe it was this: it was fun and nice to dance with Julie, but my own beautiful dances had become something of a fantasy in my past. I remembered, ached for, dances of my own. I had a plan.

So I asked my mother and I was surprised when she said yes. Take a walk. To the library, go. I lied. I would not be going to the library.

The back door closed on her song. She waltzed Bobby in the living room . . . "'Til I waltz again with you . . ." No other would hold his charms, the song went. Bobby loved getting his turn. He'd just turned three.

Opposite: Hoar frost. (Photo: Beth Obermeyer)

I pushed across the top of Mrs. Starr's horseshoe drive. The snow sifted huge against the stick trees, at about the same speed the second hand fell down the face of my Timex. How long could I stay outside in this? But I had work to do.

I fingered my angora hat and scarf into place and poked through the fur on my coat pocket, fishing for mittens. I'd cut the yarn off them this morning, the idiot strings; now I had to keep track of the darn gloves.

I checked the elastic waistband of my snow pants and snapped off the suspenders. I let them slide and never looked back. I was sure the leggings would stay up. Easing my velvet hood up, the warmth grew even.

And I did feel cared about—not totally alone—in my escapade. The warmest leggings clung to my legs, dry. Grandma Sartor had knit them,

In short order they iced up, of course.

Each foot stomped the first print wherever I went and filled in a drift when I looked back. The trees looked like hairbrushes but the snow turned the air to fog. The houses around me hid. A blizzard. In fact, I couldn't even see where the sidewalk changed to the street or where the cement walls might be. I walked clear cross town, to Rock Glen.

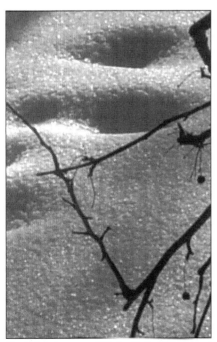

Footprints in snow. (Photo: Beth Obermeyer)

It was quite a winter, 1955. It may have taken five minutes to go every block, I didn't know. The snow shredded into cracks on my coat. A church bell rang four o'clock. The library came in view, blinking its tall white columns around the curved porch.

I was far from home, about twelve blocks, and I eased along, protected from the wind by the side of the library. A yellow quiet inside was large enough to fly a dance. Because it did have a rhythm in there. Just the way the books clamped shut and the ink pads stamped.

At that very moment Meredith was setting his Marian the Librarian, her romp in that library, but

The Mason City Library (Photo: Beth Obermeyer)

Mabel and I didn't know. I mean we all knew the library was priceless, we just didn't dance up the stairs. And anyway, I thought it was kind of for Protestants, not for me, because at Holy Family we had our own library.

A gray-uniformed man stomped the snow off his rubbers. He shoveled in a blur. My neck was hot in the wet wool scarf. I could smell the lamb, for sure. My ears burned from the clamp of the pony tail hat, on so long.

I massaged my head, through the red velvet. Better. And I had no hills by my house, but I stood looking down a huge one, at the creek. The ice below looked like black satin in the dark. The water around the ice edge sparkled. I pitched a rock to the water edge and glass sculptures shot up, disappeared. Another rock rolled down and skittered on top of center ice.

It was time.

I stood at a footbridge. It would be the footbridge where the Music Man meets his Marian before . . . but I'm getting head of my story. I leaned over one rail, then the other, side to side—whirring my arms like a plane.

I slid down the hill, wrapping my coat underneath me. Rocks in the glen slowed my slide and I clambered, spinning off skinny tall trees.

I climbed down to a log, a huge hollow log, and I sat, knees under my chin, coat wrapped around my galoshes. Squirrels flew branch to branch. I relished the alone feeling, no jitters at all. I was in a wonderland.

Music Man bridge. (Photo: Beth Obermeyer)

Almost as though on cue, the snow stopped. A sliver of a moon came out, a late afternoon thing, my spotlight. I unbuckled my galoshes. It wouldn't take long but this was important.

The frost on brush rimmed the black-blue ice. The heavy snow coated every stick, and it was as magical as I could hope. A lone dog crunched his paws in the crystals by ice edge, head bowed. Another wanderer. The lights in the houses above glittered in the dusk under the stars.

My white tap shoes sparkled in the moonlight. I jumped over the watery edge and my metal taps clinked on the ice, the sound evaporating into the air in a *tink*. It had the sound of a silver mobile. Little white lines spiraled out from my steps on top of the ice. Was it crackling? It was plain luck to stay standing but I added slides for scrape sounds. I experimented a bit with balance, rubber pads on the balls of the tap shoes.

I tried a turn and threw my head back for a spin, on the edge of a heel tap. In my mind my coat opened and flew away, and I was in my white

Winter Wonderland fantasy. (Gerard Publicity photo: Courtesy of Beth Obermeyer)

satin and fur Winter Wonderland costume, of old. The trees curved about me like frosted prairie jewelry. I was experimenting and it made me happy.

One problem with this art form: my nose could run, still could, just remembering. Cold does that.

I hummed Meredith's "S'beginning to Look A Lot Like Christmas," moved around the accents on the odd counts.

An owl hooed his falsetto, a back-up singer. But I had no audience to yay or nay. I could try anything.

I did, a circle of turns, gingerly tamping the loose screws on my taps straight down in the ice. I whirled my satin skirt out. I could hear it whip.

My legs shivered under my leggings and my hat pulled back like a hood. I slowed the whips gradually so I wouldn't be thrown by the weight. The ice did look a little wet because snowflakes disappeared as they landed.

I was on to something even if I would never use it. Mabel would not believe it.

Four choruses set, my toes curled from the cold, and I still had to get home. I huffed heat into my fingers and slid toward my boots on the creek edge.

Thrums like a cello boomed under the ice. I didn't want to join the underwater orchestra. I sat on a rock and examined my taps, hoping they didn't rust. I zipped my white galoshes, pulled my coat tight and bounded up the hill from where I'd come, pushing my scarf over my nose. My lips were chapping, my eyelashes hard with ice. Lights blinked out in houses as I passed, mysterious.

I had a Whoop-De-Doo dance of my own. Only my own shadow had copied.

Of course, a car pulled alongside, Daddy. He came looking as fathers do. I piled into the car. He didn't even wonder why I had no books.

The snow beat the windshield again and the wipers bogged down. He spun his tire chains out to better tracks. Heat came up under my coat, trapped, my cocoon.

We drove through our Mason City, past the homes of Rock Glen.

Plaque on Rock Glen sidewalk. (Courtesy of Beth Obermeyer)

I went home to marshmallows on the fire, to my house in a snow globe, it seemed.

It looked good. Dancing alone was pretty darn cold.

* * *

It was a sophisticated setting that I'd chosen to inspire me that day. Architect Frank Lloyd Wright had wanted to design the entire neighborhood but his personal life had taken him out of the country. His followers took over and today plaques on the sidewalk mark each prairie-style home.

Years later I came back to this neighborhood of the architecture of Frank Lloyd Wright and his followers, to check the sidewalk plaques, a tour. In fact, Mason City is a destination not just for its music and Music Man museum, not just for the Bil Baird puppet museum, but for two Frank Lloyd Wright structures, the Stockman house near Rock Glen where I was that day and the only Frank Lloyd Wright bank left in the world, just off the downtown park. Above the bank is a hotel, pristinely restored. Mason City saves and cherishes all it had been given.

My town had sophistication far beyond just my music. It pulled me to Rock Glen that day and it stayed with me, no doubt, raising my expectations, wherever I go in my lifetime.

Dancing at twelve. (Courtesy of Beth Obermeyer)

My mother marched to the kitchen and came back, a beer and a silver opener, flashing like a sword. She meant business. "Did you hear that?" she said. If you win, you go to New York for the *Ted Mack Amateur Hour*. Could it be bigger? Maybe we're not ready this year, but they'll do it again and again, I'm sure."

New York, my dream! "I could . . . 'Deep Purple' for sure. I could . . . well . . ." I waited.

"It might be hard to win by yourself," she said. What she didn't say was that I wasn't a cute four-year-old dancing in baby shoes. I wasn't even the compact eleven-year-old I'd been a year and a month ago. I was thirteen. Now when I danced I'd have to compete with every woman up to twenty years of age, because of my height.

"I was thinking, if . . ." Mom started. Julie stood by me, jingling her taps.

"Little kids aren't on network television," I said to Julie, just to be clear. But my mother, she just smiled.

Mrs. Baird leaned to massage my shoulder. "I've never heard you tap, Mary Beth. Why don't you dance for us? And I'll have another glass of that wine, Dr. Sartor."

Now Julie's tap shoes seemed to jingle all by themselves. "If not this year, there's always next," my mom said. Again. She was sure.

I shivered. I'd never say no to Mrs. Baird, even if I was in a horrible mood. Julie scrambled to the front entry and plopped by the archway. *To watch.*

Daddy pulled out the four-by-eight-foot masonite boards and lined them up. The last time I danced in the entry was when Mabel played the piano in the living room.

Well, where was my steam? I pulled my skirts and moved it. I flexed my tap shoes on the boards. "I'll be the music." That was obvious, I had no music. No Mabel. But I did love hearing the high clear rhythms of taps alone.

Mary Beth dances for Mrs. Baird. (Courtesy of Beth Obermeyer)

I turned as I danced, and in the big mirror over the fireplace at the opposite end of the living room—my body fattened and thinned. I fooled with sounds and slides and syncopation. Riffs and pull-backs, even frontward ones, like Paul Draper had shown Dean. Three sounds to the bar against a four-four structure, how was that? I imagined Larry Adler playing his harmonica like he did for Paul Draper.

"I especially like tap-dancing," said Mrs. Baird. My dance rattled to a close. "And that was the most beautiful dance I've ever heard," she added.

"I'm thinking about how it would look on television," said my mother. She had a point. Crowds loved the tap.

"Now Julie," Mrs. Baird said. "You try." *Mrs. Baird was just being nice to Julie, how nice.* But her last two words carried weight. "You try," she said to Julie. I dropped, cross-legged. Julie scrambled to her feet. She checked for the freckle on her right hand so she'd know to start on her right foot, that side. The little kid tapped clear, simple. She finished, bowed, to nice applause. And sat down. I was so proud of Julie.

I scrambled to her and whispered in her ear. "Do more," I said, pushing her back to her feet. "Put some hard stuff in," I said, to Julie's bugged eyes. "Show Mrs. Baird." Julie was a rattle-snap of a tapper.

Julie pushed her legs straight and bounced on her heels, that cute dimpled knee look. "That's the way I learned the dance," she hissed, her eyes on my waist. Soon I was up and at 'em, doing steps, challenging Julie to repeat.

The little girl did it back. The heels and toes I tossed in made it all a lot harder.

But the kid did it again, right back. Not even a pause, Julie snapped it back.

Maybe I should trip her up just a bit. I clicked it faster with accents.

Now the little girl bobbed her head, her hands on her hips. One extra heel in my dance snuck past her, but our crowd didn't know. The crowd now included Walter the shell-shocked veteran from the war, our lawn-mowing snow-shovel-up-a-storm man, and Hanna. Hanna'd just come back to be part of the evening. She did that sometimes.

I repeated the last steps. Julie picked it up this time, her button nose in the air. She answered every step! Spurts of applause sprinkled around us. Their hands blurred—clapping in the middle, no less.

The two of us were going to bring down the house. It was our own house, but still. Mom was on her feet, her play shoes toe-tapping in time.

I put an explosive tag-ending on and offered a hand to Julie. Julie shook it, in a hurry. Short arms shake fast. We repeated the tag ending, together.

In a way, the together-end part grated on me, all those extra sounds she was slipping underneath. Faking, a little. But it wouldn't take her long. Still, it was like if I moved I had a shadow.

But—even so—it's hard to get a standing ovation—but those that could stand did!

The applause, more applause than I could get alone, I knew, and the dance *was* snappy.

Julie looked a bit taller to me than she had. Our mother, our father, Mrs. Baird, their faces "beamed like a quarter to three." Those were Meredith words, Mason City talk.

Maybe if I cleaned up the dance, it could be fun.

Maybe Julie was a gift from heaven?

But it wouldn't be like Bil's brother helping with Bil's idea. I would have to do Julie's dance with her. Not new or exciting territory for me, not at all. But . . .

"Now that's an act," said Mrs. Baird. "And I'm going to make a prediction: Someday I'll come watch your television set, Dr. Sartor, the *Ted Mack Original Amateur Hour*. Mr. Ted Mack will spin his wheel of fortune and say . . . 'From Mason City, Iowa! Round and round they go; where they stop, nobody knows!'"

I could not believe my ears. Mrs. Baird thought a sister act was special. That meant something. And my mother's eyes stilled, large and blue, like Julie's. "Ted Mack does his show in Radio City Music Hall," she said. "That's huge."

New York!

"Maybe I just need a bigger TV studio," I said, clapping a bit now. And then I got carried away. "Maybe we *could both twirl lariats.*"

I sat down by Mrs. Baird and wrapped my arms around myself, my eyes on my own taps. My mother was thinking the Lennon Sisters, minus two, I knew.

Julie plopped on my skirt. I couldn't get away from her now if I wanted to. And I didn't want to. But I'd had so much fun, making my own dances just right.

"You could all come visit me in New York," said Mrs. Baird, onto something new . . . and then she told my mother about the move.

Daddy was done. He inched out the big Scott radio from the wall and squeezed behind the back to look at its insides. Bobby, awakened by all the noise, had climbed out of his crib and crawled behind with Daddy. Bobby loved to take things apart. It was something they had in common, something they did together.

154

It was set in con-
crete. I would dance with
Julie. That night, I walked
Julie past the grandfather
clock. I showed her my
puppet. I let her take him to
bed. Julie was a racket,
letting the puppet feet bang
on the slats up the stairs.

Did I ever have a
bedtime story for Doodles.

And for Mabel.

I was settling in on
New York.

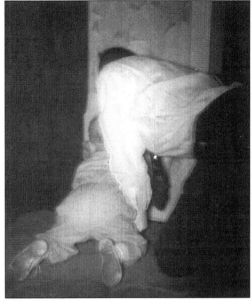

Daddy and Bobby take the radio apart. (Courtesy of
Beth Obermeyer)

31

Dancing on Ice

Months ago my Mason City Iowa had seared through the fall, hot-golden reds. Before that summer had lushed over in ripe blossoms and greens. Spring: fresh lime and sticks. I'd grown, one with the changing colors.

But winter came, monochromatic, the snow harsh and soft at once. And how it stayed, in a no man's time, that just past Valentine's Day when nothing was on the horizon, no time soon. I'd eased off that red-and-green Christmas feeling long ago. Oh, the days when I could wear my red-velvet flats with the holly on the toe to candle-lighting at church. All that— jingled out of sight. I was upon the days of galoshes and wool over-pants.

I swear it was not even snowing when I made up my mind. A hole stretched inside me and maybe it was this: it was fun and nice to dance with Julie, but my own beautiful dances had become something of a fantasy in my past. I remembered, ached for, dances of my own. I had a plan.

So I asked my mother and I was surprised when she said yes. Take a walk. To the library, go. I lied. I would not be going to the library.

The back door closed on her song. She waltzed Bobby in the living room . . . "'Til I waltz again with you . . ." No other would hold his charms, the song went. Bobby loved getting his turn. He'd just turned three.

Opposite: Hoar frost. (Photo: Beth Obermeyer)

I pushed across the top of Mrs. Starr's horseshoe drive. The snow sifted huge against the stick trees, at about the same speed the second hand fell down the face of my Timex. How long could I stay outside in this? But I had work to do.

I fingered my angora hat and scarf into place and poked through the fur on my coat pocket, fishing for mittens. I'd cut the yarn off them this morning, the idiot strings; now I had to keep track of the darn gloves.

I checked the elastic waistband of my snow pants and snapped off the suspenders. I let them slide and never looked back. I was sure the leggings would stay up. Easing my velvet hood up, the warmth grew even.

And I did feel cared about—not totally alone—in my escapade. The warmest leggings clung to my legs, dry. Grandma Sartor had knit them,

In short order they iced up, of course.

Each foot stomped the first print wherever I went and filled in a drift when I looked back. The trees looked like hairbrushes but the snow turned the air to fog. The houses around me hid. A blizzard. In fact, I couldn't even see where the sidewalk changed to the street or where the cement walls might be. I walked clear cross town, to Rock Glen.

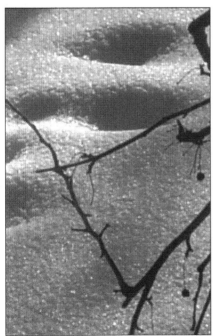

Footprints in snow. (Photo: Beth Obermeyer)

It was quite a winter, 1955. It may have taken five minutes to go every block, I didn't know. The snow shredded into cracks on my coat. A church bell rang four o'clock. The library came in view, blinking its tall white columns around the curved porch.

I was far from home, about twelve blocks, and I eased along, protected from the wind by the side of the library. A yellow quiet inside was large enough to fly a dance. Because it did have a rhythm in there. Just the way the books clamped shut and the ink pads stamped.

At that very moment Meredith was setting his Marian the Librarian, her romp in that library, but

The Mason City Library (Photo: Beth Obermeyer)

Mabel and I didn't know. I mean we all knew the library was priceless, we just didn't dance up the stairs. And anyway, I thought it was kind of for Protestants, not for me, because at Holy Family we had our own library.

A gray-uniformed man stomped the snow off his rubbers. He shoveled in a blur. My neck was hot in the wet wool scarf. I could smell the lamb, for sure. My ears burned from the clamp of the pony tail hat, on so long.

I massaged my head, through the red velvet. Better. And I had no hills by my house, but I stood looking down a huge one, at the creek. The ice below looked like black satin in the dark. The water around the ice edge sparkled. I pitched a rock to the water edge and glass sculptures shot up, disappeared. Another rock rolled down and skittered on top of center ice.

It was time.

I stood at a footbridge. It would be the footbridge where the Music Man meets his Marian before . . . but I'm getting head of my story. I leaned over one rail, then the other, side to side—whirring my arms like a plane.

I slid down the hill, wrapping my coat underneath me. Rocks in the glen slowed my slide and I clambered, spinning off skinny tall trees.

I climbed down to a log, a huge hollow log, and I sat, knees under my chin, coat wrapped around my galoshes. Squirrels flew branch to branch. I relished the alone feeling, no jitters at all. I was in a wonderland.

Music Man bridge. (Photo: Beth Obermeyer)

Almost as though on cue, the snow stopped. A sliver of a moon came out, a late afternoon thing, my spotlight. I unbuckled my galoshes. It wouldn't take long but this was important.

The frost on brush rimmed the black-blue ice. The heavy snow coated every stick, and it was as magical as I could hope. A lone dog crunched his paws in the crystals by ice edge, head bowed. Another wanderer. The lights in the houses above glittered in the dusk under the stars.

My white tap shoes sparkled in the moonlight. I jumped over the watery edge and my metal taps clinked on the ice, the sound evaporating into the air in a *tink*. It had the sound of a silver mobile. Little white lines spiraled out from my steps on top of the ice. Was it crackling? It was plain luck to stay standing but I added slides for scrape sounds. I experimented a bit with balance, rubber pads on the balls of the tap shoes.

I tried a turn and threw my head back for a spin, on the edge of a heel tap. In my mind my coat opened and flew away, and I was in my white

Winter Wonderland fantasy. (Gerard Publicity photo: Courtesy of Beth Obermeyer)

satin and fur Winter Wonderland costume, of old. The trees curved about me like frosted prairie jewelry. I was experimenting and it made me happy.

One problem with this art form: my nose could run, still could, just remembering. Cold does that.

I hummed Meredith's "S'beginning to Look A Lot Like Christmas," moved around the accents on the odd counts.

An owl hooed his falsetto, a back-up singer. But I had no audience to yay or nay. I could try anything.

I did, a circle of turns, gingerly tamping the loose screws on my taps straight down in the ice. I whirled my satin skirt out. I could hear it whip.

My legs shivered under my leggings and my hat pulled back like a hood. I slowed the whips gradually so I wouldn't be thrown by the weight. The ice did look a little wet because snowflakes disappeared as they landed.

I was on to something even if I would never use it. Mabel would not believe it.

Four choruses set, my toes curled from the cold, and I still had to get home. I huffed heat into my fingers and slid toward my boots on the creek edge.

Thrums like a cello boomed under the ice. I didn't want to join the underwater orchestra. I sat on a rock and examined my taps, hoping they didn't rust. I zipped my white galoshes, pulled my coat tight and bounded up the hill from where I'd come, pushing my scarf over my nose. My lips were chapping, my eyelashes hard with ice. Lights blinked out in houses as I passed, mysterious.

I had a Whoop-De-Doo dance of my own. Only my own shadow had copied.

Of course, a car pulled alongside, Daddy. He came looking as fathers do. I piled into the car. He didn't even wonder why I had no books.

The snow beat the windshield again and the wipers bogged down. He spun his tire chains out to better tracks. Heat came up under my coat, trapped, my cocoon.

We drove through our Mason City, past the homes of Rock Glen.

Plaque on Rock Glen sidewalk. (Courtesy of Beth Obermeyer)

I went home to marshmallows on the fire, to my house in a snow globe, it seemed.

It looked good. Dancing alone was pretty darn cold.

* * *

It was a sophisticated setting that I'd chosen to inspire me that day. Architect Frank Lloyd Wright had wanted to design the entire neighborhood but his personal life had taken him out of the country. His followers took over and today plaques on the sidewalk mark each prairie-style home.

Years later I came back to this neighborhood of the architecture of Frank Lloyd Wright and his followers, to check the sidewalk plaques, a tour. In fact, Mason City is a destination not just for its music and Music Man museum, not just for the Bil Baird puppet museum, but for two Frank Lloyd Wright structures, the Stockman house near Rock Glen where I was that day and the only Frank Lloyd Wright bank left in the world, just off the downtown park. Above the bank is a hotel, pristinely restored. Mason City saves and cherishes all it had been given.

My town had sophistication far beyond just my music. It pulled me to Rock Glen that day and it stayed with me, no doubt, raising my expectations, wherever I go in my lifetime.

A full-sized likeness of Meredith Willson stands outside his museum, Music Man Square. The opening lines to "Seventy-Six Trombones" are carved into the bulding's top rim. (Photo: Beth Obermeyer)

A detail of Frank Lloyd Wright's Stockman House, early in the renovation. (Photo: Beth Obermeyer)

Autobiographical books by Meredith Willson, fiction by him, and the biography of Meredith by John Skipper. (Photo: Beth Obermeyer)

32

The Most Heartbreaking Night of His Life

FEBRUARY 1956

While I sat in the tranquility—comparatively—of Mason City, Meredith was in a turbulent reality. I cringed when I opened Mabel's newest letter from him. All I could do was sit by her bed and hope. To get to Broadway was grit. Meredith would describe this journey in hilarious detail in his autobiography, *But He Doesn't Know the Territory*, out the end of 1957, the next year. Mabel and I would read and I would dream—the scenes—how they danced in my head.

But when Meredith Willson said he'd just had the worst night of his life, Mabel nodded and I knew. *This was God awful serious.*

It was February 1956. Meredith roamed his L.A. home, breakfast nook to music room. He was all-over miserable, every single muscle—blah. He sat at his desk and criss-crossed the revisions, a stack of papers now grown to over two feet tall. He tapped the edges of the papers, each way.

Why had Cy and Ernie dumped his *Music Man?* Meredith agonized over this. They might have produced it, if he'd had the plot ready for the time slot they'd saved. Or Cy and Ernie just didn't find the right director? The right lead? Cy and Ernie, anyway.

Ernie had hated Meredith's idea of a spastic boy lead, that was true, but Meredith did not want to quit on the character. "He'll steal every scene," they'd said, over and over. "The plot can't move forward but what that kid shows up and stops it."

But Meredith wanted to show that a kid in a wheel chair could be smart—even though in a 1912 story no one would have thought so. Shoot, even in the fifties, not a great chance.

But Ernie might be right. The more Meredith revised, the more the love story between Harold and Marian emerged—and therein might be the plot. What a stickler this kid was for him.

And—even bigger—his show was still two and a half hours too long, still four and one-half hours total. That couldn't remain that way.

The phone rang, the bells bright as the L.A. morning out his study window. That day there was no fog, just blue sky. "Jesse Lasky, MGM here. Come yet today? I've got a terrific idea for us."

Meredith's head raced. MGM? Did Jesse want to make a film of *The Music Man*? He scribbled Rini a note, "Gone to MGM. Tell you all at dinner." He jumped in his car. Rini would not believe that just when she went for a walk, that's when he ended up at MGM.

Walking through the MGM lot, Meredith was surprised to see Robert Freeman, his hair dresser. Robert raised his hand, his fingers moving like a scissors? Meredith knew he needed a haircut. Even a radio star needed the "Hairdresser to the Stars." Meredith smiled and waved. He passed the guard. He caught a ride on a golf-cart-like contraption and arrived at Jesse's office.

Jesse Lasky stood by his mahogany desk, a man of success by the look of it all. Silver desk set, brocade draperies. And unlike Ernie, Jesse moved slowly. He sat, gently tapping the cover of Meredith's book, *And There I Stood with My Piccolo*. Meredith had been in Sousa's band when he first came to New York and that book was full of it.

Meredith relaxed in the red cush chair. He crossed his legs, forgot about his hair.

"Meredith. I'm fascinated," Jesse said. He stretched his legs and shoved his hands in the pockets of his trousers. The pin-stripes stayed aligned, not a baggy-pants kind of guy. "I hear you are writing a musical about bands. I think we might work together, merge projects." Like Meredith, Lasky needed backers. "I want to do a salute to the American marching band, end with an enormous band made up of two players from each state." Jesse snapped the rubber band on a stack of letters. "These are from music educators around the country. I've got the groundwork laid."

Meredith leaned forward, air whooshing from the cushions. He flicked ashes into the cut-glass tray. If he'd learned one thing it was he won more battles by getting in the ring a lot.

"It's never been done before," Jesse said. I wonder if we could do a back-to-back show, my documentary on marching bands, your *Music Man*, then end with my giant band."

"I'd be honored to take a look . . . give whatever you think might work a try," Meredith said. Perhaps Jesse could take a look at the script? "Rini and I would be glad to sing and play it through and honored to have you at our home."

Meredith liked the way Jesse brought out his own gentlemanly ways. Most producers he had met speeded through, making Meredith feel like a rube of a country boy.

Jesse stepped from behind the desk and extended a hand, his onyx cufflinks flashing bright under the overhead chandelier.

In two days, Jesse came to the Willson home. Meredith and Rini sat at the piano, and did *The Music Man* for him. Afterwards, they sat in the living room. Jesse said he had not cheered and laughed all the way through a performance like that in a long time. "This'll be a great moving picture. I think we're a team."

"I think we might as well put all our eggs in one basket," Meredith said. "And I hope we aren't talking about the eggs in my book." Meredith had written a book, *Eggs I Have Laid*. The three laughed at the joke, walked out into the night air. The stars and moon did seem to shine just on them.

Five days later, Jesse called. "Let's do two separate pictures," he said. "Yours is already too long. Mine will be a documentary of today's wonderful state of the marching band." Jesse slowed.

Jesse's associates probably talked him down. But Meredith pushed. "It'll still be great, Jesse. Let's have our agent over—we've got the same one—why don't you have him at our home for a look-see?"

Jesse agreed, for that same night. Rini made her famous shrimp cocktail and mixed up a creamy dip for chips. In ones and twos, fourteen men arrived in all, from Jesse's office. At the fourth doorbell chime, Rini climbed the kitchen stool to the top cupboard to find more cut-crystal dishes. Meredith raced to the neighbors for more chairs. They hadn't expected so many people.

"Must be a whole lotta interest," Meredith whispered to Rini as he stuck toothpicks into slippery oysters. He opened the double doors to the music room and filled the doorway and hall with chairs. He sat at the piano. Rini rustled and swirled her full skirt with a flourish and sat close. Like back to the Vance in Mason City, Meredith mulled.

Ever optimistic, Meredith wondered. How many times would he and Rini go through the script, the songs? How many versions? What did writers do who didn't play the piano and have an opera-singer wife? At least he didn't have to hire and rehearse musicians for every audition.

Meredith started his patter, cutting here and there, to cut the length of the show way back. Rini perched on the edge of the bench and sang her songs, her piercing soprano moving easily over the beautiful melodies. Producers always loved these auditions, and Meredith turned his face sunny-side up as he went, to catch their reaction.

He paused, hands twelve inches up, over the keys, right where he always got a laugh.

Silence. He startled. His rhythm askew, he bounced to the next. Rini coughed. He knew she was surprised and not quite ready. Didn't Jesse and his friends love it? He usually saw laughs so big gold fillings glinted in the Tiffany lamp light. No one moved.

He chanted what would become the beloved train opening, no piano. If there was one thing he was sure of, it was that opening . . . *clack clack clack* his toe went, hitting the piano leg with the side of his shoe. His breath came harder, fluffing the dark hair on Rini's neck.

The men faced him like a dozen eggs in cheap cardboard crate chairs. Their yolk faces didn't even wobble. At first Jesse gave a snick here or there but to no avail. Not one shell cracked. Meredith's nose ran like the whites of eggs that he pushed to the side of the plate when he was in a bad mood.

Rini's breathing came unevenly. With no laughs, the pick-ups came faster, and she shifted her weight on the bench, off balance. She ended songs with a snort, only to Meredith's ear. She had her running-mad look. Meredith grew sad.

Rini had raced about the house before these guys came, getting her house just so. She wore her favorite taffeta cocktail dress and looked so pretty, but now red blotches showed on her cheeks and neck. Her guests acted like she and Mere were some schmaltzy act from the hicks.

At about half-way through, Rini froze still as she sang. She didn't move one quarter-inch on the bench. Meredith couldn't imagine how hard it must be for her to sing sweet as a calliope in her Rini-worst mood.

He knew she felt ridiculous, but more. She was surely embarrassed for him.

Meredith's arms, his fingers, his breathing wanted to stop so many times, but he didn't. If he knew one thing, it was to box until he was knocked out or finished the fight. His audience looked like little boys who just wanted to go play baseball, but they were forced to sit and sit.

"The end," said Meredith, in a fake triumph tone.

The men left as unannounced as they had arrived, fast before the credits rolled, so they could get their cars out of the queue. Only there were no credits, and their cars were parked on the tree-lined neighborhood streets.

Jesse, always a gentleman, stuck around. "Don't feel bad. I pushed like the devil, over all of MGM, to get *The Great Caruso* made. No one liked it, and it was a smash."

Meredith closed the door. Rini broke a dish, slinging them together. But her voice was smooth. "Oh, but, dear, you always make swell purses out of goose ears."

Meredith couldn't smile this time, not even at her unwitting miss of the language.

"Maybe they'll get back to the office and know they like it," she said. "Maybe Jesse will tell someone else about us."

Meredith didn't even get his bowling-ball-heavy hands up to her waist to kiss her good night. He died a little right there, after all those years of trying. "Honey, I'm not coming to bed. I'll bunk up on the guest bed in the study. I have to sort this all out." He backed to the den door, Rini hanging onto his hands, not able to get a word in. "Maybe I've led us down the wrong path with this crummy show," he said.

He clicked the door shut. He kicked the sofa bed to unfold. Rini appeared in a minute with clean folded pajamas.

Meredith was already undressed and curled in a ball on the bed. She pushed the pajamas onto the table and closed the door. Her footsteps tapped on the stairs, in Meredith's head, away. He counted her footprints down, like it was progress, her leaving.

She'd understand. Right now was no time for her good cheer. He reached for his pajamas and pulled them on with the least amount of movement.

His hands and feet felt enormous, like he was running a temperature, hallucinating. He pulled the top on backwards, hands so hard to lift, could never button it anyway right now. All he could do was hold the waistband out and jerk a leg in at a time. The fabric was old and worn, threadbare, familiar, used to be blue.

He wrapped his arms up around his big hot head, and breathed heavily. He nestled in the sinkhole on the bed, as he often did when he escaped, and pulled his knees to his chest, hugging himself.

Alone with his thoughts, so alone he could moan, Meredith talked to himself, as he did when he needed answers. He hummed, in cycles, like a washer spinning, he even felt the lurch, dizzy, sick to his stomach, oysters in his nose yet.

"That was the most heart-breaking night of my life," he'd say, later.

* * *

I sat by Mabel's bed and put down Meredith's new letter in disgust. "No one clapped." Mabel's face slipped down to her collar bone. I kicked that letter under the bed, changed the subject.

Once I tapped *and* played Meredith's "Good Lord Bless and Keep You" at the piano recital, I told her. "I danced and played *at the same time,* —no one clapped then. I'm still not sure what happened."

Mabel chuckled. "It's like a hymn, Mary Beth. This town is quiet after hymns. They didn't know what to expect." Mabel was pausing more between sentences than she had. She swallowed more words. "And that's okay," she said. "So what, you wanted to play "Minuet in G?" I nearly laughed off the chair. *Tap dancing to "Minuet in G!"*

In fact, one day Garrison Keillor would have me tap to "Amazing Grace," on *Prairie Home Companion.* I played Stump the Taps. Now *that's* a hymn. I wish I could have told her that.

"Meredith will bounce back," Mabel said. "Wait and see." She sure knew him better than I did. I'd never met him. Imagine.

33

Franklin Lacey

AUGUST 1956

For the first time in four and one-half years, Meredith put down *The Music Man.* He clacked each of thirty-two drafts into a file of their own and walked out the door. He was under contract to go to San Diego to conduct his music for *The California Story,* Franklin Lacey, director. Some distance from his show would be good.

The drive was stinky hot as they poked out of L.A.—too hot for a convertible—but Rini wrapped her scarf around her head, letting the tails fly over the door, her bare toes out the window. The ribbon of pavement wound ahead of them for hours until cool San Diego made Rini reach for her shawl. The temperature here was a year-round seventy degrees, a soothing fit for what felt like a vacation to Meredith.

Soon, Meredith stood in the green room of a theatre, tapping his fingers on pages of a story board of the California show taped to the wall. Franklin Lacey, skinny as a rail, towered over Meredith. Meredith always joked that Franklin was "home-made apple pie on stilts."

For the first time in the years of *The Music Man* project, Rini relaxed in the background. Her cheerleading voice was absent, not needed. Meredith's senses dulled. He was a bit lonely, but freed. "Thirteen hundred actors in this show. And dozens of horses," Franklin said, pointing to a sketch of the outdoor stage of Act One.

"Maybe you can use one dozen horses over and over?" Meredith suggested. The two men jabbed and joked and scribbled on the papers, matching Meredith's music to sets.

"Let's go take a look at the stage before the rehearsal tonight," said Franklin.

Rini tip-toed across the parking lot gravel. Her high heels scraped down between the rocks. Meredith scooped her up until they got to large stone slabs of the path. Through fragrant lavender and roses, under a deep blue dusk, they meandered towards the amphitheatre.

Settled onto high-up bleachers, Meredith and Franklin gestured and pointed at the enormous stage beneath them. Rini spotted an outdoor stand and returned with potato chips, pickles, and dogs. They munched and talked as actors drifted in, filling the bleachers closest to the stage. At seven o'clock Franklin headed down to the stage with a confident swagger. That night he would put together the well-rehearsed, thousand-plus extras with the main characters for his *California Story*.

Meredith and Rini propped their feet on the bleacher in front and leaned back on the plank. They relaxed in the cool breeze. "Good to see it before the musician's run-through," Meredith said.

"Stage left, keep front of stage clear," Franklin bellowed from the tenth row, into his bull horn. "Red shirts, more energy, cheer!" Hundreds of extras grouped. He wanted hoopla! "Louder, can't hear a word," he barked, to the main characters.

Gradually, the stage went from people scattered like confetti to blocks of bright color against the darkening California sky. The unmiked singing resounded against the hills. "Franklin's a hollerer," Meredith said, his elbow poking Rini in the ribs.

"Well, dear, blow horns do have that effect," Rini said. "Wait until *you* try to direct the orchestra's sound into the night air. Then we'll see big arm movements!"

The big night came. The show looked like it was in a bowl under a chandelier, there were so many stars twitching. Meredith stepped to the plate, in front of his musicians. His shoulders caved, over and over, the show went on for hours. His chin jutted left to right with the music, eyes closed, arms so far extended Rini would say he looked to have been shot. It felt good to use so much energy, different than composing at a piano with tiny finger moves and little head nods.

Meredith ran himself down but the sound was magnificent. He knew he'd awake in the morning, arms stiff, chest tight. But he liked when the music could run straight through, beginning to end.

A week later *The California Story* finished a successful run. The lights went out in the amphitheatre and the town glittered with night life. The crowd in the bar didn't know Meredith from the next guy. It felt good to be off the stage.

Franklin joked and chatted with Meredith and Rini in a way that made Meredith feel at home. Franklin wasn't a slick California guy nor was he fast like Ernie, but he did know his music. The two men sat across from each other, relaxed. "I hate to go home to Los Angeles without you," Meredith said. He sucked an ice cube until it melted. "I've enjoyed working with you," he said.

And with that Meredith spilled his plot story, and it sloshed forward and backward with the drinks. Franklin laughed as heartily as such a slender man could manage. "I think you've got something, Meredith," he said, with gusto.

Franklin didn't normally gush and so Meredith rushed on. His mind could not close his musical out any longer. He leveled his beloved *Music Man* all over Franklin. "This is the first I've gotten some distance from it and it feels so good," Meredith said, over a steaming corned beef sandwich.

He crunched a peppercorn in his molars. His eyes watered. "Franklin, Rini and I have a favorite place we like to go to relax. It's in the mountains outside of Los Angeles. We'd be honored if you'd come up to Idyllwild with us and listen to my script. And—I'm not bawling about my show. I've got pepper boiling up my nose." Meredith cupped his hands over his face. "Three producers say it stinks, the spastic boy stealing the scene every time, rat-a-tat."

"Meredith," Franklin said. His voice soothed. He described his lifetime in theatre and academics. He thought he could help. He said he even had taught in a school where he had "a few spastic children."

"You'll love the change," Meredith promised. "And when I get away from the big city, I'm the Mason City boy."

The next morning the convertible inched back to the outskirts of Los Angeles, like a bright-blue droning fly, on a lazy mission. Meredith and Franklin rolled their shirtsleeves and leaned their straw hats into the breeze, shouting back and forth over the rubber tires on the pavement. Rini spread head to toe across the back seat, until the highway changed to crushed rock. The car worked hard, spinning gravel as they curved up the mountain, and then it lurched to a stop.

They carried the suitcases up to the house. Meredith mixed drinks, and Rini unwrapped her shrimp and Ritz crackers she'd purchased at the little fisherman's store on the way. She stirred up her Velveeta cheese sauce and they all returned to the front porch.

The three lazily took turns pointing out the terrain below, the airport, forests, rock cliffs. As the night cooled, Meredith brought out three plaid wool jackets from the clothes tree inside and the three relaxed their sun-warmed bodies under corduroy throws.

Meredith wrapped his arms around himself and began to chant the start of his show. His voice cracked against the crackling of a far-off brush fire, a glow in the distance. He rocked the front porch rocker in one corner, then moved it to the other.

Franklin listened, nodded, cried at plot turns, cheered, and wailed. Rini's singing voice mixed with the nearby birds and some coyotes far away.

"So, what have we got here," Franklin said, at the end of the last song. He scratched his head against the backdrop of lightening bugs, like for all the world he might light his head, too. "List the characters, he said, leaning forward, like he'd make sense of it all.

"I got a love story between Harold Hill—the con-man band-instrument salesman—and Marian the Librarian," Meredith said, like it was the first time he'd realized it. "I got Mayor Shinn, the nasty likes of which Mason City never had, but there's the fiction. And a mayor's wife, Eulalie, all over the place, a social lady, plunking her voice like a ukulele."

Meredith paused, remembering Ernie's advice about conflict. His show was better from knowing Ernie, no doubt. In an important voice, he said, "I got a rival for Harold: an anvil salesman." Meredith liked that Franklin nodded. "And Tommy—the mayor was sorry to say—loved the mayor's daughter, Zaneeta." He wagged a finger, no, no.

Franklin, the former playwright, stood in front of Meredith's rocker. He towered. Meredith cowered. He so hoped Franklin could be tender and insightful with his story. "I can wade you through this jungle overnight," was what Franklin said.

Meredith stung his eyes into Franklin's face. "It's been tinkered with for years, Franklin. You got x-ray vision or something? I hope, I hope."

Rini moaned at Franklin's next words: "Who can tell the plot in the fewest words?"

"We've played this game together, and separately with countless friends," Meredith said.

"But I know my stuff," Franklin said, "and it's fresh to me. Let me try."

And Franklin proceeded to do just that. Meredith listened to every new re-routing and to some he'd heard before and rejected. Something about Franklin made Meredith see new points.

In his autobiography, Meredith would credit Franklin greatly and praise their ability to get along even while disagreeing.

The three set a pattern for that next week, walking and hiking, napping. Round about dinner they'd start their plot-chanting, again. Meredith felt like his mother was looking down, clapping at times. Surely he was getting closer to Broadway. Maybe he'd call Mabel and tell her he was almost there.

A week to the night they'd arrived, in a quiet moment over cigarettes, Meredith turned to Franklin. "Why don't you come to our house in L.A. and work with me for a spell?"

"Meredith, I think you're close," Franklin said. "Let's do it."

The next morning the three clicked their suitcases, loaded the car and swung down the mountain, thirty miles to Meredith's music room. Franklin took typewriter paper and wrapped the walls with dashes of pages, each a scene or a merger between scenes. The show moved from Meredith's head to paper, around the room like a rubber band. His head felt lighter.

Franklin showed Meredith how to chalk the scenes on a blackboard, skinny rectangles with connecting dashes. The eraser clapped the board, moving scenes about. Meredith's throat and the inside of his nose dried with chalk dust. He was surprised how much he used Ernie's advice.

"Nay!" "Yay." The two men cheered or booed every clacking scribble. Rini stayed out. She passed the crack in the double doors over and over, to the hallway and back.

"A month of this," said Rini to Meredith, three weeks later. It sounded like "Enough of this," but Meredith could not think of quitting. He was sunk deep into Mason City, where he had to be. He imagined the sweet air. He chewed gum drops, spreading crystal sugar on his lips.

The next day, always his custom, around ten in the morning, he marched off for a walk. His feet pounded the concrete street because his neighborhood had no sidewalks. Sometimes he imagined he was leading a marching band, and his right arm swung a baton up past his head and down. His knees pumped off the street like it was hot or sprung or something.

He had to ignore faces. None of their beeswax. The days and nights had no borders, Meredith was inside his music.

In his autobiography, Meredith described a day, September 10th, when a turbulence he recognized rose in his chest. He'd got up at three in the morning and worked-walked-worked all day. And Franklin came, as usual, pounding on the music room door, about four o'clock. They did "Nay" and "Yay" back and forth until dinner.

After that, Meredith didn't come out or let Franklin in. "Trouble, trouble, trouble," throbbed through him, inside the locked music room doors. Another voice inside him chanted against it, in the way he could hear lots of instruments at once when he composed.

Except, gol darn it, Meredith Willson, hello, himself in person: *Words are music when ya toss in rhythm.* The concept cleared crystal. He pounded on, feet stamping, voice hoarse, hour after hour.

He might have the centerpiece song for his musical. Franklin and Rini murmured outside the door, occasionally echoing Meredith's strains.

Meredith worked on. He'd got up at three in the morning and shooed Franklin away after dinner, in silence. Except for the pounding the piano and chanting about trouble starting with a "T" and that rhymed with "P." "P" stood for pool!

Meredith sprayed it out, a lyric with a pounding good rhythm, oh, six minutes long now. "Okay, Rin, Franklin. Get in here fast!"

Rini leaned in the doorway, color on her wet cheeks, a grin on her face. Franklin hovered at her side and thanked God or someone, hands clasped, eyes closed, lips moving along the new words, the best he could remember.

Josephine, the hired girl—the hard girl, according to Rini's pronunciation—came from the kitchen, too. She summed it up in "her English she'd not quite learned and her forgotten German," Meredith's description. "Vare yoo could vind such a actor to sing such a long scrabbling?" Meredith paused at the precious tongue twists.

"She has something there," he said. He grabbed her by the waist and whirled the surprised woman about the room, in a galloping German polka. Joan clobbered faster on the typewriter in the next room. "Clobbered" was Meredith's word. His word choice often worked as well as a photo, his talent. Meredith observed his secretary could make more money in the unemployment line in a few hours than in a month in his house. Priceless.

Franklin and Meredith hollered on, through his new lyrics, trying to hear them again before they dissolved forgotten into the sweet air. Rini sang all the way to the kitchen and returned with wheat germ and calcium and cod-liver oil and apple cider vinegar and papaya and Sanka and stone-ground toast, Meredith's usual breakfast, one combination or another according to his books.

It was the first food he'd had that day.

Meredith continued in a stupor, moving to his den to roll out consonants, h's and k's. Like a horse trotting on, turning the roller of his black Corona typewriter. Ink-blue carbon papers carpeted the corner of the den. He was hunting and pecking his typewriter with tap-dancing fingers, then racing for the music room and his piano to shout it. The rhythm slowed gradually as the three thought they had it. Somehow the song got to paper.

And Josephine once again did the unthinkable. She burst into the music room, wringing her calico apron with hands still in oven mitts. Top of her voice, she shouted: "Duh Mister Martin, *Duh* Martin!"

Rini rushed up the stairs barefoot, in underskirt and curlers. But backed right back. The long departed Ernie Martin—*the* Martin—the producer who would not produce *The Music Man*—stood in the front doorway, a sheaf of papers fluttering in the breeze. He wanted strawberry pop. His too-short pants flapped in the breeze,

All flew to the entry. Ernie's too-tight-under-the-arms yellow jacket hung forward, the back almost up to his waist. For a second Meredith thought Ernie'd never left their home, certainly not changed jackets.

Or perhaps he'd come back because he thought Meredith finished the musical?

"I tried to phone," Ernie said, profusely, without sitting. He launched into a diatribe about how Meredith could learn Broadway from him over the next year. Rini and Meredith exchanged joyful big-eyed looks. Cy and Ernie would do *The Music Man* after all? Franklin dissolved onto the piano bench looking unused to a scene like this not at all.

"Meredith," Ernie said, "I want you to do the music for my newest show *Indian Joe*. It'll be on stage by late 1957."

Not a muscle twitched. Meredith was not a man who could change gears on the turn of Ernie's twenty words. Meredith wanted to tuck his white shirt into his linen trousers—it seemed he wasn't presentable—but his hands hung limp and heavy.

His voice came out in a whisper. His dry eyes blinked only once as his mouth worked the words. He was too hung up right then on *The Music Man* to try anything.

"I thought you gave that *Music Man* thing up," Ernie said.

"Oh, fer the love of Jesus," said Josephine, pulling her scarf to mop her brow.

"*You* gave it up, Ernie." Meredith shifted weight, side to side. He felt like a little boy. Once Ernie'd said *Music Man* was, "Spec-by God-tac-cular."

"We produce *Music Man* too, end of 1958." Ernie jutted his chin.

Meredith thought he heard "honest injun" in there somewhere, funny because Ernie was full of baloney, he was sure. Rini whooshed up the steps. Meredith backed through the doors to his piano. He didn't know what else to do. He couldn't say yes to Ernie so fast, and so he sat and did his train opening, head bobbing over his shoulder at Ernie, eyes seeing nothing, stunned. But he was coming to life.

The chant was new to Ernie. But Meredith finished his blessed precious train opening to silence. "Ernie, I got too much steam up on *The Music Man*. Didn't you hear that train opening?"

Rini tore back down the steps, now in a dress, face all fixed, like she had her two bits to toss in. She closed up rank behind Ernie, hands on hips.

"Two weeks," said Ernie.

"Three weeks," Ernie said, louder. "We'll meet three weeks from Monday around eleven thirty. Twelve o'clock. And you tell me if you can do the music for *Indian Joe*. It's just the music this time, not the script and all. Much easier for you, Meredith."

"Do it," Meredith could just hear friends say. "Two Broadway shows, instead of one. Think up that." Their voices chanted in Meredith's head against the train rhythm.

Rini spoke up, real and last. "Darling," she said, swishing her skirt under the hall light. She blocked the front door. Meredith knew she thought he might leave to join Ernie. She sparked her dark eyes right at him and her iridescent black/blue skirt gleamed like fly wings. He knew she was about to fuzz. He waited.

"Darling," she said, in her way. "I sure don't want to stir you wrong, but *I* say *the heck* with it. Meredith, you are *The Music Man*."

* * *

Back at the old folk's home, I jumped to my feet. "That Rini's a genius. She's right?"

"She's part of him," Mabel said. "Without Rini, he'd be up a creek." Mabel sparked her eyes. "Lots of people would quit now. This is how we separate the men from the boys. So to speak. Meredith Willson *is not a quitter!*" Mabel's voice was insistent.

She reached for my hand. "And—neither are you, Lady Jane," she said. Her voice was softer now. But I heard her. Something about Rini made me pause, too, even though I'd never laid eyes on her.

Rini kept Meredith true to himself.

I had a friend like that in Sister Mary Franzeline, my piano teacher,

"Syncopated Clock" in Black Tux (Photo: Julie Sartor; Courtesy of Beth Obermeyer)

"Golliwogg's Cakewalk" in white organdy. Pianists, senior recital, Holy Family: Jane White, Sarann Ryan, Virginia Skram, Sheila Dougherty, assisted by vocalist Camilla McCarron and dancer, Mary Beth Sartor in "Golliwogg's Cakewalk," Debussy. (Photo: Jule Sartor; Courtesy Beth Obermeyer)

I realized. I loved my classical music. Every year she had a senior recital. Imagine, that year she rounded up four grand pianos for the stage in the church basement, for a solo recital for four senior girls.

Sister put her thumb in the dike for me, so to speak, I told Mabel.

She had the four girls play "Golliwogg's Cakewalk." She had me ask Dean to choreograph it. Ditto "Syncopated Clock." I wore pants, tails for the latter, a top hat and cane and it felt so grown up to me. My mother ruffled up pantaloons and an organdy dress for "Golliwogg's Cakewalk." Imagine, dancing to four grand pianos. They were alive with all those gold strings. It was Jane White, Sarann Ryan, Roseanne Berrie, Camilla McCarron.

That outlet, from Dean and Sister Mary Franzeline, filled me. Julie took the photos in the den with my Brownie camera, made us both happy.

I folded Mabel's letter from Meredith back into the envelope and tapped it onto the stack. I tied it with the string. She'd missed my story.

Mabel fell asleep at the drop of a hat those days.

34

Cold Call to Kermit Bloomgarden

NOVEMBER 1956

Eleven-forty-five. Meredith Willson didn't have to look at the clock in his study. Three gongs rocked his head. "Honey, I have to call Ernie in fifteen minutes and tell him what I'm going to do." Should he work on a new show, do *Music Man later*? People in-the-know knew about it, they even said it to Meredith.

Had he just come up from three weeks underwater? Ever since Ernie asked him to decide to do or not to do *Indian Joe,* Meredith had been working non-stop on *The Music Man.* He'd wanted to finish his *Music Man*—pressure—in case all his time in the next months went into *Indian Joe.* Rini leaned on the living room arch, crossing her eyes farther than most people could.

"Curtain," typed Meredith, on the last page of his script, that last word that writers swallow and spit. "C. U. R. T. A. I. N." He cleared his throat, his stomach in turmoil.

"Rini, I'm done. I finished *The Music Man.*" He crossed into the entry and banged his forehead on the arch, trying to jar himself back to the real world. He roughed up her hair with his knuckles. "Eleven fifty. I got one more idea, kid." Rini chewed the cuticle of her thumb at a furious pace.

"Frank Loesser has a huge hit. His lyrics in *Most Happy Fella* are as good as we've seen him do in years," he said. Meredith cuddled her face in his hands. "Frank says Kermit Bloomgarden is a great producer to work with."

Rini bailed to pick up Piccolo the puppy so he'd stop yapping, and she could listen. The dachshund tipped like a teeter totter on her arms.

"Well, it's a long shot, don't even know him and Bloomgarden sure won't know me." Meredith backed up to watch her reaction. "I *could* ask him if he wants to take a listen to the *The Music Man* before I get back to Cy and Ern."

"You've got ten minutes," said Rini. "Call Mr. Bloom up, go ahead. I'm sure he'll come to the phone, it's long distance." She bobbed her head, like she'd solved everything.

Meredith leaned his head on the mirror and picked up the telephone. He rallied everything in his head, all the years of *Music Man*, all the times trying to please producers. "I got nothing to lose," he said, dialing away. His legs, awakened from sitting at the typewriter, rushed blood inside. "Mr. Bloomgarden, sir," he said.

Meredith spewered his story, spinning in the phone cord, this way on one sentence, back on the next. "I have this musical, was gonna be produced by Cy and Ernie, now they want me to do a different show and I have to tell them by noon. Today. Would you take a listen to *The Music Man?*" He felt like a little boy pleading with his mother. His voice had as much gusto as Ern's, maybe more.

And, he was contrary. He couldn't switch gears to *Indian Joe*, and he'd stand up for himself till the cows came home. Anyway, he didn't believe Ernie'd get to *The Music Man*. He didn't last time.

"Do I know you?" Mr. Bloomgarden said. He suggested Meredith send him the book.

Meredith huffed at the mirror, steamed over from his sputtering. He swiped it clear and encouraged his reflection. "Well, no, sir, the book won't do, not at all. This show is rhythms, no rhymes, that turn into the story and the music is the beat of the words. And it just so happens, my wife and I do a great sit-down piano vocal, can do it for you, anytime." Piccolo skidded at his feet, wanted to go out.

Meredith couldn't believe this blooming producer opened up to a phone call. The producer "must of put the phone under his arm"—something caused static anyway. It muffled a shout and what he shouted hurt. Mr. Bloomgarden called Meredith a cowboy!

Meredith talked on, long hard and loud, his entire body pleading. He shouted. "I wrote a bang beatin' musical . . ." He rattled. "A whale of a belt of a show." He paused, wondering if Mr. Bloomgarden was still on the line. He heard his own breathing.

Sometimes Meredith was glad the hall light reflected on his thick glasses, hid his eyes from Rini. His eyes could grab the disappointment first if Kermit said no and then he'd say it better to Rini. His weak knees readied to roll back and die into his grave of dusty old radio shows if Kermit Mr. Bloomgarden pushed the receiver button.

Meredith dropped to the floor, cross-legged. Rini covered her mouth. Meredith lay back and his head hit the floor hard, his legs sproinging straight.

"I'll give you all the time you want any night this week, Mr. Willson. It sounds interesting."

Meredith's eyes flew open. This is not just any chopped liver producer either. This is the real McCoy—*Bloomgarden*. He pumped one fist to let Rini know all was good.

"How about Wednesday?" Mr. Bloomgarden said.

Meredith removed his glasses and mopped his eyes, breathing yes.

The Mr. Bloomgarden said, "Fine, Wednesday night at Herb Greene's apartment."

Herb Greene's? *The famous conductor?*

"Two Hundred West Fifty-Eighth Street. Twelve midnight. Give Herb a chance to get home from conducting *Most Happy Fella*." Rini jumped on Meredith, the better to hear.

Meredith said something proper to accept—he couldn't hear his own words in his roaring head—and he hoped he sounded appreciative. He hugged his phone arm around his Rini. He stood for one more call.

"Ern! I got tied up, can't make today's meeting. See, this producer *Kerm Bloomgarden*, going to take a listen to *The Music Man* on Wednesday. So we need to wait."

"Fine, come over to our office when you finish Wednesday." Ernie's voice slowed toward the end of the sentence, more of an earnest Ernie by the last word. A thoughtful slower Ernie.

"I might be late Wednesday morning. *The Music Man* is long . . ." He didn't want to say the audition was at midnight.

"You don't say," said Ernie, right on the beat. It was so Ernie.

Meredith and Rini rocked the entry.

35

Meredith and Kermit

DECEMBER 19, 1956

On a white loveseat in the lobby of New York City's Waldorf Hotel, Meredith and Rini waited for the stroke of midnight, with all the drama of a Cinderella story. A cab ride away and they'd walk in the door at Herb Greene-the-conductor's apartment, to meet Kermit Bloomgarden, *the* producer.

Rini rolled her eyes up into her head, which was a long way when you had Rini's orbs. Meredith closed his eyes. Usually, the calm of his life was Rini but the moment of his lifetime was upon him. He felt every nerve in his body, each like a pin prick. Whatever went down tonight, he'd either turn back into a radio show talker or into a Broadway star.

If this Kermit Bloomgarden didn't like his *Music Man*, then he didn't know what.

Meredith was the dinger going up the pole at the fair and he'd either hit the darn bell or not. If he didn't, his quarter was spent.

He'd had ten tries at getting this thing produced, at least.

His thoughts raced, over-lapped, the past, his boyhood, his mother, all the years writing this show. He had to get free of his frenetic mind, chug through on a high—nail this night.

And what a chiller it was. He walked to the cab, his face stinging from the pelts of drizzle. They could kill themselves off right now if they slipped on the glare ice. It didn't do this so much in Mason City where the temps stayed well below freezing much of the winter. But this New York stuff brought snow that melted as it landed, only to turn to ice, all within a night and day. "Just can't trust New York," he said to Rini, bowing his head to miss the roof of the cab. "Mason City's snow would be crunchy sparkle-glitter in the moonlight."

Rini pulled her chinchilla collar to her nose. "Well, since you're going to get rich telling New York and the world about Mason City—I am very pleased you like Mason City's snowfalls."

Up the cement steps of the brownstone they teetered, each gripping their own handrail as they pivoted on the ice. "God help us, this feels like that night we auditioned at Cy and Ernie's."

"Surely we've learned something in our long trip to Broadway," Rini said, pressing her back to the door. She planted cold lips on his and and stayed til his glasses steamed.

"People in warm climes don't get kisses like that," Meredith said. He held her, hoping to plug her warmth and love into his psyche, a stunning sensation when in God's Frigidaire.

Mrs. Greene pulled open the door, a sophisticated lady with shiny dark hair pulled straight back. Her voice hushed, like they were kids up past bedtime. The Willsons shed their melting coats like pros. She let them stare, she was a suave hostess. "You're looking at the actual posters from shows Herb's been part of: *Guys and Dolls, Can Can, Silk Stockings, Most Happy Fella.*

Music Man, said Meredith's heart. "Leave room for the *Music Man* poster," said Rini.

Meredith settled on the grand piano in the spacious living room, "A pip it is," he said. He'd crossed a room suitable to be a sound stage. The recording equipment stacked like bookshelves. He figured the bedrooms had to be postage-stamped with a bed and that's it.

"And Cole Porter gave Herb the electric organ." Meredith, no sissy, gave not a glance.

"Do you play too?" Rini asked Mrs. Greene. Rini had a way of bonding—and by gosh didn't she find it with Mrs. Greene in fifteen seconds. Mrs. Greene was a concert pianist.

Meredith hid behind the piano, warming up his cold hands on Rini's waist. He was admiring Rini's cute reflection in the window, distracting himself from nerves, when Herb Greene arrived in the living room arch, a mid-thirties kid in a soft white leather-lustrous coat. Meredith imagined himself in a box just over the Broadway stage. This Herb was the guy with the stick in the pit below, the conductor that would do Meredith's downbeat. All a mind game.

Herb, the conductor, got even more charming. In Meredith's book, *But He Doesn't Know the Territory*, he'd described Greene as sucking a pickle like he thought it was an ice cream cone. Maybe because it was coated with snow. Maybe his coat wasn't even white, just covered with snow. Meredith loved his flair. The guy's independence relaxed him somehow.

With every tick of the grandfather clock, a new person drifted in the door. This was no funeral visitation like when Jesse Lasky's gang came to hear their audition. Meredith didn't know any of them but they had to be important.

Mr. Bloomgarten came last. "Howdado," he said, like everyone had told Meredith he would. In his late forties, Bloom gave the gathering that famous Bloomgarden look. Meredith had heard of that, too. "Could tunnel right through an alp," Thornton Wilder once said.

"Let's go. It's late. Such a night," Mr. Bloom said. As though on cue, the radiators hissed. Meredith's breath felt like dry heat and his mouth dried up like cotton balls were soaking under his lips. And, his lips stuck to his teeth.

Sleet tinkled the window, a music overture he didn't write or expect. A guy with a stovepipe schlipped the window up. Noise from below rattled, honked in.

According to Meredith's autobiography, he gathered his stuff. He asked Mr. Greene to shut the window because he had "a ton of lyrics here and if you can't hear them . . ." Nope they all agreed. They had to smoke.

But Herb crossed the room and shut the window, massaging Meredith's shoulder on the way back to his seat. Meredith started his precious train opening, about talk, talk, bicker, talk.

"No, it ain't, no it ain't." Rini screeched, like the train coming into the station.

Even with the window shut, the audience missed the next lines. Herb honored Meredith and Rini with a "Happy hoot of a yelping belt," Meredith said later, "covering up the start of one of my best lines."

Who else could make rhythms and sense of words like hogshead, cask and demijohn? Sugar barrel, pickle barrel, milk pan?

Meredith had never welcomed a belly laugh like he did Herb's, and he changed his darn-scared volume to relaxed and louder, trying hard as hell to be smooth. The Iowa showman inside him knew the tone was set with Herb's laugh. He'd blast it right through the glass of the window all the way through the city of New York. At least a block away.

When you're in, you're in, that's all he wrote, went through Meredith's head. Rini swished that taffeta skirt, good news because if Rini got mad again, like she did at Jesse Lasky's—well now—Meredith said he would rather just die right there. But Meredith knew she knew too—they were about as close to Broadway right now as they'd ever been.

The next morning, nine o'clock, the phone rang in their suite at the Waldorf. Mere reached his go-to-meeting, pin-stripe flannel pajama sleeve to the white and gold phone. He froze in wide-awake silence, the veins on his wrist throbbed, waiting for the words he wanted to hear.

"Haven't been to bed yet," said Mr. Bloomgarden. "Can you come right over?"

Meredith couldn't believe that he and Rini had slept well. He couldn't believe either that Kermit wasn't intimidating and suspenseful. All his cards were on the table. "Whatta man, out of producer heaven," said Rini, hugging Meredith until her satin spaghetti strap broke on her nightgown. She closed her eyes with a smile, stored her eyebrows under her bangs.

Meredith and Rini went to Kermit's office. Full well they knew they were looking out the window at the back of the block-long billboard—between Forty-Fifth and Forty-Sixth Street on Broadway—the block-long *Baby Doll* in her crib.

Mr. Bloomgarden's first words, starting from his first intake of breath, made Meredith cry. Meredith'd never felt so professional and worthy and classy and talented and important, clearly not a rube. He was Iowa in New York, apparently with just what the U.S. of A. wanted.

Mr. Bloomgarden's words didn't start fast, they didn't spray, they didn't say *maybe*, or *I think*, or *if*. Meredith raised out of his chair as the sentence started, hanging on the arms at the same time, in case his optimism was not right.

"Meredith," Mr. Bloomgarden spoke, his eyes honest, his hands folded. Rini's ankle wrapped tight around her Meredith's leg. Could they believe him?

"Meredith. May I have the privilege of producing your beautiful play?"

Saving Julie. "Watermelon Weather." (Courtesy of Beth Obermeyer)

36

A Tale of Two Sisters

SUMMER 1957

Meredith's news had reverberated through Mason City, word of mouth. It made Mabel cry. She cried at everything these days, just one eye, happy or sad. Surely Meredith's new producer would not be a false alarm, we told each other. But if Meredith could be canceled once in *The New York Times*, Mabel and I knew we were not in control. But we could hope. Meredith wrote he was full speed ahead. "Words holler at me."

The *Globe Gazette* went into action with the news. Now everyone knew.

Inspired, Julie and I worked hard. Julie was a different little girl than I was. She was just so smart. She thought ahead and worried about every little thing that could happen on a stage. Anyone knows that in live entertainment, things just happen. But, no, Julie worried away. Mabel mostly listened.

"I never worry, but now I worry that she'll worry, because she blinks when she worries."

Mabel's brain worked. She got that last sentence.

And my dad didn't like that Julie worried, not at all. But when we pulled off that first Iowa "Watermelon Weather," the audience went nuts. Julie jumped from her end pose onto my lap. Even the cast on the stage stopped to clap. And Julie got it. She could stay on her feet and do it.

We had a ball after that, at fairs, dancing at official events in the area. If we succeeded we could get all the way to New York, if we just could win that one fair contest. My secret wish, and I could hardly mouth this, was this: if I did get to New York, I *could meet Mr. Meredith Willson himself in person.* With any luck, *The Music Man* would be getting to Broadway, right down the street from the Ted Mack show. Then I'd have a story for Mabel!

I have to say I imagined meeting him often. They say if you don't imagine yourself in an idyllic situation, you won't know what to do when it happens, or even recognize that it is happening or *could* happen. But I was just a kid, one of many Mabel had cheered over the years. But one of the ones who stayed with her. Mom saw to that, even if I felt we were tapping faster, and leaving an ever-slower Mabel behind.

I imagined Meredith knew who I was even if Mabel didn't talk to him as much. He still sent his brief notes. He might know who I was, a tap dancer in Mason City. Even though, in reality, to that time my only real personal connection to Meredith was that I used to color my sheet music, Mabel's, too, and I did one for him, with morning glories all over the round note heads. But that was as close as I got.

I loved the path Julie and I were taking, where it took us over three years. When "Watermelon Weather,"got our feet wet and salved Julie's nerves, we were out there. Julie had one hard dance for a little girl. I learned her dance, faster than the other way around. She was, after all, still "the baby" in my mind.

Mrs. Sartor's first of four *Music Man* costumes. (Art Reynolds Publicity photo; Courtesy of Beth Obermeyer)

190

I even got a solo of sorts when the Society for the Preservation and Encouragement of Barbershop Quartet Singing in America (SPEBSQSA), asked me to stand at the front edge of the stage through the SPEBSQSA show, held in Mason City. I turned the cards announcing each quartet, a tradition left over from Vaudeville. My mother made me the first of four *Music Man* costumes.

"Copy Cat Shadow" at the Fourth of July, Clear Lake. The contest winners (in order of placement), Bill Riley, KRNT-TV, emcee: Colleen Taylor, singer; Mary Beth and Julie Sartor, dancers; Donna Nelson, singer; Linda Meinecke, dance; Carmel McDaid, singer, and Ron Klipping, singer. (Courtesy of *Clear Lake Mirror*)

The Music Man was already rumored to have the first barbershop quartet ever to be in a Broadway musical. That put Mason City on the map.

The next summer Julie and I tried our first competition. I was fourteen, and little Julie was a whopping bitty seven-year-old. We did a song and dance, "Copy Cat Shadow," where we started with our tap challenge, a story dance from Dean, and then did a difficult routine, a combination of her new dance and my old ones. I suppose his ballet line was in the dance, too. Julie was up to it. Daddy spliced our Danny Hoctor dancing school record, "Copy Cat Shadow," with his 78 rpm version of "Me and My Shadow" onto his reel-to-reel, then made a record of it, with his record maker.

"Western Swing," for the Fourth—in our practice room. (Courtesy of Beth Obermeyer)

We placed second. We were thrilled. I could take contests in stride by then because Julie and I were just getting our feet wet.

And then we went back the next year and did a Western Tap, with Mrs. Diggins on the piano. The dance was not hard and traveled like a freight train. We danced the challenge again, shook hands and stormed the crowd. I found tiny cap guns in the dime store. Mrs. Poppy helped me. She knew her stuff, and the tiny pistols added a bang to the finale on the turns. We won the whole thing that summer on the stage on Clear Lake, on the Fourth of July! Mrs. Diggins had a bit of arthritis in her hands by then. But not a stroke. She would play for decades to come.

Daddy tried to give Mabel music, a transistor radio, the biggest new invention. She could plug it in her ear and not bother other residents in the home. He said music would be like medicine to her, bring her out, keep her interacting. Everytime I visited I tuned it to a new station. Mabel liked all kinds of music but not rock and roll. The radio cost $39.95, roughly $200 if it were today.

She was worth it.

Julie and I were rolling! We headed to the Hancock County Fair, the biggest contest yet. First Prize: that trip to New York to be on *Ted Mack*. Okay, fifty years later no one knows who Ted Mack was, and his show. But the country did then, believe me. It was the late fifties.

37

Mason City to the Emerald City

Oh, those Western costumes. White felt spats, boleros, and skirts with every edge trimmed in silver sequins, satin blouses with a glittery paisley print. It all stayed on the dining room table for months, like paper dolls on lace.

We went to the Hancock County Fair. We saw, we conquered, that simple. We were among hundreds auditioning, then worked our way into the final twenty.

To First Place! We were on our way to the *"Ted Mack Original Amateur Hour,* New York City!

But like Meredith, we'd barely just begun.

I scrunched the stiff nylon net under the costume. The smell always got me, kind of like a hot iron had fused it, reminding me of stage lights. "God bless nylon net," my mother always said. The cotton net would have wilted at the first try-outs.

My mother was the world expert on petticoats.

Our mother, not just *my* mother.

"I hope the humidity isn't so high that the crepe paper lariat loses its stretch," she said. White leather tap shoes with silver Capezio taps, so scratched, broken in. The worst thing in the world was new stiff tap shoes. So Julie and I each had at least two pairs going. White socks slipped over and protected a third pair, back-up to the back-up pair.

The big day came. Off to New York. Daddy came through the front door, jingling his keys, slapping his flat feet. Under the big white arch of the entry, he crooned to the chandelier.

My mother flopped in a chair like she'd tear her hair out. She was trying to get us moving and here he sat, into his newspaper. She clicked the white dancing-out suitcase shut. "Time to go," she said. "Get going early. Today's a scorcher!"

"Oh, lookie here," Daddy said, adjusting his glasses. "The article on the Kossuth County Fair. Let's see, let's see." He snapped the newspaper on his knee. "It says 'The Sartor Sisters in a western dance routine.' Oh my. 'A pair of the best-known dancers in the state.'" He smiled over his glasses at me, then at Julie. He didn't dare look at Mom.

He looked through the bottom part of his glasses. "Ah, yes, Governor's Days. Here's your picture with Governor Herschel Loveless. It says, 'Judging from the governor's broad grin, he enjoyed the little session with the two attractive young women.'" Daddy chuckled. "A lot more pleasant for our governor to smile with two little girls than to defend his vetoes."

Mary Beth and Julie with Iowa Governor Herschel Loveless. (Courtesy of *Clear Lake Mirror*)

Mom set her chin. She was a Democrat. Dad was a Republican.

"Look at this," he continued, reading. "'Accusations that he's depriving Iowa's young of a higher education by vetoing the building appropriations for the state schools brought this question from the governor.'" He threw his head back. "Were they just born this year? And what were my two little Republicans doing dancing for the Dumb-o-crats?" he asked. "The Guv says 'all of those preparing for college educations were born during the eighteen years the Republicans controlled the Legislature and governor's chair.'"

Mom tried to wrap it up. "Al Gerardi was in charge of entertainment. He only asked three other acts."

"Arrrgh." My dad read on. "Just listen to this. 'Iowa's income last year was two-billion dollars from agriculture and four-billion dollars from other industry.' The Guv said, 'we must move toward a balanced industrial-agricultural economy. If we do not get more of the processing dollar, Iowa will lose 200,000 in population in the next five years as has been forecast by a national magazine.'"

"Anyway." Mom interrupted. "We aren't *all* Republicans here, you know." She stared her best. This conversation was old hat. "We can talk about this in the car," she said.

My father was going to wail out his voting story, I just knew it. Why he stalled sometimes, nobody knew. I don't think he did it on purpose. It's just that he was away from the hospital, enjoying being on home time.

Away he went. "How could I forget," he said. "Twenty years ago, I came all the way home from the hospital, in Chicago traffic, to pick you up so we'd have two votes, and who did you vote for?" He threw his face to the ceiling. "The Democrat! We canceled each other out!"

He tipped his head at her. "We should have had two good votes. I might as well have stayed at the hospital." He clowned, strangling his throat with his hands.

She raised her chin. "What's a vote if not a vote I'm thinking." She reached for her straw hat and adjusted last Easter's starched fabric dahlias. "Bring the paper with you," she said, as clearly as she could, around the hatpin in her mouth.

"How many fairs did we go to this summer?" Daddy said. "And look here, we missed this one: and *this* was the one! A Two-Day Auto Show at the North Iowa Fairgrounds." Was she listening? He wasn't leaving yet.

Mom's polished-cotton skirt flipped a summer garden around her knees as she collected everything. Daddy jumped his eyes to his finger on the paper.

Mom was always early. Daddy was always late.

"Oh, ya. Here we go. Oh, this is big." He continued reading. "'On Tuesday, "Fezz" Fritsche, King of Goose Town, and his eight-piece band will entertain.' Wait, wait, wait. Here we go. 'The big attraction will be the glistening new cars on display. Fritz Olson will have General Motors foreign made Opel, as well as the Le Sabre, Invicta, and Electra.'"

"Mary Beth can read it aloud as we drive," Mom said.

"Now where were we going?" Now he was teasing! "Oh yes. New York."

I headed out the door because Mom'd already started down the front sidewalk to the car, Bobby alongside. Julie trailed. We were almost launched. Everyone at the Old Folks Home knew to tune in the television for Mabel. Daddy made sure Mabel had her own TV, but she could only watch it if none of her roommates got upset. But they all knew Julie and me.

Daddy was last out of the house that day, but he was the door locker anyway.

If you leave in chaos, always think hard, double check, go over your list.

38

The Pennsylvania Turnpike

The Burma Shave signs clicked by the car window in a comforting rhythm, one six-stick poem, then another. Are we almost there?" Julie was just wondering.

We hit the brand new Pennsylvania Turnpike. We flew on the one-way lanes. Special exits led right to gas stations and restaurants. You didn't even drive through towns, and we thought that was slick. "Don't leave anything or forget something in a bathroom. I can't turn around on this thing," Daddy said.

We stayed in motels, right on the pike. Soon we'd have a good time in New York, have a nice hotel, take a boat ride, see museums, Daddy promised. But my mother would want naps and practicing, of that I was certain.

Mom leaned back on her seat. "It seems as though we've forgotten something, but what would it be?" I had no idea what she might have forgotten, but I'd sure been a hero for life if I had. But I didn't even know what clothes I had or which suitcase they were in. Anyway, the car was packed three days ago.

We chanted the states, our route, like a jump-rope sing-song: "I-, Ill-; In-, O-, West Virginia, Pennsylvania, New Jersey, New York!"

Daddy always saved mealtime for restaurants that looked like houses. "You can be sure the food is good if a family makes it. You can never tell what you're walking into otherwise," he said. "It could be a bar, a hang-out or a nice family operation, you just don't know." We always ate California hamburgers and French fries. Daddy always got milk toast.

He also thought it best to stop early before all the motel rooms were taken. "We don't want to have to stay in a cabin, and these new motels are pretty far apart." We always had to work hard at waking Bobby. Daddy gave him a big dose of sleeping medicine so he wouldn't get car sick.

One day, at the end of the driving day, Mom inspected the cases in the trunk of the car. "I just know I forgot something. I don't like to leave home, I guess. I just like to wake up to my own toaster."

Soon, I knew for sure the drive would take three full days. We'd heard about that for weeks. I lifted my long hair onto the shelf by the rear window while we cruised. It was hot.

Mom chewed on her fingers, elbowed the open window ledge. She turned down the sun visor and looked at us in the back seat. In our matching shorts outfits, what could we need?

"Oh!" My mother screamed, bloody murder.

My father put a mesh shoe on the brake. "What?" He glanced at the whizzing traffic on his left. "What? Don't scream when I'm driving on the turnpike for heaven's sake."

"Our Sunday clothes! They're hanging in the front closet at home! That's what we forgot!" Mom said. My mother stopped shouting to sob.

I sat way up. "What will I wear to go see the Rockettes?"

"My suit too?" Daddy asked. He rocked on the seat, eyes ahead.

"My cowgirl costume?" asked Julie. She jumped up and landed cross-legged.

"Oh, no, it's not *that* terrible. We've got the costumes. And we can't go back, right?" My mother slumped on the seat, hands over her face.

Daddy leaned onto the steering wheel like he did to ease the pressure on his back. It turned out the "Sunday clothes" included everything but our traveling suits.

"Here's what we do," he said, after a bit. "Call Hanna and ask her to box up the clothes. When we visit Cunninghams after New York, the clothes will be there." Cunninghams were our old neighbors, now in Short Hills, New Jersey.

"But the Rockettes show is the night we get there," I wailed.

"Hanna can use the metal box Daddy used to mail laundry home when on a trip," Mom said. "We'll be only one night in New York till it's there. Wouldn't you know it'd be that night. "No one knows us anyway." Mom leaned back and stared at the little cut-out stars in the car ceiling.

I unzipped my gold reptile notebook and jotted all this in my journal. I pulled out the Rockette folder and smoothed the page, my favorite page. A cute boy in a red and gold uniform had a white-gloved hand on the arm of a beautiful girl, seating her for the show.

I was going to be that girl in my white cotton-satin dress with the iris painted on the bodice tucks and up the skirt hem. Now the movie star usher might not even notice me. Heck, for sure he wouldn't. I'd be in pedal pushers and cropped top. Girls never wore pants out. Never.

Maybe he would have come backstage to see me at Ted Mack's, that's what I'd thought. He had never known a girl from Mason City. He would watch me dance and wait behind the gold curtain, by the gold curtain ropes and tassels. Shoot! My trip was ruined. I *was*, had planned, on going home and telling everyone in high school about that boy.

39

The Sidewalks of New York

D o not talk to me from now on. This New York traffic is not what I'm used to. I need to concentrate." Daddy talked out of the side of his mouth toward us. He leaned over the steering wheel, perspiration drips caught in his hairline. An orchestra of car horns blared.

"Roll your windows up," he said. "It's hot, I know, but people walk right up to your car, and you just don't know what they want. Like look at these guys, up ahead two cars." I cranked and jerked my window handle, up.

"Shine, sir? A nickel." The fellow's red bandana squeaked on our glass and his fists pounded the window in a rhythm. His lips and nose grew big against the glass.

Daddy put the car in neutral and revved the engine like a hot rodder. Steam poured through the cracks of the hood. He was still two cars from the light. Julie cowered in her corner and wailed. She looked like a squeak toy, rubber tongue wagging.

"For crying out loud, quiet her down," Daddy shouted, at my mother. Mom grabbed a hanky from her bodice pocket and smoothed it on her lap. She turned on her knees to face the back seat, folding the fabric in a blur. "*Shush*, I'll make babies in a cradle."

New York pennant.

"I'm car sick," said Julie, slapping the hanky across her face.

"Sit forward where you can see the road, and you'll feel better," said the doctor driver. Julie dragged her leg toward the center of the car, pushing into my space.

"Don't do it all over me," I said, turning the little girl to the front with a shove.

We'd been in the car eight hours every day for four days, was all, today with just a short stop for lunch. I wondered if this was what Mom was expecting in New York. The sounds outside the car mulled. "It stinks," said Julie, wiggling her nose. The smells batted around the inside of the car like balloons.

"Your dad knows what he's doing in a big city," Mom said.

The store windows lined up as far as I could see, like facets of a giant rhinestone. That's all I thought I'd see in New York: movie stars in rhinestones. Instead, I saw *everything*.

"Don't touch my leg." Julie screamed and slapped her hand on my back. When she kicked her good leg, I slammed the arm rest on her hand.

"I'm going to stop this car and give you both a good spanking." Daddy shouted into the steering wheel like a maniac. He rocked back and forth. "I'm driving screaming meanies, that's what."

Baby Bobby slept through it all. On Daddy's new-for-the-trip Italian straw hat.

40

The Times at the Hotel

H ere's our hotel," my dad said, finally, his voice tired, eighty-three blocks later by my count. We peered at the faded words on a buckled-board sign above the entry of a building.

My mother frowned at the only unblinking sign in town. "This doesn't look good," she said. The building, at least the first ten stories I could see, had open windows and yellowed shades. Stained curtain linings hung out like tongues, gasping to escape. Julie rolled in a ball and lowered her head to see. She could've looked out my window and seen the same on the other side of the street.

Daddy maneuvered alongside cars at the curb. "This is what they call double parking. It's what they have to do in big cities." He stepped into zinging traffic and keyed the trunk open.

Mom woke up Bobby and stepped out of the car with him and soon our beige linen valises were on the curb. Daddy dropped his head back and squinted at the building, top to bottom. He wrinkled his nose. His upper lip pulled tight. He didn't say what he was thinking.

"We have a reservation—it's where all the acts on Venita's bus are staying," Mom said. All the rest of the acts were on a bus, probably still driving straight through, from all over the Midwest. We climbed onto the sidewalk, one stiff leg, then another.

"Move the Caddie," a man hollered at my dad. What a way to talk to my father.

Fancy ladies walked by on high heels, charm bracelets big as hubcaps, fat skin sticking out of their bras in the middle. My reflection was skinny on the dirty window. In the hotel we went.

"Why does the elevator smell?" Julie asked. She dropped her packages and pinched her nose.

"Fish," Mom said. "People must cook in their rooms. We don't eat fish," she said.

I said, well, we eat tuna and salmon. That's fish.

"There are no tuna and salmons in Iowa," she said. "We eat *canned* fish. That's not real fish," she added. My mother marched to the middle of the elevator: "Don't touch the walls," she said. About twenty more people climbed in.

Mom opened Room 636. I rushed to get out of the cigarette smoke. Puke. Two single beds, a sun-bleached chest. A door opened to a smaller room with a closet and two twin beds.

There was no room to stand in the room because the biggest fastest beetle bug I'd ever seen was running the narrow strip of a carpet. "Oh, God help us," my mother said, careening onto the bed. And my mother did try to stomp the bug, from her perch. She did and then she had to kick off her play shoe.

She eased her skirt up her pale legs, so pale they looked like the white marble slab of the nightstand. How light-skinned she looked, compared to New York. Her foot was already swelling from bumping the bed and she tucked it under her and rubbed her corn-colored hair. Julie snuggled onto her stomach. Bobby was under the bed, after the bug.

Half an hour in the heat, and Daddy hung his head in the door. "I ran into Venita. We'll meet her at the audition tomorrow. Get your things and let's go!" We took turns walking to the edge of the room and out.

"Be careful what you say," Mom said, like we'd not heard that before. "It's just like watching a show. You don't know whose mother and father are sitting behind you." I heard a different language behind every door we passed so I don't know what difference it made.

41

The Limp. Our Gimp

W hat's the trouble?" Daddy scooped up Julie. She reached for Mom.

"My leg-eg. It hurts. I can't step," she said. My parents gave each other a this-is-no-good look.

Daddy stood Julie in a patch of light from a window and dropped his cigarette into a metal slot on a stand. The pedestal ashtray rocked back and forth. I checked. Its pillow base was full of gravel.

Daddy massaged Julie's whole leg, calf to thigh and back. Julie's hair bow slid down the side of her cheek. A round man snored in a leather chair by a radio. Our Miss Brooks shouted from behind the radio screen: "Mr. Boynton," the nasal voice pined. "Whatever is the matter?"

"Ow," Julie answered, looking for the voice. She "ow"ed on out the door, one every step. Mom carried Bobby. My daddy the doctor said she'd walk it off, rode in the car too long. I lapped in front of Julie and back. Mom stood Bobby in front of her. He collapsed cross-legged.

"Let's take a cab the few blocks to Rockefeller Center and have a look-see," Daddy said. In the cab. Out we scrambled, hanging our heads back. A three-story high 50,000-gallon waterfall rushed real water down a sign, just like on the brochure.

"What if Julie can't dance tomorrow? Does she have polio?" I had to know. Bobby didn't have to dance. No use asking about him. He was tottering too.

"Stop talking about it," Daddy the doctor said. "It isn't anything she can't walk off if she stops thinking about it. Did you look up, Julie?"

Were we shrinking? I thought I'd tip over backwards looking. Julie threw her head back and cried like a baby, right under the seven-story blinking Pepsi Cola bottle.

The sidewalk throbbed under my feet, the heat of blinking signs made me shiver. Shadows already played on our faces and it wasn't even supper. New York didn't have good light like Mason City. For that reason, or maybe that we didn't have our good clothes, or maybe we had no smiles yet, with the sore leg, we took no photos.

Julie was not faking. She would never do that, even though she was cranky and tired. Our Julie was a pro. Horns honked at us and we crossed the middle of Fifty-second. I leaned on my dad. "Make her walk," I pleaded. What if she couldn't dance? He could fix anything.

"Look at the huge bottle cap," he said to us, jiggling her. Julie laid her head on his shoulder, legs dangling. On he talked. "Until a year ago, those bottles were seven-story statues of people without clothes, a man and a woman. Did you ever see anything like it?"

"No." I said. I supported my head back with my hands. "If the statues were inside our building and went up through the rooms, we would have the statue's shoulders in our room. Right?" I was the only normal person in the whole family. No one else looked.

"That's my brand," he said, pointing at the sign. A huge man's head on a billboard puffed smoke rings, next to a Camel package. "Count the rings."

"Ten," Julie said, after the puffs stopped. He said she was right. "My leg still hurts," she said.

"Look at the spastic kid," said a teen-ager. Daddy picked Julie up, *one more time*, and we headed towards the hotel. *Meredith would love this.* He wanted a crippled kid for a big part in his *Music Man.* His producer was right: steal the show.

42

The Savoy Hilton

Stay put," Daddy said to Julie, dropping her onto a davenport near the front door, back in our lobby. The eye-burning cigarette fog wasn't quite as thick there. I plopped across from her and paged a *Life Magazine,* one slick page after another. Queen Elizabeth unfolded on a double spread, parading in her crown, waving from a big white car.

"Let's go. Car's here," Daddy announced after a short bit. We jumped to our feet. I brushed graham cracker crumbs off Julie's mint-green sunsuit bottom. Two round grease spots didn't budge. "It's baby oil," I said to Mom, sniffing my fingers. "Where's the beach around here?"

Julie limped like a Tiny Tim without any cheer. I was so engrossed in cleaning her up and worrying about her leg that I was the last to land on the sidewalk.

A white car—the length of two cars—slid open its doors. A black doorman, New York had more than one, extended a white-gloved hand.

My mother bowed into a car so big she had to stoop and waddle across the back seat, pulling Bobby behind her. I crawled in next, so fast my momentum could have leapfrogged me out the other door. Daddy handed Julie in last.

Two seats in the back of the big car faced each other! We had parents on one side, children on the other. Bobby started to perk up. *Now* I was glad we brought him. I'd never been away from him.

A tight perfect red rose bobbed in a skinny vase on each door side. It smelled like my back yard. "Help yourself to pop or cordials," said the driver. His white glove waved it so. A glass window closed behind him. My dad pulled out two Buds and three Orange Crushes from a refrigerator!

"How did we get this car?" my mother said. We all waited for my father to answer.

"Don and Marie." Don and Marie (he didn't say Donnie and Marie!) were our old neighbors next door, but they moved to Short Hills, New Jersey. We would visit them the next week. "They called the Hilton and reserved the Penthouse. How do you like them apples?" he said.

My dad hitched his trousers and spread his long legs, feet planted in the wide aisle. I did the same. One good thing about pants: legs didn't sweat against each other and I could sprawl them all over the place.

"Do you believe this?" Daddy said Don and Marie were paying for our new rooms. He shook his head as though he couldn't believe they could spend that much money. Don owned a chain of dimestores now. "They want to show us the very best time, and they can spend it, I guess."

"How nice" my mother said. She crossed her legs and angled her foot back and forth, as though she didn't realize she had on such pretty shoes. I bet she felt much better about not having her best clothes, now that she had a beautiful hotel and limo.

Julie knew a good mood when she saw one and slid cross-legged down to the soft carpet, Bobby beside her. She was right: Mom didn't even notice her kids were all over the floor.

I was sure this could not be the street we arrived on scarcely an hour ago. No one jumped on the hood. Montovani strings played music fit for Sandra Dee, from tiny speakers. Fans whirred in the four corners.

Daylight was beginning to go. Lights spun past the windows. On cue, we spilled out of the big car.

A uniformed man led us twenty-five floors up and down a long hallway. He unlocked large double white and gold doors. We dented the blue carpet with each step—the floor seemed to have a quilt underneath. "Holy cow," I whispered.

The man in the soldier costume approached the next set of doors. The entry we passed through was as big as our old hotel room! A five-foot gold cat was on the right. The man jingled a key that sounded like money and spread the next doors as though the Rockettes were kicking inside.

Julie stayed behind, stroking the cat, top to bottom, until it tipped but not on her and it didn't break.

The man bowed. His white teeth sparkled. He pushed an electric switch and pulled a curtain on our stage. The window on the opposite wall was the biggest I'd ever seen.

Out and below was the city of New York. I could see lots of streets at once, dizzying. All the windows had lights, and the bottom floors of the buildings blinked like a hundred strobe lights. Our window had a balcony of trailing flowers and a white metal rail.

"Do Elizabeth Taylor and Nicky Hilton stay in this room?" my mother asked. No one answered but it made sense. Hilton. The man opened yet another set of gold double doors. The brass door knob clicked: "*ka-thick, ka-thick,*" like

Savoy Hilton penthouse. (Postcard courtesy of Beth Obermeyer)

it fit the plate perfectly. The most beautiful bedroom I had ever seen lay beyond. How could I describe it in my journal? I could never exaggerate this.

Mom sat on a heart-shaped seat. The man pushed four paneled mirrors. The closet beyond the mirrors had a hardwood floor, big as my bedroom at home. I knew before she said it. "You can practice your dance in the closet!"

A second man entered and unpacked our nightgowns. No one would ever believe what was happening to me in the summer of 1957.

Get this: "You have a roof garden, first door down the hall. You can have your dinner brought there, if you like."

43

Time to Go

The clink of tap shoes clattered off the hangers, mirrors and shelves of the walk-in closet at the Savoy Hilton. I imagined it was my own dance studio in New York City. Julie was on her feet that morning but her eyes blinked with every sound, her elbows locked to her waist, fists rolled like boxing gloves.

"I'm going to give her some Phenobarbital again tonight so she sleeps," Daddy said.

I scrunched down to see Julie's straight-line little mouth, her bugged eyes, under the brim of her hat. "I think my leg just went to sleep,"

Mother's prayers for what would be best for us: to St. Jude, patron saint of the impossible, holy card; her prayer books; Infant of Prague and Pope Pius XII medals. (Photo: Beth Obermeyer)

Julie said. Actually my own leg didn't feel that great. We really did sit in that car for a very long time. Would my *fouette* turns buckle me?

Mom lowered onto the satin bed and fumbled in her purse for her prayer book. She thumbed through for the blue card, the one with a prayer to St. Jude, patron saint of the impossible. She slipped it in the neckline of her print dress and buttoned the white collar. Her pretty face looked skittish, her usual confident jaw was not set.

She never dreamed she'd be wearing her house dress to Radio City Music Hall. That probably was it.

But wear it she did, right under the marquee. It blazed as we walked in the door, past the chandeliers, sculptures and draperies, to the enormous curved steps. We stopped talking. Up we went, circling like bumper cars, Julie paddling on one leg. Bobby crawling and scrambling.

I always pictured the stairway to heaven looked like that. The brass rail was cool and smooth. Julie hung over the rail. Her eyes rolled astray, awry, like cat-eye marbles. She was rattled. She slept through most of the show, Bobby slept through it all.

I saw the Rockettes. They were good. But what would it be like to have thirty-five more just like you? Their costumes were exactly the same. Daddy said I was not going to be a Rockette or a Playboy Bunny, either. I was going to college and get educated and that was that.

The next day we were wide awake, ready. The frosted glass door to the audition room stood open. An accordion wheezed in one corner; across the room, a contestant with buggy eyes puffed and tapped her cheeks, getting "America the Beautiful" from the air exploding from her lips. (I couldn't believe it.) In the middle of the room, six folk dancers clapped and stomped around ten-foot bamboo poles laid on the floor like hopscotch lines. "A kid could get trampled in here," Julie said, sliding to sit. Her voice squeaked.

"I think you're acting the most grown-up of anyone in this whole room," I whispered in her ear.

Daddy paced, pointed to pictures of Connie Francis, Pat Boone, and Elvis Presley. "All losers, not one of them won *Ted Mack*. That's what it says." I'm sure that was supposed to make us feel good when or if we flunked the audition. Because really, everybody in the country wanted to be on this show.

A woman at a desk adjusted her glasses on a chain and crooked her finger at us. We padded in our socks over the black linoleum. "You're number 732. We're on 671. Do not leave the room without permission. The bathroom is down the hall. Keep track of the numbers."

The woman slapped our form to the side and buried her curly bangs and fingers in a box of index cards. "Sit, sit, sit," she said, fast like they did in New York. She wiggled her gum in her mouth. She kept a spare piece stuck on the side of her Rolodex.

I fully intended to analyze all the other acts. But under my chair, out of the corner of my eye, I saw the Weejun loafer. The shoe was connected to a boy, about sixteen. He sat by me, sat sideways, my direction. He'd directed us into the room. My elbow still felt his grip. He patiently flicked bits of glitter from beneath his fingernail, like he didn't notice me.

The beautiful boy leaned his head—black wavy hair, just like Daddy's—on the wallpaper, hair that looked like hair, not oiled grass like some boys. That's why he could get away with leaning it on the wallpaper, of course. He was slick.

His navy linen vest hung loose over his gabardine trousers. It could be the boy on the Rockettes brochure!

"Relax," he said."You're two hours from auditioning. They spend minutes per act. More if they're interested. Then they trim the act to one minute thirty seconds, *if* they pick you."

Huh?

All the acts have to fit in one-half hour, he explained, with a flip of his fingers. "I've worked here two years. My mom plays the piano in there, and I can tell you that's how it's done." He absent-mindedly studied the girls with the black straight hair, who were still prancing over bamboo sticks. *Wouldn't you think they would have their dance down by now?*

At the same time I mulled. How did mom and I miss that? Acts could only be a minute and a half. We had watched *Ted Mack* for five years, every week, since we got our television.

"Ricky," the boy said, nodding to introduce himself to me and my mother. He leaned into the corner wall and braced his knees against my leg. I flexed my leg muscles. *He was watching me.* My breathing slowed. I separated the felt fringe on the bottom of my skirt and curled the strips, one at a time, glancing at him from under my cowgirl hat.

His fingernail was pink with the cutest white edge and little moon on the end. The bottom of my stomach fluttered but he couldn't know that.

"What's a head hitter?" I asked. He'd said we had one here.

"Coffee?" he said, whispering in my ear. I said no thank you.

"Want to come get a drink of water in the hallway? It's stuffy in here."

Not as stuffy as my parents, it seemed in the moment. I'd never been invited into the next room by a boy.

44

Not Fair!

Boy, was I dumb. He didn't want coffee. *He wanted me to go out into the hallway with him!* "A drink of water," I said to Mom. "With Ricky. He sort of works here." I felt, oh, one hundred pair of performer eyes, following us.

Ricky slipped behind the table in the hall and opened another opaque windowed door you couldn't see through. I turned sideways, slipped past him. He lowered in a black leather chair and put his feet on the desk. "What's your job?" I asked. He looked like a boss. "Is this your office? Are we supposed to be in here?"

"I'm an assistant to the show. I come to the auditions and get to know ones we think might be on the show. During the show I'm back stage to help if anything goes wrong. Relax." Ricky talked fast with clipped New Yorker words. "Sit down," he said.

He certainly was paying attention to me. "How do you know who might be on the show before the auditions?" I asked.

"Good question," he said. "Venita's got a list for her group. They're always really good. But there's just so many slots left in the show, maybe none. So if there's already a singer on the show, and you sing, you're out of luck."

"But singers came all the way from Iowa on the bus." I sat up, pulling my skirt from the chair back. "Is there a dancer already on the show?"

"Yup. But. Venita's checked your name on her audition list. That might mean something." Ricky shrugged, like it was the best he could do.

I knew exactly what my Meredith would say, so I said it right at him: "Bare-faced, double-shuffle, two-bit thumb-rigger."

Ricky scratched his top knot. I think he thought I swore at him. I leaned my head back. This was a mess. I tried to keep tears inside my lower lids. "I've got to tell my mom. Venita *knows* who is already on the show?"

Ricky jumped onto the desk and landed by my chair. "No, no, no. Not a word. You're not supposed to know this. I never should have told you. Oh, no, you're gonna cry. You're supposed to be tough. Don't you do auditions all the time?"

"Everything's going wrong," I said. Maybe this would be the breakdown my dad thought Julie might have. My head throbbed and words stuttered out. "Julie's leg's not good." I told him the leg story.

"Gosh, you sound just like Dorothy in the *Wizard of Oz* when she gets to Oz and finds out the wizard's a fake. You've even got sequin shoes. Can I see what your taps looks like? Put your shoe up on the desk?"

I thought of home for the first time. Dorothy sure liked home after Oz. Bubbles popped out of my nose. I felt stupid. "I want to go back to the room." If I put my shoe on the desk my satin bloomers would show.

Ricky leaned down. I smelled the Dreft laundry soap on his shirt. His breathing was like Smith Brothers cherry cough drops. "Okay, I won't tell my mom. Promise," I said. I blubbered.

"Know what?" he said. "You're right. I'm not supposed to bring you here. You go back and I'll come back in a while, like I ran an errand." He grinned. "You look beautiful sitting in that chair. The skirt goes around you in a circle, like a flower."

I took a big breath to get back to normal. I'd never had a boy my age say anything so nice. "We've probably been here fifteen minutes. Will I be in trouble?"

"Not if your parents don't say anything. Doris at the desk will never notice. She doesn't care. She just watches her numbers, day after day after day." He stretched his arms overhead. "Break a leg, kiddo. Hey, maybe the other dancer they've already got for the show will break a leg. Better give me your phone number just in case there's a horrible accident backstage Sunday night." His eyes pleaded with me to laugh. Like he'd be Mr. Nice Guy and break the girl's leg for me. Probably best not tell my mother about Venita's list or all about New York City boys.

I wish she had taken a photo of Ricky. My mother did not take photos of boys.

45

The Audition

Blink, went the last chord on Addie's piano. Our dance spun to an end, and the audition room cycled three more times before my eyes. Incandescent light bulbs flew like yellow-tailed kites, as they always did after so many spot turns.

Julie was a world-class trouper. The little girl shuffled her dance and held the lunge on her sore leg, smiling the smile that said this was the most fun a little girl could have. The smile that just might get us on *Ted Mack*. I conceded to myself: little kids can steal a show.

The *Ted Mack* lady didn't clap, she didn't smile. *Please don't say "Thank you, Harold will show you the way out."* That's what all the performers said Mrs. Mayme'd said, all morning, to one act every five minutes. None of them got on the show. The men on either side of the powerful lady leaned heads over their papers, scribbling. And the lady's face, it screwed up "like the criss-cross sections on a cinnamon roll." Meredith would say that.

Perspiration burned the inside of my eyelids. Mrs. Mayme rattled her charm bracelet and raised her eyebrows to Addie the piano lady. "I've never heard "Turkey in the Straw" that fast. And—the dance is too long." She got louder, like a bear waking from a long winter. "Cut the waltz!"

We nodded our heads off, still breathing fast from the dance. "Do we do it again?" said Julie in a loud whisper, eyes to my waist, eyes round as silver dollars. Addie thumbed her music pages. Mayme rubbed her

215

forehead, tapping her pencil like the second hand on the clock. The balls of my feet burned on the web of my fish net tights.

The room, the room I had been waiting for all my life, seemed to get smaller until it looked a lot like the cafeteria at Holy Family School, except it had rows of outlets and musical instruments and it stung my nose with sweat, not old milk. My mother didn't get to come in this room. She wouldn't have liked it anyway.

"'Oh, Dem Golden Slippers,'" Addie said, waving some music, over the upright.

Mrs. Mayme rocked her head impatiently, eye on the huge clock. Addie played a few measures and the judge lady tapped her high heeled pump under the table. The guy on her left copied information to a green form.

"Know that one?" Addie asked me. "Come look at the music. We won't change the tempo, just the music." Mayme tapped the side of her hand on the table in a steady rhythm. "Right. We'll check it for time, from the top," she said, slamming the button on her clock. "Without the little one for now."

"Not me?" asked Julie? She was a crackerjack.

"Another country heard from," Mayme said. She turned her entire body on her chair at Julie. Julie did a lame four-legged scramble for the corner. Her satin bloomers flashed in the harsh light. She slammed her bottom to the wall.

The lady twiddled her pencil, like she might break it. "Leg bother you today, kiddo?" She'd noticed, and I thought Julie put a lot into it!

I explained about the long ride in the car. "She can do the dance once. That's all it takes."

"Mary, try the dance alone," Mayme said, to me. "I ran for the wall to enter stage left.

"No, no, no." Mayme screwed her face and clipped the words, impatient. The second hand on the clock jerked along. "Ever watch the show?" she asked me. "Mr. Mack interviews you and you start from center." Her eyes turned mean.

The door cracked open. Ricky hung his head in and his face said it all. He didn't expect Julie to be snoozing in the corner and Mayme yelling at me.

But Addie, winked, at me. "See?" she said. "It can go two/four instead of four/four, two counts to the measure instead of four. Much easier on the fiddlers in the orchestra."

Mayme didn't watch the dance at all, just clicked the knob on the clock again and at the last second. Piano Addie got the length right!

Mayme slashed her pencil across the form, folded it in half and stapled it to the green form. She waved the paper and nodded to Ricky. "Go, go, go," she said, shooing us with her hand, pulling the next form from the pile. Our audition was over. But what exactly happened? Were we in or out?

Daddy would say: Is you is? Or is you ain't?

Julie scrambled to her feet. She pulled her eyelashes, pulled the lid away from her eye. I took her hand. Mayme stretched. She needed a quick nap. We exited.

I waited for Venita to look at the form, to know for sure. Ricky pinched my waist as I passed. He gathered the lariats like he was doing any old job for any old contestant.

My mother half-stood now, snatching at sliding papers from her lap, eyes huge. Her mouth was ready to smile or ready to snap shut, depending on the news. Whichever it was, we would discuss it far into the night, I knew. My mother wanted to win as much as I did and Julie did.

My dad leaned over his feet, hands loosely folded on his knees. Julie hobbled across the tile to his lap. "How did it go?" he asked, turning her onto his knee by her waist.

"I don't know." Julie snuggled. Daddy was good with little kids, his thing.

46

Bobby and Those Hats

Venita's hand opened wide for the green paper—she really
cared. We were on her bus load after all. She held it at a
distance. Her blue eyes drooped, under gold-shadowed lids,
over black mascara tracks—but oh my. She beamed like a grandmother.
She wrapped an arm around me and her eyes spun like *I Love Lucy,* and
she acted like her too, as she reached her other hand to our mom.

"Mom, I think we got on. I think we did," I said, siding up to her.
We followed Venita. What would she say? She dropped her silver lighter onto
the table, retrieved a pop lid for ashes. She was taking forever. "I audition and
do shows all year just to have one of my winners get on *Ted Mack,*" she said.
"I'm so pleased. You're on the show, if you can stay another week."

Daddy bounced up to shake Venita's hand. "Pleased to work with
you," he said. Julie whizzed her lame legs past each other like they itched.
Mom hugged Julie.

Our dance was about to go on television across the United States
of America and now I knew how big that was. At least the half we'd driven
across. And I'd met a boy who was probably a movie star, now that I
thought about it, and he was going to be backstage at the show.

"This is pretty amazing," Venita began. "They already had a dancer
for this week, you know," she said, smiling. The smoke floated on her
words. Her red lips looked almost as if Julie had colored her in a coloring
book. "Things just sometimes fall together," Venita said. "Never say never."

218

And then I knew. She looked like a Bil Baird puppet, that's what it was. Her hair was black, her skin was white-white, her cheeks really red, lashes like brushes.

Maybe Venita Rich was magic!

And that's when we remembered. We left Bobby sleeping in a chair in the waiting room. We found him shaded in the huge hat Daddy had folded from a newspaper.

47

Made It!

My mother and I flew in circles, down the hallway, over the big staircase, to the door, into the limo. "We made *Ted Mack*," we screamed. Inside the car the story of the audition got told, fast and big. "Julie, did you cry?" Mom said, her head flung back on the seat. Julie shook her head. Mostly Mom was incredulous that they'd cut the dance and changed the music.

Daddy watched the passing buildings and filed his nails. I had never seen him *ride* in a car before. He always drove. But he was still in charge. "What should we do?" he said. "We have all day." He reached in his coat pocket for brochures about New York.

"Let's go to Bond's, the big department store," I said. "Every day 3,490 people shop there. And buy a ready-made dress? Could I? A New York fashion? *I could pick it myself?*"

"The Science Museum. You've never been to one," Daddy said. "Central Park? The Statue of Liberty."

Mom thought the carriage ride and boat sounded perfect. "We can talk all about the audition. If we're back before five o'clock, we can look around Bond's. And here we are." The hotel.

"The Lennon Sisters?" a hysterical voice screamed, filling the wide doorway of the limo. I ducked my cowgirl hat through the opening. Three women pressed us. "It's Kathy, the second youngest. Is that Janet in the car?" A woman clamped her toes on the curb, blocking us, pushing paper and pencil in my face. The doorman removed his top hat and pushed his cane against the women, making a walkway.

"Hustle!" Daddy said, ignoring the fuss. "We've got just one day in New York and we have to make it good. Tomorrow is the show, and we head for Don and Marie's the next morning. I'll wait in the lobby and get a beer," he said.

"Daddy, are we rich?" I just wondered.

48

Rehearsal: The Ted Mack Original Amateur Hour

f this is the Ted Mack show, where's Ted Mack?" Julie asked this question, all day long, ten different ways. Julie and I had been waiting alone in our room with the star on it in Radio City Music Hall in New York City, since eight in the morning. Each act had its own room. Just the contestants, no more. Today was rehearsal and the live performance for *The Ted Mack Amateur Hour*. Both. And it was almost dinnertime and we hadn't done a thing.

We'd never smelled a pastrami sandwich before, much less eaten one. We spoke up right away, soon as it came. "This pickle tastes like pee," Julie said, sniffing.

"Kosher dill," the lady said. Julie said she only liked pickles made out of bread and butter.

"Bread and butter pickles," I said, explaining. "They're sweeter."

The lady frowned. "Want cheese cake?"

"Velveeta cake?" asked Julie. Everything was all mixed up.

"I like ice cream in Dixie cups," Julie said, crossing her arms protectively over her stomach. "With movie star pictures inside the lid," she went on. "I collect Lucy and my sister likes Debbie Reynolds."

"I'm not a deli, ladies."

Julie backed to the corner and slid down to a squat. "Well, at home—when we eat out—it's 'hamburger, hot dog or nothing.'" She blinked, more than usual. "Where's my mother?" she asked the lady, like she had been, about every half hour, whenever the lady passed our door, all day. Julie was used to a nap but I had no idea how to get her to take one. A dark room, her stuffed ducks, not to mention her mother or Hanna.

But mothers weren't allowed backstage, not in New York.

And now it was dinnertime and the lady was taking us to rehearse. "So what did you two eat? Nothing? That's not smart." The woman checked her watch. "Let's go, picky-picky."

Fifty-seven clicks down the hallway, I peeked around the curtain at the stage. I pulled the back of my leotard down over my underpants. Julie didn't own a leotard. She had on a blue seersucker sun suit. Her hair straggled under her barrette, in front and in back of her ear, that look. Mom would have left Julie's hair pin-curled in the Star Room.

The big gold curtain pulled, not straight, but under a huge gold arch by enormous columns. It was large enough for thirty-six Rockettes. I didn't have any more words for big. New York used them all up: Empire State Building—"Tall," Statue of Liberty—"Holy Cow." The waterfall . . .

But I didn't have anyone to talk to anyway unless I counted Julie. I couldn't understand the New Yorkers.

Julie squatted, chin on her knee. "I'm hungry," she said. My stomach roared. We were used to noon as our big meal, like pot roast, brown potatoes, cottage cheese, black cherry Jello salad—then nothing between meals—then a light supper. Mom always had butterscotch candy—sugar energy. I put my tongue on the little spot on the roof of my mouth where I sucked candy hard.

"Center stage, dearies. You're next." Our lady of the red vest pushed my back with one hand, pulled Julie with the other.

A man stripped masking tape from a roll and stuck it to the wood stage floor, a place for each of us. We stood by it. Another man held a light meter to our faces. Julie had no idea.

Camera men whipped huge cable tails behind them with one foot. Stage hands clustered on either side of the stage, smoking and whispering. I kept Julie's dimpled elbow in one hand.

The orchestra tooted random sounds in a pit. An occasional phrase of our music surfaced. "Yikes, not the right tempo at all," I whispered. Musicians leaned sideways at each other's music and shuffled their own pages. One player inspected a fingernail, just diddling.

The conductor tapped his stick, his white shirt inflated, and his arm came down. Three big long notes roared. *What was that?" Our introduction?*

Whir. The music rushed along with the blood inside my wrists. It was the song Addie played at the audition. Were the musicians rehearsing? Or were we supposed to be dancing? I locked my knees and tightened my grasp on Julie's arm. My throat burned.

"Yeeks." I snapped my leotard, a nervous habit. "We missed our intro," I yelled, at Julie, over the music.

"What?" Julie flexed her legs. I hummed the three big orchestra horn notes—all on the count of "1" in two/four time—fast as I could. Perspiration beads gathered on my bangs, magnifying the glint of the horns.

We were used to a different intro, way longer counts one through eight. I played a piano, I got it.

Now there was no horn on the count of eight. And "Eight" was the count that started Julie. I tried to count it.

The conductor shouted, loud enough to start dancers on Mars. He sang: "Oh-one, two-Dem, one-two, one . . ."

I tipped Julie's face to me. Julie's eyes rolled sideways toward the conductor.

"Julie." I hung onto her. I hummed the horns and stamped the start. Julie sucked her shoulder strap.

The conductor straight-armed the podium and shot a look. The music halted. His face said it all: these little girls can't even start their dance. To be fair, hardly any small children were ever on this show. If they were going to change the music, that was why.

Julie was a sharp cookie, but she had no idea why she was off. I was plain old embarrassed.

"One more time." The stage director shouted while the conductor talked to a bunch of horns. No one cared what our old music had been before it was changed at the audition.

I leveled at the conductor. "I can help her in our dressing room. I get it."

The conductor's arm came down. I took Julie's hand down on the stamp, nearly squeezed it off, and pulled it up, little girl too, on the hop. The dance launched. We *sailed.* Way up-tempo!

We lunged. The dance ended.

No one seemed to notice. Heads riveted to the side stage, over gasps and squeals. Not twenty feet away, on the stage, Mr. Ted Mack walked to his chair at a desk, straightened his suit and held still for a final powder. A pink puff touched the shine on his forehead.

He didn't smile. He didn't talk. We must be the last to rehearse. Ted Mack chatted with each act, found a joke with each, and moved on. He went so fast. What will be our joke? Will he tease about the trouble with the music?

Soon we were center stage, waiting, all he had left. "All the way from Mason City, Iowa," Mr. Mack said. "What do you want to do after you graduate, Mary Beth?"

"Oh, Mr. Mack, I want to go on to college."

"Very nice," he said, looking at his paper. "And what would you like to do, Julie?"

"Oh, Mr. Mack, I just want to get married." She didn't even pause.

Julie made Mr. Ted Mack laugh. People in shadows laughed out loud. The same people who couldn't clap for our dance five minutes ago.

"Wrap," shouted the stage director. *Now* he smiled. When we did something stupid!

49

A Telegram from Governor Herschel Loveless

But where was Ricky? I thought I would have seen him by then. Maybe he didn't know what room.

"The real trouble," I said, and Julie seemed to follow: "The rock-and-roll band. They're up for their third win."

"No Business Like Show Business" came through the walls, up from the orchestra pit. It was 8:30. The show must be starting. We were in costume.

"Geritol!" shouted the TV in the hall. Now we were in business.

Folks, do you ever get that tired out run-down feeling? Well, maybe you need to run down to the drug store and get a pick-me-up. Geritol will make those bones move like new again. Give you the energy to get up and vote for our talented young people. So get by your phone and be ready at the end of the show. Or write out a postcard.

Our dance was number three out of six, just before commercial. They'd moved us up in order. The bamboo pole dancers and the rock band needed set-up time and so they got the spots after the commercials. A knock on the door rattled a familiar tap rhythm.

I put my face to the crack and opened the door a tiny bit.

I was face-to-face with Ricky! "Oh! My!"

Julie jumped in circles, hands over her mouth.

Ricky leaned into the room. He smiled a delicious smile. His eyes up this close were the color of my mother's aquamarine ring. His hair waved like

226

Tommy Huffstetler, the famous cowboy singer from Manly, Iowa. He held out a telegram. "Can I come in?" he said. "I'm not really supposed to be here."

"What? Who is it from?"

"Congratulations STOP All Iowa will be watching STOP Iowa is proud of you STOP Herschel Loveless, Governor, State of Iowa."

"Who told him we're on the show?"

"Public Relations Department of NBC," Ricky said. "They tell all the newspapers and television stations in Iowa if they have someone from Iowa on the show."

He squeezed Julie's arm. "Running errands. I have to go get water for Mr. Mack." Ricky peeled out the door.

Almost immediately, the door opened again. It was the woman who had been taking us in and out of the room all day. She held the door. She led us through the hall, like we were ponies.

"Volare . . ." A magnificent young singing voice from the stage.

Julie, fingered the fringe on my skirt. Her fingers were cold on my leg, tickled. We peeked at the stage from the side. Tiers of seats in the audience were filled with people. It looked even bigger with an audience.

I dropped to one knee, my face in Julie's. "Remember: Horn. Horn. Horn-Stamp: HOLD." I didn't want to her over-think. I wanted her to stop blinking.

The second Western Union telegram from the governor. (Courtesy of Beth Obermeyer)

50

Meredith Watches Ted Mack

Meanwhile, in the same town but still far away—because New York City was a very big town—Meredith sprawled in his den, a spacious sublet on Thirty-fifth Street, New York. Rini found the place when *The Music Man* got close to on Broadway.

Meredith was still delirious about *The Music Man,* even though the plot was long out of his typewriter. He worked on the lyrics constantly. It would be November before he felt they were completely right, at his out-of-town opening, Philadelphia, only a month before the Broadway opening.

"Hell's bells," he'd tell Mabel. "I left so much to fix in Philadelphia." He had so much to go, and that amid casting calls for chorus and dancers.

"Meredith," Rini called, from the next room of the sublet. "Can you hear me? Come look at this. Mason City girls are on *Ted Mack.* Quick."

"Where are you?" he called. "I forgot where the television is. This house is so quiet." And what a treat that was. Back in LA, neighbors were in the midst of a big addition to their house. "I hated that electric drizzle." Rini had moped. Electric drill was what she meant, of course.

Ted Mack?" he said. "I once had a radio program, we ran a season opposite *Major Bowes,* it evolved to *Ted Mack.* Split the ratings half and half." He'd take a look, if Rini thought so. She did, after all, discover their Winthrop Paroo for the show, on *Name That Tune.* The bonus was that when Eddie Hodges came to audition, he had flame-red hair! You couldn't see that on television, but Rini just knew. So good for *The Music Man* that Rin watched TV.

"Listen! They're starting their dance without music," she said.

"One does it, the other answers," he said.

Rini danced alongside the television, pink curlers bobbing on her head. She frowned at her feet, underskirt whizzing around her legs. "Tap dancing must be American. Nothing like this in Russia."

Meredith exercised his shoulders; his body had writer's cramp far beyond his fingers. "Betcha Mabel knows these two." He massaged the deep dents on his nose. "Great costumes." He dropped in his easy chair, rolling his shirt sleeves. "You know, tap-dancing is as American as Barbershop Quartet singing. Listen to that sound. I imagine the tap dancing is as good in Mason City as anywhere."

"The Barbershop Quartets are good in Mason City," Rini said.

"Oh, ya. The ones you see in old tin-pan alley movies—like *Meet Me in St. Louis*—aren't the real thing. "Bicycle Built for Two" is too regular a tune, a one-in-a-bar waltz clog, doesn't give the give-and-take, not the harmony challenge for a real barbershop. No group would be caught dead with a piano along. No, sir." Meredith liked to get huffy about this.

The Sartor Sisters on *Ted Mack* as seen through the television screen. (Courtesy of Beth Obermeyer)

"Sh-sh-sh dear. Look. Listen! Like jazz music."

"I hear the give 'n' take," Meredith said. "They must be here in the city. The *Ted Mack* show is over at Radio City Music Hall."

"For crying out loud, they're taking that orchestra at a clip."

"Think that little one is making the sounds too?" Rini said.

"There's her solo. She's right on top of it. Look at her click away. How old is she? Oh, turns, big one's turning."

"Are there cowgirls in Iowa?" Rini stood by Meredith's chair, hands on hips. She chewed her thumbnail, listening to the applause. "I've got an idea. Invite them over, take some pictures. For Mabel!"

Meredith raked his hair. "Better yet. We're auditioning dancers for *The Music Man*. Let the little girls come 'n' watch? It's the open-call-for-dancers audition. They'd love that." It'd be the cherry on the soda.

Meredith pulled a black leather pad from his pocket. "I'm glad we caught this. Where's Josephine? Have her leave a message for the whole family. Tell them Monday, tomorrow, Imperial Theatre, 1:30 p.m. 'til it's over, probably midnight." He scribbled and eased the page under an ashtray on the end table. He padded back to the den, to his characters and their songs, a shuffle added to his gait.

51

The Dance Flies through the Air on National Television

The spotlight came at us like a cone. From its needle end at the top of the Radio City Music Hall Theatre, it landed on our stage at the *Ted Mack Original Amateur Hour*. In the center of the swinging yellow light, we whirled our final twenty-four.

Arms in a pinwheel—we whipped the air. Finally, sixteen chene turns to center front stage, the last drum roll to the horns. It didn't make my blood boil but it was heating up the audience. I'd done these steps since I was eight, just not this fast.

We had gotten to national television, had the experience of New York City and how they did things. I was about as far as I could go.

A man waited on the front edge of the stage at the end of the chain of turns, behind the camera, arms up like a butterfly. I smiled into the glass eye of the television camera. Not easy, I found. It didn't smile back.

The man's arms said "Hold-hold-hold-hold"—then down they came, like a mousetrap. We posed, frozen in spinning lights and crackling applause.

Two fingers—for Camera Two—and he swung his arms like a New York policeman, from us to Ted Mack. The camera light in front of us switched to red. "Off."

The conductor and the musicians in the pit deflated, arms and instruments, out of sight.

A guy rushed us off the stage like he was a push broom, past a guy waving his "Applause" sign at the audience.

Our bow didn't affect the applause, the card guy did. "All the way from Mason City, Iowa . . . be sure to vote. Operators are ready to take your call. Central 981, Radio City Station, right now."

"And if there are any nine-year-old bachelors out there, well," Mr. Mack winked, "call back in nine years." Ted Mack, well-known for his corny-but-funny jokes, shook his head as though he couldn't believe it. He stretched to the large wheel on his right and spun it. "Round and round she goes and where she stops, nobody knows."

We skidded to a slowdown at the curtain, under the backstage monitor, elated but alone. I hugged Julie a long moment. "Now I can say it," I whispered under the little cowgirl's curls. Julie opened her blue eyes wide. I could see the NBC spotlight reflected in the prisms. "Break a leg, Julie." We convulsed and careened, to stand by the stage door.

"I'd hate to make you any happier," a voice behind me said. I turned. Ricky was straight as a stop sign. He rotated in my vision because I was still spinning inside.

Ricky's face still jumped side to side but the edges were getting cleaner. His black forehead curl stopped. It's just what happens—when the series of turns end, the world throbs.

"Big phone call, kiddo."

"Me? Who'd call *me*?"

"Meredith Willson. Know him? His secretary, Josephine. He invited . . ." Ricky paused. "He invited *you* to the open auditions for his Broadway show. Tomorrow, Imperial Theatre, 1:30, end around midnight, usually."

"Me? Just me? To be in his show?" My heart thumped.

"No, pretty girl. Have to be eighteen. And the young speaking roles are equity." Ricky pushed me out of the light. Julie followed me like a tail.

"He invited you to watch the auditions. Just you, the producer, director, Meredith. A few other guys. Choreographer. And hundreds of dancers, twenty at a time. Lucky, lucky, lucky."

I put my hands over my face, eyes.

"You'll go, of course. I'll meet you there."

"Really? Can I have the note? So I can show my mom and dad?" I slashed my arm to break Julie's grasp.

Ricky unfolded my hand. He gave me the note, in his handwriting.

I pressed the note to my lips.

52

Can I?

The limo from the Savoy Hilton waited at the curb in front of Radio City Music Hall. Our family climbed in, ready to pop.

"Yeeee—Yahoo." I crowed. I was on TV, national TV. Now Mabel could be proud.

"I did it right, didn't I? I got the introduction," Julie said, leaning forward on the seat, feet kicking, face grinning. Daddy tinkled the cans in the silver ice bucket, massaged a beer.

"The interview went perfectly," said Mom. I fished in my hat box for the governor's telegram. I read it aloud. So much glee.

"Look what else." I waved Ricky's message and told them about the invitation. "I'm invited! Daddy, can you give me a ride?"

"By yourself?" he asked. Daddy squeezed his beer can flat and pushed it down the ice bucket. Bobby scrambled to the floor of the limo and retrieved it, to push it like a race car, with great sound effects.

Now a siren.

"I just sit in the back of the theatre and watch and you pick me up at midnight," I shouted, over Bobby's din.

"What?" My dad folded his arms and leaned back. "Now why would Meredith do that? You sit right by him? No, not likely. Until midnight? Just you? Not us?"

"Bethie's got a boyfriend," Julie sing-songed. "I saw him."

"I'll introduce myself when I get there, show my telegram, and do what I'm told. I can go, can't I?" I expected a yes.

"Me too?" Julie asked. I dutifully checked the message again and handed it to Julie. "Your name isn't on the invitation. You're probably too little."

"Oh, I think it's wonderful," said my mother, corralling Bobby to sit. Her eyes spun. "You must go. What should you wear?" She knew.

"Until midnight? In a theatre in New York?" Daddy shook his head again. "I'll have to come in and look around before I leave you."

"You can't park at the curb in New York City, can you?" I had thought this out.

"She'll be fine. Watch her go in. She'll wave when all is right," Mom said.

But Daddy knew best, always, especially when it came to teen-age daughters. "Absolutely not," he said.

City lights flashed over me like spotlights. "No?" I repeated, stunned. My family went silent, waiting.

But my dad never repeated himself.

53

I So Wanted to Go

I would have finally met the music man. I'd come so close, and it would have been a doozie. But that would be the end of my story.

The next afternoon, as we packed and readied for some sightseeing, the phone rang. It was for me. "M.B.," the voice said. "Where are you?" he asked. "I'm at the theatre."

I knew it was Ricky. I so wanted to go. "My dad said no."

"Oh, kiddo, I was sure you could come. Are you sick?"

"I can't come alone."

"I'm at the theatre now. Tell him I'm here and will meet you."

"I can't," I said. It was done.

"Okay. I called that one wrong. Should I describe it?"

"Sure." My heart ached as I listened. He said hundreds of girls in leotards and shorts drifted past him. He was in the phone booth in the lobby. They were all there for *The Music Man* audition. I so wanted to soak up how New York dancers looked and acted. I could hear their high heels, slung over calloused and taped feet—dancers' feet—their calf muscles pulled tight in that mysterious way women's legs do on high heels—clicking through the lobby.

I was on tiptoe and I stretched the phone cord, idle. I checked my Lady Elgin. It was five to one. "An usher just propped the theatre doors open," he said. They're bumping to get down the aisle now, to the side stage stair."

"Do they mostly have pony tails?" I asked, gathering my hair into one clump.

"Yes, the young ones, and cotton bags, bouncing side to side on their bottoms," he said. "Some have seen better days."

For some reason, I pictured a balloon, shiny and full of air, then shriveled, wrinkled, the rubber yellow with age. The sweet dancers of the world must wear down when New York is finished.

"What are *you* wearing?" I asked.

"My turquoise short-sleeved T-shirt, sleeves rolled, black trousers."

Oh, my. This was *way American Bandstand.*

I could just see his straw loafers. I'd never seen anything like it and never would again. His smile would have filled a movie screen. His breath, that Black Jack gum.

"You could have brought shorts and I would have sat in the back row and watched you audition," he said, breaking my heart. "Big idea for a girl from Iowa."

"Meredith's a boy from Iowa and he's got bigger ideas 'n' you," I said.

"No, wait," he said. "I'm not teasing. I mean, you've never been to New York and all."

Wait till I get back home, I thought. Everyone would notice I'd changed.

"M.B.? I can't say all of that 'Mary Beth,'" he said. He was probably grinning like Bobby Darrin.

I pushed the back of my hair way up, like Sandra Dee, probably. Cheeping chatter seared through the phone. High-pitches bounced on those lobby surfaces. "What's the lobby look like?" I asked.

"Mirrors, columns, marble, glass.

I tied the sash from my dress tight on my pony tail, yanking the satin so tight I cracked my crazy bone on the phone. I wouldn't have fit in anyway. New York girls had bigger sun tans than me, way up their legs and down their tops. I saw them at the audition for *Ted Mack.*

"Numbers 100 to 120, on stage for Group Number One," came the voice in the theatre. "Onna's an assistant choreographer on another show," whispered Ricky.

I bet she had eye pencil on. The piano and Onna's miked voice came across the wires. Onna showed a tap combination. The dancers sounded like one herd after another. They must do this all the time. I sunk in a chair and hung tight to the arms.

The moments hung heavy on the end of a phone.

Well, that was about it. Ricky said it would be five hours before the last group of twenty hit the stage. They were doing single, double, triple, double-triple time steps with breaks at first, buffalos, a scissors step, trenches. Barrel turns, stuff I learned from Mr. Patten. The pianist played "Swannee River," an easy clip.

"Ricky?"

"They're going to sing," he said. "Start with stage left, sing four measures, one girl at a time. "On the Sunny Side of the Street." Onna's voice echoed.

Meredith Willson spoke now. I could hear him. Meredith, the photo on Mabel's wall, the black-and-white photo I'd gazed into, spellbound—from the time I was six—was speaking.

Onna barked. "Turns. Chene turns, stage left to stage right, a new girl every four measures." Turns were cutting the men from the boys, so to speak. "Pique turns. Single, double, triple." The dancers laughed for the first time, out loud, as they cheeped the song and pecked the funny dance. These girls probably learned new steps every day, did them for an hour and learned more after lunch.

I wanted to go home and dance by myself in the pink rec room walls. I'd turn up the music until all they'd hear in the den was the roar of the bass, and I'd make up my own steps. I'd do them for live Iowa audiences.

"Dancers got through the first cut because they were looking for 'fresh-faced, innocent, corn-fed girls,'" Ricky was saying. "You have that look."

"I'd get picked for my corny face?"

"Well, those without the look, even the good ones, got cut fast."

"Now don't get mad at me," Ricky said. "Meredith invited all four of you to come and watch. In the message I put only your name so we could have some fun. Your dad would never have known unless he talked to Meredith."

"Oh! Get out of here. No! Meredith will think we didn't come. He would have seen my whole family sitting in the theatre."

"Okay, so I think fast," he said. Headlights from the street simmered over the glass and metal and marble of our Hilton room. I closed my eyes and slid further down the wall until my elbows and shoulder blades were on the scratchy carpet. But I had to smile. I knew one thing or I'd get up and run. Ricky was a friend, even if he screwed up Meredith's invitation. When I got home, I could write Ricky a letter and he'd read it and care.

Something fluttered in the corner of my eye, a change in light. My arms and legs solidified in an instant, like ice under skin. Daddy was outside the door, leaning in, a black silhouette. My dad's feet sounded like sandpaper as he moved across the marble floor. I watched his flat feet close in under the chair next to me. He sat and put his hand on my arm.

I thought he'd be mad at me, on the phone for what seemed hours. But he wasn't this time and lucky it was so. I couldn't hear what Ricky was saying. He was talking to someone.

"M.B.," Ricky said at last. "I asked Meredith about Mabel." Tell you what, Meredith had said. He said he was sorry we couldn't come and to tell Mabel he'd mail more photos. And he'd like to talk more . . . say hello for him . . .

And with that Ricky was gone. Daddy said he was glad I talked to my friend, but it was time to go to Coney Island. "I'm sorry I couldn't let you go to the theatre, not by yourself."

I was back to the security of my father. I felt all buttoned up, back in my family. Daddy said home would feel good and that was all good.

However.

I might never meet the Music Man.

Hell's bells.

54

Home Again, Home Again

I raced the two blocks to Mabel's, hair flying, a real teen-ager in my new size-five blue plaid dress. I could wear it back to school. It was from Bond's in New York. I got to pick it out myself.

We didn't win the vote-in contest at *Ted Mack* but we didn't think we would. A rock band had won for two weeks and this was their third and last week. Anyway we got to New York. The Kiwanis and the Knights of Columbus had banded together at Labor Day picnics, sent in votes. Kids in neighborhoods all over town went door to door to remind people to vote.

We'd had a great week with the Cunninghams in Short Hills, New Jersey, reminiscing about the old days in Mason City when we lived side by side, the duplex, 317 Fifth Street Northwest.

Bobby meticulously un-screwed the taps from our shoes. Nobody cared. He was our take-apart guy, and he usually put it all back.

I called to Mabel. My voice echoed through the hallway, and I skidded to her side. "So how was it in New York?" Mabel asked. "You ended up with different music on the show?"

I went on forever about the audition, Addie the accompanist, Radio City Music Hall, Ted Mack, the Empire State Building. And Julie and Bobby

Bobby taking things apart. (Photo: Mary Beth Sartor with her Brownie camera)

sitting too long in the car, the stiff legs. I only remembered the good about the last part, it seemed. I didn't mention Ricky, but I did say Meredith watched us on television.

But I slowed as I talked. Something was missing in my story. Was it the crowd when we danced? Not that they were New Yorkers. They probably came from everywhere, like us. New Yorkers talked too fast but it wasn't that. And it wasn't because the dance had been cut, to different music, we were troopers.

I told her they couldn't clap when they wanted to, about the man with the signs. And we didn't smile to the people. We smiled to a TV camera. She caught what I meant. What that woman could show with half a face. "We had to keep track of when the camera was lighted green and dance to it. Even when we talked to Mr. Mack, the camera was between us." Who knew I'd get to New York and miss . . .the *hands in the middle!*

I nailed it: "I just didn't feel the same about dancing on Ted Mack as I did in *Varieties*. It wasn't my own dance, for one. It was one that fit with Julie and I just did it, like one, two, three."

"Something will come along," Mabel said. "Time goes by. You'll have programs to dance at college. Julie will find something here as she grows." But something new had not come along for a very long time, not for me.

The audiences got a gimmick. Sisters. I got New York.

"It was a new experience for you," Mabel said. "You've just begun. Fold it in."

"Mom says everything I ever learn or do I will use someday, even if I don't see how, right now. But, Mabel, where do old dancers go? When they're thirty? They might as well die!"

"Nonsense," said Mabel. "They're not unhappy. They don't want what you want. They hear music and wear cherry-colored ribbons in their hair—and—they feel twine pull beneath their skin in time, for all time."

I had to mull that awhile.

And then I remembered. "Mabel. Meredith said he'll come home soon and he'll visit you." I thought Mabel would cheer.

"Of course, he will," said Mabel. "Meredith always comes home."

Is that what I really wanted? To come home again? Do my own dance.

Well, I was still glad I got to go to the Emerald City even if it was made of concrete in shadow.

Somehow it just wasn't the whole banana.

55

The Challenge for the Chamber at the Hanford

F all came and went, nothing special. Kids at school were into groups, just one group in a class as small as twenty-one. Daddy said teens were about peers, liked to lump together.

But then a rather elegant thing happened.

The director of Music for the Chamber of Commerce called. It was December 15. Could the Sartor Sisters appear at their Christmas party at the Hanford Hotel? The Wedgewood Room. It was important when the Chamber invited.

Mom went to work. In days two red velvet Santa costumes hung, one on each dining room corner cabinet, white fur on the skirts, the petticoats, the hats, the cuffs.

We danced our hearts out, got hands in the middle, not just polite but proud hands.

In the bag at the Chamber of Commerce Christmas Party. (Courtesy of the *Mason City Globe Gazette*)

241

A live audience, the back and forth. The *Globe* photographer snapped our picture and the next day we were in the paper. It was kind of a funny photo though. For fun, we'd made an entrance with me pulling a sleigh with a bag of toys on it. I started to dance. Julie popped up out of the bag. Except that's the moment of the photo, Julie standing with a bag over her, head to toe. Julie didn't care. She laughed. Had it been me pictured in the newspaper . . . in a bag . . .

56

The Test for The Music Man

November 1957

Meredith rubbed his face. It hadn't taken even a year to get the musical together and to Philadelphia for its trial run. Meredith's baby—his musical—had been poked open in the first three days of rehearsal at the Shubert Theatre, Pennsylvania. And Meredith had been warned: these trappings, the costumes, the sets, the orchestra can subtract as much as they add. For one thing, on its first big night in Philadelphia, he couldn't hear two out of three words. Meredith would stick his big fingers in every hole he could.

Apparently the struggle was far from over. "Isn't this why we do the show in Philadelphia before we take it to Broadway? Sit and take notes?"

Robert Preston, the lead, cast as the Music Man, raised an eyebrow: "From where I stood, the first act felt long. How did it feel where you were?"

"Longer," said Director Tec, Morton Da Costa. Kermit Bloomgarden, Producer declared it so. They waited in the hotel suite for the opening night reviews.

Wheat-colored press review papers drifted in, some good, some bad. "Holy Honk!" Meredith said. "We're okay, right?" Who was going to pay eight-eighty a ticket?

At three o'clock in the morning, Meredith's team ganged up on him. "We've got a good review for a bad show," they said, in agreement.

"Go to bed," Meredith heard. "We'll get the magic back tomorrow," Bob Preston promised. He was still in his white suit.

And that wasn't all. John Shubert—how many shows had *he* seen in the Shubert Theatre—lowered the boom: "Try to get hold of Ray Bolger, yet tonight. Only thing that will save the show."

Replace the lead? Meredith was incredulous.

Replace Robert Preston, the lead, by nightfall?

Day Two: The next morning, Meredith left the Warwick Hotel early. He wandered back stage to check the sound, with the persistence of a guy who wrote an "umpedump" number of drafts, as he liked to say.

Three center mikes in the footlight trough were dead. All those lyrics, swallowed in cotton.

Get ahold of a sound expert!

"One speaker working, Mr. Willson," the tech said. "When four speakers should be working, two front, two to the cast. Well, you got two, one hung backwards, voice to the wall."

Meredith headed for the auditorium and zoned onto the stage, pressing his cheeks with four big fingers and a thumb. The rehearsal began.

Spats, the braided and coiled hair, the bustles, the braces, the petticoats, yards and yards of broadcloth. He missed the sexier look of dancers in skimpy practice clothes. Maybe erotic purity came across through the period costumes? Somehow? He pulled his trouser legs straight away from the knee, loose from his body, and eased into a seat.

Too tight shoes, sharp bones in bodices were being fixed in a costume room backstage, he was told. *Okay, forget this.* Not his problem.

Day Three: True, Meredith knew, the opening train did not look the same as at that jewel box of a theatre, the Barrymore, New York, when they had no costumes, sets, orchestra. Even the program manager knew: "Didn't the train used to stop, then start? It's just a rush now."

How could that be? Meredith roamed the aisles, the balcony, sat in every row of the cavernous theatre, dazed. Fixing an impression you can't touch is tricky. It can be in the lights, the speakers, angle of the stage, plenty of hot sharp things you can trip over. He'd fixed those.

Day Four: Somebody said—he didn't even know who said what anymore. "The show is cornball but the lyrics world class." Those words rang in his ears.

That night he paced the back row, during the rehearsal. The train opening, not right yet. "Tec," the director, sat down next to him. Meredith nudged him. "Only difference between now and before . . . the orchestra. Drop the orchestra?" Their eyes swung with the train.

Day Five: Night, the opening was just with the rehearsal piano. Tonight they had an audience. His lyrics emerged. But people were still paging through their programs through the train opening, as though this was still the overture of the orchestra. "Nuts."

Day Six: Meredith had the orchestra stop the overture, when the train screeched to a halt. Nothing new there, orchestras had been crashing trains for decades. But now—the show started with only the voices, in the rhythm of a train. No one had ever made a train go with voices and chants. *Some magic seeped in.*

Better, Meredith sensed. "Better with a but," he said with a snort. An irritated woman in the back row turned and glared. "Shhh."

Still, he nudged Tec. "We're amusing, but we're not *killing*." Meredith wanted the audience to convulse, to clap wildly at the end, their mouths agape. Meredith's eyes jumped with the flashes of the train windows.

Day Seven: New idea. "Let the lights in the train windows swing slowly at first, gain momentum, the bodies lurch in time, the voices go slow to fast, *that* will make the train start up." The set, the train, of course, would not move. The light effect would make it seem so.

Meredith roamed the Shubert Theatre like a ghost all week, stopped eating two days, added a beard. He could feel the hollows under his eyes. "Lazarus," was his nick-name, from Bob Preston, the star, the lead, the music man. He'd called to Meredith mid-kick from the stage. At last Meredith had a nickname, well-earned, he figured. He probably did look risen from the dead. Small piece, bit by bit, Meredith nailed details.

But he still had a klunker. He'd tinkered for weeks with Marian's lovely song in the second act. For ten days, Barbara Cook barely stirred a quiver from the audience, even though she'd slayed them before Philie.

Ten times Meredith headed for the Ladies' Room to get a new tact, sat in a stall, his best bet at privacy. Ten times the professional Barbara Cook hit the stage and tried each new version of the song, never asking why it wasn't right. She did as he asked.

Meredith sat in the stall for the nth time. He should bring a pillow for the toilet seat if he didn't get this right soon. His head cycled the songs in the show that led to the problem song, her "My White Knight."

Bang, crash, each ditty had the audience. He had the Train-chant opening, he had "Iowa Stubborn," "Trouble," "76 Trombones," "Pick a Little" . . . now . . . why not her ballad? Why didn't the audience care?

Late on Day Seven: Ballad. Ballad. *Hold your horses, you old duffer.* He didn't know his own horsepower. "It's a b-a-l-l-a-d." Meredith bumped his head on the coat hook on the bathroom door.

You're a composer, he said to himself, because you didn't play the piano that well. Well, you're more than that, you wrote a *ballad*. That's it.

Stop the show cold and let her sing her ballad.

"Dump the pepped-up start verses," he shouted, elbowing his way through dancers to the hallway.

"Barbara," he shrieked, running his dead legs. Barbara Cook turned, gracious, by the orchestra pit, cooperative as ever. "I've got it," he said. "My mistake. I thought we needed to bridge from the peppy songs. No one noticed you. If you just start with the ballad, slow and easy, you'll get your comin's. The audience will slide all over your voice. You'll own this show, girl!"

The biggest issue of all, however, was to come. It hit just one week from the end of the Philadelphia run. Bob Preston, the lead, his vocal chords, they quit, one week out from Broadway.

"Don't worry," Robert said to Rini, who had warned him about straining his voice. "Rinitchka, my voice is made of rawhide," he said. But Rini knew. Robert Preston was an actor. Who could sing. He had no experience wearing out his vocal chords.

"Bob's a first-class hollerer," Meredith said, optimistically.

The Saturday matinee, Act One, Robert's voice started to go. By night, his understudy took his place, in one of those miracles of show business. After months of running one rehearsal to the next, Larry was on. The cast took assigned places as prompters. Larry pulled it off.

The next Monday, Bob was in bed until show-time. Back with a throat spray and a promise, he did the show, through the last week in Philadelphia.

And the very last night in Philadelphia, Barbara Cook's song swung off the stage, just the way Meredith wanted.

Her song took hold of the audience.

Taken by surprise, Meredith floated his spirit home to Mason City. In Barbara Cook's place stood his mother, apron over light-blue pin-stripes, ruffled collar to her ears!

Somehow, he'd written his mother into his story, and he hadn't even known. The emotion filled his cheeks with blubber, his nose with sudden snot, his eyes with gush.

Like his mother, the character comes to town, teaches Sunday school and piano, stands for her "few nice things" and she has a not-too-normal kid of her own to boot, plays the piccolo.

Wellll, write what you know!

He headed for the Men's Room for tissue. He'd thought when he got to Philadelphia that his show was good to go.

Go to Broadway, Mama.

57

Meredith Is on Broadway

DECEMBER 19TH, 1957

Mabel and I waited. It wasn't long. Meredith called and gave us a blow-by-blow. We felt like we went to Broadway with him. Of course, I'd never met the man, but still.

Meredith pounded his feet in rhythm with his heart. He marched to the door of the Majestic Theatre. Rini's red faille dress spun like an open parasol on his arm.

It was the Broadway opening night of *The Music Man*. On heels half as tall as the calves of her legs, Rin lifted her step. She did not like to be short. Meredith knew she'd like to be tall. He strained to talk about nothing at this important moment, so aware of the cameras, the looks.

"Liz Taylor's got short legs too, Rin, and she has half your sunny disposition."

"I'll bet she can't sing *Happy Birthday* like me, either." She'd done a whopping good rendition, exactly one month ago. She sang "Happy Birthday," on preview night in Philadelphia. His fifty-fifth and one-half birthday. He'd melted down to his red socks.

Meredith knew they were acting in reverse tonight. He was inflating her for a change, in the midst of all the beautiful stars in designer dresses. They settled in their seats well before the crowd, away from the lobby melee, on the far left side, nearest the red exit. They could make a quick exit if they had to. They pressed hands together, cold and wet from anxiety. Meredith squirmed on his black scissor-tail coat.

"So, Meredith, tell me now?" Rini leaned back on the velvet chair. "How many drafts did you really write, front to back?" Her voice shook as she pulled his soul out through his eyes.

"Forty-some odd. Next show I write will go faster."

"How many . . . ?"

"Rini." Meredith faked exasperation: "I wrote twenty-two new songs 'tween Philadelphia and Broadway opening tonight and we're using eighteen." He fumbled his program.

"And all together . . . you wrote . . ."

"Okay, all together I wrote . . ." He folded his program in half.

Rini: "How many of the forty songs came out of the trunk, already written?"

"Three." He knew what she was doing. She was keeping him talking and occupied.

"And fifty-three experimental rhythm poems that didn't rhyme," Meredith said, happy now to play her game. Rini leaned forward, like she hadn't heard this before.

Meredith wearied of chatter. He blurted: "Last night's preview performance was lousy."

"Dress rehearsals are always lousy for a great show, you know that. Between you and Tec and Onna, a list of problems. The cast heard you. They'll be on top of it tonight. Pros."

"We've got a brave little army back there, behind the curtain," Meredith said.

Rini quieted, let him simmer.

"Nothing I can do now, anyway," Meredith said, curling his program corners. The horns in the orchestra pit gleamed.

Clicking heels in the aisles faded to polite coughs, candy-wrapper crackles. Lights went down and Meredith's breathing grew shallow. Rini leaned her head on his shoulder, her opening night diamond lorgnette lit as if wired in her shoulder. It was her opening night gift from him.

Herb's baton pointed skyward. Meredith's jaw lowered with it, his tongue dry. He removed his glasses. Over the next two hours, his heart beat four/four, three/four, five/eight, two/four, just as his musical score prescribed. His lips moved with every word he'd penned.

His eager cast rolled, flawless.

He didn't leave his seat for intermission and so Rini talked on.

The finale roared over them. Every person in his town roared forward, off the stage, down the aisles, it seemed. The Boys Band led, grandiose, suddenly making music. Mayor Shin, Ulele, Marian, Mrs. Paroo, every townsperson paraded, dancing singing.

Meredith swelled. Everyone in his town made the music, every age, every shape.

The curtain closed. Applause soothed his eardrums until they numbed and the stage disappeared behind the standing first few rows of people. More rows stood, front to back, rising like a wave. The applause grew and throbbed like a corn thrasher.

Meredith Willson. He and everyone in his town brought down the house.

* * *

Almost six decades later, The Music Man has been on Broadway multiple times, enjoying the initial run of 1,375 performances. It won five Tony Awards and the cast album took a Grammy. The second Broadway run was in 2000 with 699 performances. In 2003, it became a TV movie. It is a show of choice of theaters and high schools worldwide. Every role is a pip.

The song titles are so beloved, most everyone can rattle the opening lines on the spot.

The man is in our psyche, his music for forever. And that the music never dies would have been very good news to me in 1957.

58

The World's Music Dies—
Tragedy at the Surf Ballroom

FEBRUARY 1959

A year went by, and Mason City reveled in the joy of being River City, Iowa. While Meredith was working on getting the Music Man on celluloid, and Julie and I were adding solos to go with our Sartor Sisters performances, our territory in Northern Iowa went down in history in a way no one could have predicted. My greatest fear reared its head again. We were capable of killing the music of the world.

Paralyzing news came from the big Scott radio in the living room at 801 North Jefferson, into the hot house air. Somehow, the waves on the burlwood radio cabinet stayed still.

"Four persons, at least three of them nationally known rock 'n' roll singers, died early this morning in a plane crash five miles north of Clear Lake after a long-awaited concert at the Surf Ballroom. The plane was discovered about 9:30 a.m. on the Albert Juhl farm. The search was delayed hours by the fog.

The burlwood radio. (Courtesy of Beth Obermeyer)

It was made when the plane didn't arrive in Fargo for their next appearance. The bodies cannot be moved until Dr. Smiley, coroner, inspects the site."

I pushed my science experiment posters aside and sprawled, head against the sofa. The project never made it to school. My mother drifted onto her chair. My dad leaned on the archway. No eyes met. The songs were about "Oh, Don-n-na, Oh Don-n-na . . ." And "Peggy Sue, I love you . . ." And "Chantilly lace!" The pretty face, the pony tail, hangin' down.

I was seventeen. The music went round and round my head until it died.

The music died? Absolutely: the whole man died, three of them yet. Gone were Buddy Holly, Ritchie Valens, and the Big Bopper. And their pilot.

My mom headed to the telephone to talk it over with Helen Casey, a few doors down. My dad headed to his den and closed the doors. He hated when people died needlessly. He worked so hard to keep patients alive. (The only time I ever saw tears in his eyes was when we watched the planes go into the World Trade Center. He was ninety-five.)

I grabbed my coat and my pony tail hat from the hall tree. I jerked my galoshes over my loafers. I backed out the side door and worked to get traction on the ice.

I reached the school curb, laid a mitten on the hood of a Chevy. The windows were steamed, and I knew the car was full of shocked kids. I chugged to the double school doors. Inside, on the ground floor, first graders whirled and skidded from the lunchroom. Their voices sang.

But up the next stairway was different. A cluster of pleated skirts and kick pleats on straight skirts huddled. Duck tails and flips bunched like flowers. Boys voices mumbled, nudged by girl sobs. Joe Duray, senior class president, pushed his Buddy Holly glasses against his forehead, his reflection in the trophy case window. Across the waxed floor, Linda Moline fingered her collar, one of those dickies that never stayed in place. She swayed the finest Big Bopper pony tail in Mason City.

I didn't belong to any group to just walk up to and hug and cry. Nothing like this ever happened in Mason City or Clear Lake. How were any of us supposed to know what to do? Famous boppers belonged to other places and crashed in planes on the news.

I still had George M. Cohan and Irving Berlin, my music. And I had Meredith, who did not like Rock and Roll, not one bit. The news made me sad for my friends. Their Drive-in, Hi-Dive, jitterbugging at the Surf—this was their music that died.

I hung my coat and hat and peeled my boots. I lowered the seat of my desk and pulled my skirts into the seat. The hall bell rang. The girls' room door whooshed in and out, emptying.

This was not just—the show is over. This wasn't someone leaving town. Or a stroke. These men died and their music making with them. I felt as though somehow we hadn't taken very good care of the music. Music, so darned important.

And I had already been paranoid about losing the music. This pretty much did it.

Meredith Willson, celebrity judge, picking Iowa State University Yearbook beauty. (Iowa State University Yearbook, 1962; Courtesy of Beth Obermeyer)

59

Mr. Ruby's Exotic Idea

MAY TO JUNE 1962

Three years passed. My connection to Meredith didn't stop with the news of Broadway, or him watching Ted Mack, or with luck or whatever magic it was that I had going—the sugar in the air, a be-ribboned Baird puppet, a flying fairy. I was home for the summer from college. He was still on my mind, that Meredith. I so wanted to meet him.

I still cared. I'd even had yet another near-hit with Meredith. I was picked at college to be a finalist for yearbook beauty. A celebrity would choose from eight selected by the student body. The celebrity was Meredith Willson. I imagined him, spreading our photos on his desk.

But he didn't pick me. Being from the same home town, it might have been messy if he had.

Two years later I was a finalist again. Norman Rockwell was the celebrity and he picked me! Which just went to show—I don't even know what. Never say never? I did get an autographed photo both times.

Norman Rockwell, celebrity judge for the Iowa State University Yearbook beauty. (Iowa State University Yearbook, 1964; Courtesy of Beth Obermeyer)

Mary Beth Sartor, Bomb Beauty. (Photo: Tom Murray, Iowa State University Yearbook, 1964; Courtesy of Beth Obermeyer)

But soon another town legend came through the door at 801 North Jefferson Street. He was searching for the costume maker's daughter—that would be me. He picked my mom to make the costume and I lucked out.

Warren Ruby, an art teacher at the public high school, was looking for a Hollywood-worthy costume to ride the first float in the biggest Band Festival ever in Mason City. It was for the biggest Meredith Willson celebration yet. Mason City would host the film premiere of *The Music Man.* Meredith would bring its stars with him.

"This is what I envision," the brilliant Mr. Ruby said. He had done sets for just about everything, in Mason City. Mom and I perched, edge of our chairs. He sat on the sofa, his suspenders, his tie, regal. He unrolled a plan. The paper crackled. The sketch unfurled.

A golden woman stretched tall, breasts tipped to the sky, hair flying behind—like she'd

Hanna Heizelman. (Courtesy of Beth Obermeyer)

blasted off. "She looks like she's on a ship's hull," I said.

"She's a *bare naked lady,*" said my mother, her voice high.

"Gold, completely gold," said Mr. Ruby.

"Ye Gods!" came from the kitchen, like a finale, from Hanna. A crash of glass added crescendo, goblets in the sink, I'd guess. Hanna was a professional, never broke a glass, that just showed how bizarre this was.

Mr. Ruby tapped his finger on the plan. The gold beauty's arm—raised like the statue of liberty. She had a drum behind her, twice her height. Guard girls raised six-foot horns at each side.

They, however, were clothed like Vatican guards, pleated skirts down to the knees, tasseled boots up to the knees, in billowing white satin sleeves, large-plumed hats.

"We'll spray everything on the float gold, an air pump, to get this effect," Mr. Ruby said, still striking the goddess with the tip of his finger.

"Except the buglers," I said. I shivered.

"This is Mary Beth?" My mother pulled her arms to her chest, like she was cold, too.

"Yes, and this is my daughter, by the drum," he added.

"Your daughter wears a costume. My daughter does not," Mom said.

"Mary Beth will shine gold like metal. It will read like a costume." He meant a leotard.

"Her costume has to be just like this drawing?"

"Well, this is only a sketch, but in this mood, yes."

"I do have gold fabric," Mom said. "It's gold *la-may*," she said, enunciating.

"I'm sure my mother will know what to do. Her fabric has metallic threads. She's been saving it for something big." I didn't want my mother to have to brag for herself. I pictured myself, a spool wound in gold threads.

"For God *sakes*," came from the kitchen again. Mr. Ruby smoothed his white tucked-shirt into his trousers, his forehead shining. He'd been a man in a hurry, but now he slowed.

"Sleek is key, front of the parade," he said, encouragingly. "Even her hair must be gold. Hollywood." He inspected me over his glasses and lifted his painted sketch once more. The man had vision, couldn't kick him for that.

And I did trust him. He was brilliant, a true artiste. But I scooted closer to my mother.

Mom set her jaw, straight and square. "Hollywood." She said. "But we live right here, in Mason City. I'll do my best." She'd done New York, after all. But she didn't sound all that certain. She tipped her head at the drawing. I'd never seen my mother in a mood like that.

And I understood her twitch. She was being pushed to do something not at all her idea. Everything was always all her idea. She rolled the drawings quickly and they rattled.

"Dr. Sartor is home for lunch. I think we have this down, Mr. Ruby." She handed him the drawings. "I won't need them. I'll remember the essence." She was polite but hurried.

Mr. Ruby snatched at his rolling plans. He no sooner clasped one than another cart-wheeled away. We helped him corral them and watched him all the way to his car.

And then I got it, his idea. "Mom, I'd be like an Oscar statuette—for Meredith's movie!"

"The crowd wouldn't know who you were, face and hair gold. Why ride on a float as someone else?" Exactly. We headed for the kitchen. Hanna shook her pan, the noodles topsy-turvy in the broth. The ham bone toppled like a baton.

"What gold lamè fabric, Mom?" I asked. She hadn't bought it yet. It was at Teener's Theatrical in Minneapolis. She'd seen it.

Mom's blue eyes clicked, first to Hanna, then to me. "This will also be your costume for the Miss Mason City pageant," that's what she said.

"Oh," said Hanna. "Mary Beth, you could be Miss Mason City while you're at it."

60

More to It

I hadn't seen that coming. My mother was faster than Tom Obermeyer's Corvette.

"A beauty pageant?"

"Of course," she said. "Miss Mason City. Remember, this isn't any old queen. This is queen of our town. It's different: this one requires talent." Hanna was sure, too. And I respected Hanna's opinion. Daddy said she was like a scientist, knew all the ingredients in cleaners, in general she knew exactly how to make everything look right.

"But I didn't have to stand in a swim suit at college for Bomb Beauty. (Iowa State no longer has Bomb Beauties. The name probably dated to the war.) "Contestants do quarter-turns—each way for thirty seconds. Why do they do that?"

"Easy," my father said. "They're checking for bowed legs and shoulder blades-like-wings. Grey's *Anatomy* 101.'"

"They'll list my measurements, right on the program. They did when Kay Lannon got it."

"You'd be the third girl on our block to get it," Mom said. "Jane Casey back there a ways too. So our block would have three Miss Mason Cities, five doctors and twelve nuns." Of course, it was a double-sized block.

"I'm not Miss Mason City yet," I said.

"There's a current event question, if you're a finalist," my father reminded.

"We'll have to read your father's *Newsweek*." My mother took over the soup and skimmed endlessly at the scum on the top.

"I know what's going on in current events; I major in *journalism*," I said.

Geez Louise.

Daddy checked the high cupboard for his favorite soup crackers. He tipped a box down from the shelf and began surgery on the lid with the folding knife from his shirt pocket. "Journalism is a man's job," he said. "I don't trust journalists. Shifty opinions. I like the facts."

I sank down in my chair at the table. My mother paused at the head of the table. We sopped Wonder Bread in soup broth. The noodles were amazing, and we all told Hanna they were. The sound of the Holy Family playground bell jangled through the screen from just past the church. The pepper danced atop the broth. It all blurred, muffled, like someone put a lid on the pot.

At the window a flipping and freezing fairy folded to come through a hole in the screen. It exploded into irridescent pink and blue, flew over the table, sprinkling sugar. I blew the air and the sugar glittered! Did the pixie not take its place on the curved shelf just inside the window? I sighed. Maybe.

I had sat in that chair ten years before, watching my father focus on our mealtime. He'd adjusted the knot on his bib just the same, so it'd fit, slide over his nose, down to cover his tie, just the right length, just the same.

I was a new kid, but the same kid.

61

The Music Man Dance

Hours later, in my pink-stucco practice room, I listened to my *Music Man* record. I lounged on the hide-a-bed, and picked at a metallic thread in the upholstery.

"Shipoopi. The girl who's hard to get." A gold metallic costume. The silvery mirror pulled. This would be my own dance.

I thumbed through my mother's alphabetical file of 78-rpm records, grown to 700. I dropped a brittle 45-rpm onto the fat spindle. I sorted my hair up off my black leotard. I was alone, just my body and music.

I twitched to the quick tempo and Meredith's quirky words. I looked like a centipede, stretching, dipping to warm-up, but soon the mirror on the wall reflected the dance, slow and half-extended at first. Now it was "Seventy-Six Trombones."

A hat, I needed a prop. Not pointe shoes or ballet shoes or tap shoes: I'd wear gold tennies. The rubber soles would give great traction for landings and spins.

The sewing machine in the den above whirred to my *Music Man* music.

From the beginning of my memory, from five years old on, I knew when all parts of an idea came together. Soon my *Music Man* dance was written in sweat. I knew a smash.

I snapped off the fluorescent lights and went through the words. This *was* the dance. I'd get two more records tomorrow at Carleton Stewart, back-ups, so I could scratch this one to death.

The hum of that sewing machine jelled with the motor inside me, just like the old days. Me and my mother churned together towards the parade and the pageant.

I danced for hours. The cracks between the mirror squares made my body parts jump apart and back. Over and over I spun, spot turns, renversé turns, grande tours. I added a tag ending forward, straight to the mirror. I cooled down, that joyful stretch of pain pulled to taffy.

One good thing about Miss Mason City, even if I didn't put it in words at the time. I'd just choreographed my own dance. It was just so nice, my job.

62

Mrs. Sartor's Music Man Costume Number Three

The lilacs breezed in the screens on three sides of the den. I sat cross-legged, knees under my chin. What would my mother create?

Whatever she wanted. She leaned over the sewing bench, warping a three foot circle of metallic fabric, up then down, like a sound wave over a tutu of gold net. She nearly chewed off her tongue, and she scratched her arms on the metal edge.

The scene moved to the basement, by the wash tub. She wound the gold tutu into a cylinder the size of a pipe, secured it with black electrical tape, and dipped the cut end into LePage's butterscotch-colored glue, then into a pie dish of glass glitter.

"Yikes," I said. I slipped into the costume and pulled a loose-fitting Fels Naptha bag over my head. The air was tight at first, but nothing compared to the fumes when my mother began pumping glue, then pressing glitter, onto the gold lamè fabric. My arms and body felt the wet sog. Mom whisked the bag off my head and blinked her eyes. "This'll work," she said. "Stay still. Directions say the glue will dry in twenty minutes."

And the LePage's glue did dry. My mother unwrapped the tape from the bound petticoat. By the light of a lone basement bulb, the glittered edges of the petticoat unfurled into a tipped and twinkling chrysanthemum. The petticoat slipped under the metallic skirt. In a storm window leaning on the basement wall, I saw—a golden girl. "Oh, Mom," I breathed.

"Ten hours 'til parade time."

My mom was a lesson in doing things her way, confidence.

63

The Biggest North Iowa Band Festival Since 1958

I was in place on the first float in *The Music Man* parade. The silver globes on cameras popped like so many metal suns. *Flash. Ssst.* Spastic light whooshed sound like butter on a fry pan, as newspaper men twisted the hot bulbs—spit on fingers—and pocketed them, ten feet beneath me.

A huge drum rose behind me, blue and white tissue paper tufted into chicken wire. Buglers reigned on either side. Fringe on the side of the float swished all the way to the ground, covering the tires of the flatbed, a tremendous improvement on past floats. I'd heard Warner Brothers had spent big money, $100,000, on this premiere parade.

But would I see Meredith?

The two girls behind me laughed and squealed, lips to raised horns. They'd hold those horns in the air for—they didn't know how long. Katy kept one hand between the metal and her teeth for protection. Floats jiggled.

I braced as the driver of the convertible inched forward to the start point. It was hard to stand without a post for support on a moving flatbed, let alone in a pose. I experimented with balance, pointed my gold baton skyward, back arched, face to the sky.

Warren Ruby surprised me, coming from behind. My hand tightened on the sticky glittery baton. I hoped he'd like my mother's version of his sprayed-gold idea. He backpedaled to the lamp post and did a long shrill whistle. "Spec-tac-u-lar," he said. "How *did* your mother get fabric to look like—molded metal?"

Oh. I wish my mother could hear Mr. Ruby! My costume broke two of his rules, we all knew—it had a skirt and a petticoat. But gold it was, and statuesque, definitely. I dropped my pose, stretched as best I could, cast in metal as I was. My mom had outdone herself.

I took a deep breath under the gold threads and flat sequins of the bodice. It clung and curved, steel and sparkle. My chest moved like gelatin underneath. Mr. Ruby said it was alive and gold at the same time. "Your mother is a talented lady."

I touched the hot golden skirt, a metallic circle in the morning sun. I had to inhale in my chest to avoid the sharp cut of the circle at my waist. Nothing to eat for breakfast or I'd taste it. I ran a gold fingernail up my fish-net tights, metallic gold over legs. I flexed the balls of my feet. My leather boots crinkled like crepe paper under layers of paint. The tassels swung, hard as sleigh bells from glue and glitter. Glitter chips crusted through my hair.

"Can you twirl the baton?" he asked. I did, the glass-sharp glitter scraping the palms of my hands pink.

"Not much," I said. "I'm not that functional." I laughed and my cheeks cracked. To deal with wind, I'd cemented the curls on my cheeks and forehead in place with clear nail-polish. Glitter grit under my smile.

Mr. Ruby waved good-bye. His daughter and her friend and I cheered back. They looked spectacular in satin capes and shorts.

I could see now, forward over the top of the Mason City High School band. Behind us were empty convertibles. All we waited for was Meredith and the stars of *The Music Man* to get in their convertibles.

If someone looked down on the globe of a world from a thousand miles up, this street in Mason City curled like ribbon, the millions of cheering arms and fingers on either side like confetti. Detroit must have been pathetic with envy by day's end.

About one hundred marching bands were assembled on side streets, practically to the edge of town, ready to fall in line. Rudd, Britt, Algona? How many floats? Who knew with the Hollywood budget and all. Meredith really did it this time.

My float turned the corner. We wove back and forth, nearing the start, the float and band blending, waiting. I wondered—if I ran into him— would he recognize me?

Just last night, through the blue sky above us, Meredith had circled in his plane, truly coming home, complete with his beloved *Music Man* film in a can. It was his baby, come home to its town.

Maybe it would just have to do. Meredith was within spitting distance. Wiggle and spit, one of Meredith's sayings.

Warren Ruby's Band Festival Float, *Music Man* Premiere Parade, Mason City, with Mrs. Sartor's Music Man costume #3 out front. (Courtesy of the *Mason City Globe Gazette*)

64

The World Film Premiere, Mason City, Iowa

Meredith soared into the Mason City airport, over cornfields. Crops were on their way to knee-high. Houses and barns looked like thumb tacks. Seated with him were all the stars, the producers.

Out the window of the airplane, down on the side, huge block letters proclaimed: "The United Airlines *Music Man* Special." The buzz and hum of the small plane roared in his ears.

"Marketing genius, Meredith, having this in your home town," said Tec, in the seat across from him. Meredith lurched his big frame into the aisle of the plane and caught his balance, anxious to see the townspeople below who waited at the gate.

What Meredith had really wanted was to have special movie sets made, shoot *The Music Man* in Mason City. But Warner Brothers said, "No, too expensive. Need wider streets for the big dance numbers." Disappointing. But he did get to keep Robert Preston in the lead part. Meredith clapped him on the back. "You're the only Harold Hill," he said, above the roar of the plane.

"Frank Sinatra or Cary Grant, wouldn'ta been the same," Preston said, leaning his tall frame to the window. "Look at the crowd, and we aren't outta the airport."

"We're all startin' to talk like you, Meredith," said Tec, standing in the aisle by Meredith. "You've converted us like it's religion." Fresh air blasted down the aisle from the opened door. They were on the ground.

267

Rini hugged him from the back, a long meaningful hug, her hands pressing long on his heart. The red carpet ribboned down the runway from the plane. Mason City was in the mood. Ten years of *Music Man* energy surged through his body.

"*The Music Man* is gonna happen right where it belongs," he said, his eyes moist, hard to control. Every breath he took, his eyes filled. He marveled at the movie stars coming down the plane stairs with him. Shirley Jones in her pale yellow suit with the demure tie at the neck, a rhinestone clip glittering in her blond hair.

Tec and Robert Preston—all the men dressed-up in suits and shirts and ties.

Ron Howard, just a boy, jumped the stair. His freckled face talked and turned like Howdy Doody, his red hair shining. Meredith had so wanted a boy about ten, a very smart boy—in a wheel chair—in the show. Instead Ronnie learned to lisp for the movie and played a self-conscious boy who overcame his embarrassment. He was never precocious, just a talented kid.

"I gotta say," said Morton. "We have to see this town, what all this fuss has been about. Anyway, hard work's done. Film finished before Shirley's baby arrived." She had been pregnant and growing through the filming. The last day of filming, baby Patrick Cassidy kicked Robert Preston in the belly, when Shirley hugged him on the footbridge. "Can't believe no one guessed before that," Meredith said.

"I hope Mason City gives us a good review," said Rini. She had to tip-toe on the stairs so that her tiny heels would not slip through the slits on the steps in the warm whipping breeze.

"We're here three days, plenty of time for you all to win them over," said Meredith, laughing to all the crew. "They're not pushovers here in Mason City, you know. You're gonna have to blow them over."

Meredith so wanted to show the Californians how Iowa was.

Arthur Godfrey bumped down the stairs. His job: to announce arrivals at the Palace Theatre as they came to the premiere. "MGM spared nothing," said Tec. "The biggest premiere since *Gone with the Wind*, Atlanta."

"And I don't think all this is wasted on the citizenry. Only thing that makes me sad," Meredith said, shouting to Godfrey over the racket: "The Mason City citizens won't get to see the film, well maybe the mayor and a dozen or so. We have the entire theatre filled with guests from outta town. My only downer."

Newspaper strips of stars in the *Mason City Globe Gazette*, the day after the 1962 Band Festival Parade. (Beth Obermeyer photo; Courtesy of the *Mason City Globe Gazette*)

"Oh, darling, remember there's the parade," said Rini. "They'll see all the stars in person, no one else gets to do that."

"We're gonna have a tommorow. We'll be slippin' butter on corn on the cob, crumblin' chicken drumsticks and thighs and wings, passing bowls and bowls of potato salad," said Meredith. They began to shake hands of dignitaries down a line. Godfrey smacked his lips and touseled Ronnie Howard's hair. "Hear that, Red?" he said.

Meredith hugged his way through the tiny airport, his planeload of stars behind him. He climbed into a light-blue Buick convertible with Rini.

He would go on grasping hands through the next days. He would laugh with people until his ribs hurt. He didn't have any work to do between then and when he left town, just the schedule to follow. All he had to do was be at the events and love the people, easy for him, no cares anymore, not for Meredith. He had people to get it all in place.

Finally, Meredith's convertible headed for the big parade, to go south to north on the Main Street of Mason City. A reporter stuck a mike over the door: "Meredith, it's seventy-six degrees. You've got seventy-six thousand people watching the parade. And you're with a band with seventy-six trombones. What do you think of that?"

"That's three times the population of Mason City." Meredith's car slipped into place. He stood in the back seat, peering back over the parade.

The Mason City High School band stood in red and black uniforms behind him, perfect rows, one of the most spectacular bands he had ever seen. The lines were straight as the feathers standing on the Mohawk drum-major's headdress. A gleaming baton flickered like a tiara. The band puffed their chests like robins.

"Whatta band! Whatta band! Whatta band!" Meredith shouted, as the magnificent band played his songs. The parade wound on. Finally, unable to sit and wave any longer, he swung over the convertible door and raced past the bulging crowd to the front of the band. He swarmed the gasping drum major and turned him to face the band. The two pranced backwards to the lush horns.

That Meredith took the baton was not surprising. He'd done this in previous festivals. The young drum major spun forward to march ahead, his arms propelling him higher. Meredith pumped the baton and watched the magnificent band come with him, followed by dozens of the world's finest bands, he knew. He pranced, his knees high as he could muster.

Meredith Willson directs the Mason City High School Marching Band at the film premiere parade, the North Iowa Band Festival, the lead float with the drum and majorette close behind. (Courtesy of the *Mason City Globe Gazette*)

Behind the band, Meredith could see a float with an enormous drum, a bugler on either side, a golden majorette glistening in the sun, baton held high. When the float stopped, when the band played, she spun in circles as on a music box, freezing like an Oscar statuette when the float started to move. The buglers to either side of her hoisted horns in sync. She looked like an Oscar in a petticoat. Would Meredith and his film win one?

He cheered at the crowd. It popped like popcorn. He gave the baton back to the young man and sprinted back to the open door of the car. Rini leaned her head back, against the seat. "Isn't this something?" Meredith was delirious in a blaze of sunshine.

65

Meredith at the Palace

The next he knew—his hands pounding from hundreds of handshakes—Meredith was outside the Palace Theatre. Arthur Godfrey announced each guest as they entered. It was a Who's Who, his planeload of stars and every important columnist and movie mogul. He had no idea who was missing.

He passed through the doors with a thump on the World's Largest Drum, made especially for the premiere, twice the height of the doorway. Painted on the side, Mr. Toot tipped his trombone.

He'd been in this theatre many times as a boy, head tipped back to read posters. Now he drifted through the lobby, nothing to see but the ceiling and lights. A lawn of blond and gray. Some brown heads bobbled but it looked like dandelions gone wild in a yard.

A uniformed usher guided Meredith and Rini to their premiere seats, close to the front, where they'd always dreamed they would be. Only this time, it was his show. But unlike Broadway, the show was in a can, and the stars were relaxed, seeing their performance for the first time. Rini laid her head on Meredith's shoulder.

He gazed on the white screen with the red velvet curtains to the side. Many Saturday matinees had been shown here. He'd watched silent films with Mabel playing the piano. She'd rippled scary chords.

He'd studied films in this theatre his entire life—the color, the music, the dance, the rhythm. Everything, he chuckled, but the plot. If only he'd noticed the plot.

The screen flickered to life, awash in color, swirling in his music, chanting his words. He felt like a wizard. He had no more wishes for this life. He squeezed Rini's hand, dry, cool.

Mabel most certainly was applauding this moment, that she couldn't attend.

Meredith smiled. He had an idea that would knock Mabel's socks off.

66

It's a Wrap

My dad turned the knobs on his TV. Doug Sherwin's voice came over the air. The television news was what we had left. "Seats for the premiere were tight, you know that," my dad said. "We're not the only locals who didn't get invited."

"It's just a film," my mother said. "It'll be in the movie theatre for a regular run for everyone to see. We had a bigger moment this morning."

At least I'd *seen* Meredith.

"If you weren't downtown today, you missed the most important parade on the planet," said Mr. Sherwin. He gave the details and the camera changed to the parade. My gold costume flashed on the screen like fireworks. My kick divided the screen, top to bottom, in one straight line, a toe at the top and a toe at the bottom, a perfect circle of petticoat in the center.

"A split screen," my dad chuckled. The camera panned the float to the drum behind me, up to its top, down Katy and her magnificent bugle. Next was the Mason City band, stripes of red and black, prancing through their intricate pattern. "Wow," my dad said. "Look at that band! They don't make bands like that in Hollywood. Now *that* is great playing."

I was so hyper I could barely listen. The national news had it again at ten o'clock. "Good old Arthur Godfrey, look at that redhead running right through our crowd," my dad said. He knelt by the screen and adjusted the picture a little sharper.

Kick! (Courtesy of Beth Obermeyer)   Flip! (Courtesy of Beth Obermeyer)

Doug Sherwin sounded like Ed Sullivan, listing the names of so many stars. Robert Preston waved to the screams of the crowd. Shirley Jones waved, shaking the lace on her sleeve, like she recognized person after person. The little red-haired boy bounced from one side of the convertible seat to the other, accepting cotton candy and eating it, too.

Arthur Godfrey jumped back in his car. Meredith Willson marched up the avenue, the drum major of the band strutting alongside, minus his baton.

Meredith and Mr. Godfrey would not stay put. Their every move caused ripple over ripple in the crowd. The drum behind me read: "Music Man Band Festival World Competition." "And the parade was just the warm-up for the big night, tonight's world film premiere," the announcer said.

My father snapped the television off, and my parents went to the kitchen. The sound of metal caps snapping from beer bottles and the whoosh of foam ended the day.

When I was twelve I lay in the fresh spring grass in my front yard. My father's television antenna, the pride of his life, soared higher than the church steeple. I'd wished then that my dance could fly through the air—

on television. I never dreamed it would fly away from Mason City, to national television.

And then it struck me. I had just *danced* in the Band Festival Parade! It was beyond my little-girl dream. Okay, on a float when it stopped. Sometimes dreams come true in ways we never could predict. But if we don't dream, we won't recognize when they come true, Mom said.

And Julie—she was not destined to trailer along. Julie would go to Iowa State University, too, and graduate magna cum laude in 1971. I wish she could write her story—part was in front of us the night of the band festival. Arthur Godfrey was in the big parade. Later Julie would be his crowning jewel on national television, on the *Arthur Godfrey College Talent Show.* She would also become Miss Mason City 1969, a runner-up to Miss Iowa and win the talent contest, dancing. When she was thirty-nine she was named Iowa State's Outstanding Young Alum, 1984.

"We're down to the glue in your hair," Daddy said, his eyes twinkling.

I patted my shellacked bangs. "I hope it comes out," I said.

"It better," my mom said. "The Miss Mason City pageant is two nights away."

67

The Miss Mason City Pageant
Miss River City, 1962

In September, 1954, my Mom and I had watched and cheered, picked and pointed at the Miss America pageant, on television for the first time. "I want to dance Miss Mason City," I'd shouted to Mom, during the talent portion. The Revlon commercials gave a break, and I'd mimed on tiptoe, for high heels. My mother had sorted rhinestones from limestones from sequins. Mom remembered.

And now I was at the Mason City High School auditorium for the pageant. I closed the door of Daddy's car. It inched away.

My mother folded my new *Music Man* costume—the second in two weeks—over her arm. Families swarmed up the steps, hands pink to farmer-red, ready to clap.

Threads of clouds wavered overhead like a dome of net. When I saw clouds like that in Mason City I imagined music notes caught in the cross fibers, unable to get out. Music had to stay in the town of *The Music Man*. I pulled off my heels and bounded up the stairs.

Two hours later, formal dress competition over, I followed a dozen women in pastel swim suits over the planks of the stage. "A quarter turn right, please," Ken Kew, the KGLO TV announcer, said. I tugged the front panel of my swimsuit over the tops of my legs. It inched up every step. The scent of rubber from stretch fabric, the bones in the tucked side seams— the audience foot-stamped, cheered, a static sound. Swimsuit judging was over.

Like marbles on granite stairs, we girls sprinted on heels, to change into talent. Bodies around me bent and stood between the school desks, arms snatching for talent costumes. I joined the stooping and standing. We were like so many pink flamingoes.

68

There We Are

Mom paced in a circle, twisting her red stone ring. Backstage I stretched, a fifteen minute warm up. Talent was fifty per cent, a rule. I ducked the whip of the gold curtain, and started on the snap of the spotlight.

I went with the spasm of Meredith's music. I hoped my dance had the steam of *The Music Man*. My end stopped without a skid.

Mr. Kew called Maryls's name as Miss Congeniality and she grinned and hugged us. He opened a silver envelope so fast, I knew I'd know who was Miss Mason City by my next breath. I wondered in the second if he remembered that his mother baby-sat for me when I was two. I even knew how he got his glass eye—something had kicked up out of the lawn mower when he was a boy.

Mindy Wagner, last year's Miss Mason City, stepped from behind the stage. She wasn't being judged this time. Her tiara didn't fall off or even waiver, when she bowed. Ann Good from KGLO radio sang *There She Is*, just like Bert Parks. The organ roared.

Gusts of night fresh air rushed up the big stairway from the front double doors of the building. My dad flashed his tiny pocket flashlight in the audience, so I'd know where he was.

And then the tiara pronged through my hair.

"And there you have it," said Mr. Kew. "Miss Mason City, 1962, in the year of *The Music Man*. I was honored beyond words to represent such a town. But I heard those words.

The year of *The Music Man*. That *Music Man*.

I'd come close, so close. I had him in view in the parade, but still. I had not met my Music Man. Wouldn't you think?

Mary Beth Sartor, Miss Mason City, 1962, in the year of *The Music Man*. (Publicity photo. (Art Reynolds Publicity; Courtesy of Beth Obermeyer)

Part IV

The Miracle of Music:
The Music Seed

69

To Mabel's

What happened next defied science, even Daddy the doctor said it was so. And it didn't even happen just once. But that's getting ahead of the story.

Genevieve peeked in Mabel's door at the nursing home. "It's Miss Mason City, Mabel, here to see you," she said.

I landed on Mabel's bed, a lump in my throat. Daddy had said Mabel was running down. I tucked the puppet beside her and gave her a hug. "See the photos of the premiere in the paper?"

Mabel's eyes stared ahead, her mouth slacked. Her throat rattled, not really an answer and the smell of Smith Brothers cough drops rolled off her lower lip, welcome in this room of soft body scents. I massaged Mabel's right hand, the good one. It didn't respond, limp and thin.

Her dry eyes stared at the door to the room. Was she watching for Meredith or just hanging on a breath? I propped her up, the way I'd seen my dad do, shifting the *Globe* articles all about her. She was feather light.

"I'll read the paper," Genevieve said. She did, loud, read about Fourth of July decorations one could make from chicken feathers. "Mabel, can you hear me?" Genevieve said.

Mabel closed her eyes. Everyone had a bad day but this seemed more.

I pushed the soft part of the puppet towards Mabel, angled where Mabel could see him. That clackhead, Lilacchio, was great company on lonely days. Mabel had to come back. She'd waited years for this to happen, had so much faith in Meredith. I snitched a cookie. "It's two o'clock," I whispered to Genevieve.

"If anyone can get to her, Meredith can," she said. "She'll know him, I know she will. But you know, you do have to go. Meredith has gotten so big, no one else is allowed when he's here or the whole town would be here."

I said I understood. Anyway, this was special, between Meredith and Mabel. I gave Genevieve a hug and a camera. "Be sure to take the photo?" Genevieve squeezed my hand. We were already in tears, afraid the best part of the story could never get told.

From the car, I watched. Soon Meredith Willson alighted from the back door of a car. He took leaping steps over the walkway, damp from a spring rain, his spectator wingtips flashing. He'd left his rubbers home, I guess.

70

Mabel and Meredith

Meredith's arms tingled and his chest tightened. Rini was already at the airport with the suitcases.

All the same, he had time to lean over the rail of the nursing home. A mouse disappeared under the porch. He wished he could do just that, disappear into Mason City, no one would notice. He had everything he wanted. He'd made a show about his entire town making music. He'd been on Broadway, made his film, a huge success. Now everyone knew about his Mason City.

At this point he got mixed up, not knowing if the town created him or if he created the town, probably the former. He felt one with this town.

The porch door closed behind him. A frail man with strong eyes smiled and nodded. Meredith beamed and gave the man's rocker a small push as he passed. "Pleased t' see-ya," the man said.

Every person in Mason City knew him, of course, but Meredith was specially pleased. This man had saved the memory of his visits. Meredith, brushed his feet on the rag rug. He remembered his mother tying such knots. He hated to move.

"Mabel, Mabel, where's my gal?" he said, his voice a boom. The shout bounced off the the wall, the dining room to the right, the small bedrooms to his left.

More than one voice answered. "Hi there." "Yes?" *Harumph.*

Genevieve leaned from Mabel's room. "Mr. Willson?" She did a nervous tiptoe.

"She barely even knows me," the nurse said. "But I read your letters. Mabel thinks you're tops." She patted his sleeve, approving. "All she's ever wanted was to see you get to Broadway, and now the film, too. Oh, my."

Meredith studied his shoes, felt like a little boy. "I'm lucky, kid. I'm so lucky," he said, squeezing her arm right back.

Meredith had to small talk. He was waiting for a special delivery. "I'll never forget when Squiz Hazelton came to town with his band; Ralph and Mabel and I traveled with them, I was a kid with my piccolo. Squiz' base drum on his back, in the heart of a blizzard. If you ever saw a guy tap-dance on ice, this was it, for about two blocks until we caught him."

A young man pushed a cart through the door, one hand on top of a large box, the rolling sound heavy on hardwood. "It's all ready, sir. I've never seen anything like it, if I say so myself." He brushed his sweaty hands on tweedy pants.

"Well, let's take a look," Meredith said, securing the box with one hand, yanking flaps to open. It had been his idea way back when Mabel first had her stroke. It's just that he needed the money to get the job done. He thrust his arms, one side then the other, inside the box. "One, two, three, four, five, yup that'll do her." This moment was inspired and he couldn't wait to see it unfold. "Music with it?"

Residents wheeled and shuffled to the hall, drawn by his enthusiasm. "Let me see," pleaded a patient, her head shining in the late sun. Another twisted his hanky, his eyes and mouth wide. "Ah-ah-ah," said a woman, pounding the heel of her hand on her chair arm. Meredith nodded, one to another. He always liked this audience.

The messenger tugged out a sheaf of music from the box.

Genevieve peered in, her whole head disappearing under the flaps. "Oh, Mr. Willson," she said, coming up for air. She helped Meredith lift, and lower the treasure to the cart. She smoothed her well-washed hands over tucks on her starched uniform.

Meredith caught himself, watching her hands. He didn't mean to stare but he was trying to read her. It was the way she caterpillared her hands over each other, giving away her nervousness. Something was biting at her.

"You know, fella, she may not remember you. And that would be such a shame, being Meredith Willson and all."

Meredith headed to Mabel's room, to a scene he thought he had written. Maybe not. He moved to her side and dropped to one knee. *He didn't want to look down on her*. He wanted to look into her eyes.

She was smaller since his last visit. She balanced on the chair as though on the crest of a roller coaster. Her famous smile was in half. "Is her hearing aid on?" Meredith asked, whispering. He could not take his eyes from her face.

Genevieve pushed the smallest piano ever, over the linoleum, stopping then lurching on the seams. The full-sized keyboard jiggled, as it was hoisted up and over a low table in front of Mabel's chair. It was made to roll over a bed, this was make do. Mabel hovered. It seemed to be all she would do.

Meredith held her hand. It wasn't going to move, he could see that, but he thought it might feel good if she had it secure. An aide brought a Kleenex.

She seemed ready. It was in God's hands.

Meredith reached across the keyboard. He walked his fingers back and forth, the same three notes, one-two-three.

Mabel clamped her mouth, nodded side to side, went back to gazing. Her legs slid forward in the chair and she collapsed her back. She was swaying in and out of attention. She rocked toward the keyboard like a rag doll, her breathing shallow.

Meredith smiled. If ever Mabel found her words, they'd be—oh, well, thank you ver-much. Those words were automatic all her life. "C'mon Mabel. It's my 'G'Night My Someone,'" he pleaded. "Get the right hand a-goin'," Meredith whispered, onto her cheek.

Mabel's expression was not an old look, but a proud ageless look. In fact she had never looked more beautiful. Her hair was a white cloud about smooth cheeks. The red lipstick and rouge of old had done her no favors. If only the Mabel inside would respond.

"You never know, she might," Genevieve offered. In a classic nursing home lift, she came from behind, pushed her hands under Mabel's arms, and hoisted her up in the chair. Mabel's head didn't bobble but neither did she speak. Meredith stared hard at Mabel, intense. He plunked three notes, the same three over and over. It was the intro to "Good Night My Someone."

Mabel followed with her eyes.

He headed on into the melody, two measures, over and over. And over. Never had a downbeat lasted so long.

Mabel's right hand lifted. Thumb down it pummeled, and it struck a note. Her index finger plunked next, right where Meredith had started his melody. Meredith continued his three notes, setting a waltz time, waiting. And the melody of "Goodnight My Someone" came back from her hand, pacing him now. He could follow.

She didn't finger as in her earlier days, but she shifted her thumb and next finger wherever she needed to go.

Not a clap or another laugh or a word interrupted, even though the doorway to the room and the hallway had filled. Everyone in the house who could walk or roll or be rolled was out there.

Mabel and Meredith stopped playing. Mabel ran her hand over the tops of the white keys, the cracks, the black keys, the bumps. Perhaps the piano was talking to her?

When does music leave a body?

Last, he was sure.

Genevieve flashed their photo with a pop and a sizzle.

Meredith pushed his large black glasses back up his slippery cheeks.

Meredith gives Mabel her piano at the nursing home. (Courtesy of Beth Obermeyer)

He was certain as a button hook in a loop. Mabel's music would transcend age and time—and her body.

* * *

Genevieve told me the story. Mabel had awakened to music. Her music was still there. Mabel responding to nothing and then only to music—had a seed been planted in her, to stay as long as she lived? I remembered all the days I'd wandered about the nursing home like Ichabod Crane, so sad the music had died.

I was so young. Everything had seemed normal.

But this made me cry. Mabel played, Meredith played, or maybe the reverse order.

I went home to my mother. She would not believe my story. My dad—maybe he would?

Oh, Dr. Sartor, he believed.

* * *

A few years and Mabel went to live near her son in Colorado. She died there. Meredith proclaimed her Mason City's Music Woman and sent a floral arrangement. It looked like a measure of music, black wires for staff lines, red roses for notes. The curve of my heart that held Mabel and her music started to warm.

Was it just the magic between Meredith and Mabel that made
Mabel play the music again, in the nursing home?

Certainly a one-time thing, I thought at the time. I was wrong.

Mabel had died three states west. My mother brought her closer to me when she made a list of all the Iowa towns where Mabel had gone with me to do our dance (Mom and Daddy, too). As I read them I swelled. I had my own chart of towns, just like in *The Music Man.* My list was sentimental: Algona, Ames, Bancroft, Belmond, Britt, Buffalo Center, Charles City, Clear Lake, Des Moines, Dougherty, Dows, Emmetsburg, Estherville, Forest City, Garner, Joice, Hampton, Kensett, Mason City, Orchard, Osage, Plymouth, Rock Falls, Rockford, Rockwell, Rockwell City, Rudd, Sheffield, Swaledale, Swea City, Titonka, Wall Lake, Wesley, as well as St. Paul, Minneapolis, and Albert Lea.
Adams and Austin. Our towns.

71

Twenty Years Later
FINALE
OCTOBER 12, 1981

Two decades passed. My mother always said I would never waste anything that I learned, even if it seemed a waste of time—something I'd only use once or only do as a child, or as a teen. Baton twirling. Tap dancing. Enter a speech contest. A jingle-writing competition. Even if I knocked myself out and came in second. She said it would all come together some day, a bit at a time, perhaps, and it wouldn't even be measured in a contest. Follow the moonbeams, she seemed to say.

My experiences piled up. I did get to solo, alongside Garrison Keillor, with the Butch Thompson Tap Orchestra, on *Prairie Home Companion.* Christopher Plummer, the Minnesota Orchestra accompanying, Sir Neville Marriner conducting. With Gregory Hines, to promote his film, *Tap!*

The biggest tap challenge was to perform Morton Gould's *The Tap Concerto,* a twenty-minute piece in four movements, Henry Charles Smith conducting the Minnesota Orchestra.

Fifteen years of that and I started my own event company. On my first big opportunity—I copied the end of the *Music Man* film. I put 1,801 of the townspeople of the Twin Cities on the busiest thoroughfare, to open an arts center. It was not a wine and cheese event, and they were not the Rockettes. They were ordinary people, and I told them they could do it if they believed. But they had to have tap shoes and dress in red, white, and blue. They went into the Guinness book.

Three more decades and I wrote the book about it, *The Biggest Dance,* published by North Star Press.

And *Big!,* also published by North Star Press, about the solos with celebrities and six more world records by the people.

It was in directing one of those world records that wrapped my life in a bow.

I sat at my desk, reached for my pen, lined up my paper and just wrote away, 1981. Meredith by then would be almost eighty? It was worth a try.

"Dear Meredith," I wrote. "Would you consider directing the World's Largest Marching Band?" The sponsors for the band were the Greater Minneapolis Chamber of Commerce and the Downtown Council. I didn't even know at the time that the president of the Chamber of Commerce was native to Mason City, Jack Bailey. I don't know if he knew I was from Mason City. We were both just acting like it.

But Meredith declined my invitation to conduct. He suggested I find the best band director in the area. I did, Dr. Frank Bencriscutto, director of bands at the University of Minnesota. I wrote to Meredith again. No again.

I followed with five more letters. The same result: polite answers, letters, some signed by him, some by an assistant. "The Music Man cannot fit this event into his schedule."

I sent the 1962 snapshot of Mabel Kelso and Meredith, on the day he presented the miniature piano to her in the nursing home. I sent scenes I had written, depicting our days in Mason City. He said he loved the story I was writing.

World's Largest Marching Band logo. (Courtesy of Dayton's Department Store, 1981, and the Downtown Council, Minneapolis)

But still he said no. A seven-times "No." He could not come.

Why was he saying no? What could be more perfect? I tried a new approach. I sent Meredith my news releases, press kit, a logo and a bib, that all twenty-two marching bands (sixteen back-up bands) would wear. Numbers for Guinness for their backs. Could he conduct "Seventy Six Trombones," Peavey Plaza at the end of the parade?

293

And. Ride in a convertible down the parade route while Dr. Ben, the area's finest band director, directed the 2,512 musicians, from a cherry picker? And, oh—the Northwestern Bank's weather ball at the top of the city skyline would blink in time with the music.

The answer came. Dayton's Department store had done us proud, putting my news releases in a shiny white cover folder with a three-color logo, just for our band. But it was the way I worded that last request that made the difference.

"Yes," Meredith's letter said. "I am pleased that it now appears I *will* be able to be in Minneapolis for the World's Largest Marching Band. Please arrange an air ticket that is open-ended. *Do not arrange any post events.*"

That last sentence would reveal its meaning.

The Twin Cities got in gear, in a tremendous state of excitement. The day came. Maureen Wright—Director of Special Events at Dayton's—and I—rushed through the Minneapolis airport.

The high school marching band, ready to welcome Meredith, was caught in the airport metal detector. But the plane was a little late and all fell into order. The Minneapolis Chamber of Commerce and

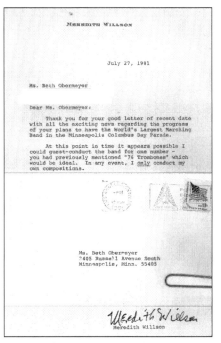

Meredith's letter: Yes! (Courtesy of Beth Obermeyer)

Downtown Council members arrived by the tarmac, honored by such an appearance, two and more hours north of Mason City as we were. Important people from United, the airline who had flown him in, lined up. Would I, would I finally meet the Music Man, at least shake his hand?

Meredith stepped off the plane with Rosemary, his wife of fourteen years at his side. Rini, Meredith's previous wife, who had soldiered by his side through a decade of writing, and saw *The Music Man* to Broadway, had died of cancer, a few years after the film premiere in Mason City. Rosemary had been his secretary in his early professional years. They had married, a decade by then.

Meredith came through the tunnel to the airport singing. "Five-hundred and six trombones led the big parade!" Out the door he popped, his voice echoing against the terminal walls. My daughter, Kristin, eleven, peeked from behind, uncertain at the noise of the plane and Meredith's voice. Her puppet's wooden feet kicked into my legs, his head into my ribs.

It was Rosemary, not Meredith who met us greeters. Meredith adjusted to the bright light. But then Rosemary took Meredith's elbow. She whispered into his ear.

His eyes widened behind those glasses, they sparked as she spoke. She had something small in her hand. It was the photo of Meredith and Mabel that I had sent him, taken when he'd presented Mabel with the miniature piano.

Meredith studied it, his face frozen just for a moment. He tucked it into his pocket and gave it a pat. He walked a straight line, towards me.

He stopped abruptly, as though to ask me to dance.

Mary Beth meets the Music Man, Meredith Willson. (Photo: Philip Prowse; Courtesy of Downtown Council, Minneapolis, and Beth Obermeyer)

Meredith Willson extended his hand.

In a stroke of turn-of the-century gentlemanliness I had never before experienced—he took my hand into his own. His eyes held mine.

Meredith Willson bowed and kissed my hand! Everyone else disappeared and Meredith danced with just me. A camera flashed. His hand squeezed mine until I had my moment.

He turned abruptly. He crossed the room to his one true love. He seemed to embrace the entire marching band, shook hands across the row.

Had he never seen or heard a band before? He stood, feet spread as though to take flight. They played on and on; he applauded wildly when they paused, huge arm claps, until the band could play no more.

I met my Music Man, himself, in person.

72

A Miracle for the Record Books

The next day, the three-block-long band lined itself onto the stair-stepped Peavey Plaza to rehearse. Two-hundred forty-six trombones filled the square in their center where the fountain had been drained. I waited for my Meredith, trying to be on my feet. I would rather have stayed in my daze but we had work to do.

About us, the remaining fall leaves, no more than sheer parchment, dangled on stems wispy as spider threads. And they glittered in early morning street light. At last Meredith arrived. Maureen and I guided him from his limo to his perch, thirty feet above the crowd. His glasses flashed the bright concert lights at the massive band beneath. Tom Duffey from the Downtown Council placed himself horizontal on the ledge beneath, his trench coat slapping in the crisp fall breeze.

Meredith shifted his weight and narrowed his eyes to see where our kids in anticipation fused—shoulder to shoulder, red town to blue town, gold braid to red-plumed helmets. Exactly 2,512 soldiers

Readied, actually thirty-four high school bands. They came from the Canadian border on the north to Iowa on the south. Their colorful flags rimmed the square, rippling.

Perhaps distracting?

Because "oh," is what Meredith finally said. More words came on a shiver.

But he didn't start the band. He twisted the button on his coat like a metronome, back and forth. Again and again, in the charged air. For a long moment, the leaves on trees were the only thing moving.

His thin frame swayed. Could the wind blow him off his perch?

The seconds passed in eternal drama, as we waited for Meredith. "Are these Iowa kids?" he said, to no one in particular. Rosemary stood at the side of the fountain top, bobbing her smooth pageboy, encouraging him . . . *please take over, honey, start the band* . . . she seemed to say.

The crowd stuffed and pulsed to infinity into the surrounding downtown streets. The musicians gulped the crisp night air, ready to blow. *Good Morning America* and *Today* cameramen shifted their mighty cameras, shoulder to shoulder.

I thought about the irony. I'd gone from meeting the Music Man for only the first time to being in charge of his image, in just twenty-four hours. I could not let this moment make a fool of the Music Man, not after my lifetime of loving him.

Fortunately, that best band director Meredith had suggested we find made his move. Dr. Frank Bencriscutto, the University of Minnesota's director of bands, knelt on one knee, at Meredith's feet. Dr. Ben raised his baton and dropped it with a slice.

And thank the stars and garters! Mabel would have said that. Meredith's arm shot to twelve o'clock. And the downswing of the famous arm rocked downtown.

The famous introduction of his "Seventy-Six Trombones," this time with 1,000 horns, drum rolled and delivered. Meredith's face inflated, an awareness.

The bass of the music shook the sky and his shoulders twitched in time. His solid chin set. "Give, give," he said in a pleading voice. His cheeks colored bright. And that would have been enough considering what we'd seen so far.

But his elbows picked up the thunder. Small controlled moves, jutted accents with after-shocks. He seemed to be writing the music all over again.

Cameras spun dials. Hands across downtown reached for their caps and slid them off their heads, a gesture not seen for decades. Slowly, hats in the crowd went down sides of heads, as though not to disturb the man in charge.

Meredith Willson guest-conducts the World's Largest Marching Band (Courtesy of *Skyway News*, Minneapolis)

Meredith's wiring sparked as he ate more and more space. His knees were fluid, his feet shifted and the man who barely could shuffle onto the podium—music rolled from his spine to his fingertips. It whip-lashed from his chin to his topknot. It banged his forehead.

The music inflated the Music Man to a full range of motion and enthusiasm and musicality.

The music made him timeless one more time and gave his old body no limits. The world awoke at his feet and he most certainly knew it.

"Whatta band. Whatta band. Whatta band," he chanted.

In that moment it sounded a lot like—whadya talk, whadya talk, whadya talk.

I saw the miracle of music again.

That night Meredith's face sputtered and glowed with silver light on television sets in darkened rooms around the world. I watched the phenomenon on my television, my fingers over my mouth. My eyes lost focus to see the music circled in the man, our world icon, never to stop. Even my heart still thumped with the rhythm.

I wasn't six years old anymore and star struck. I wasn't twelve years old collecting moonbeams. I wasn't twenty, at home with my parents when the music awakened Mabel.

I was thirty-nine. I was part of the American experience. I'd lived *The Music Man*.

Early the next day, *Good Morning America* brought us to the world. They kept the camera on Meredith's face, his cheeks shuddering as he chanted. They did not show when he stopped after a bit, mid-chorus, and walked to the side, into the arms of his wife. He wanted to go home to Mason City.

*   *   *

Two months later, in a last appearance, Meredith directed the University of Iowa Band at the Rosebowl in the song he'd written for them, the "Iowa Fight Song." He told *The Des Moines Register* that leading the Iowa band would be "one of the biggest things that ever happened to me. I don't know how it all came about but I'm doing it . . . God has really blessed me. I get down on my knees and say thanks for every one of the nice things that have happened."

I watched that Rosebowl on television. As Meredith climbed the ladder to direct, as he hesitated, each step seemed an eternity. But I knew he could do it. And I knew, he wanted to go home.

Meredith died June 16, 1984. He is home now, in Mason City, Iowa. The granite block in the Elmwood Cemetery reads:

MEREDITH
THE MUSIC MAN
May the Good Lord Bless and Keep You
1902 – 1984

Taps

And that is the beautiful end to my love story of Mason City, Mabel and Meredith and Mary Beth. And my Mother. In the Music.

In the time of song and lilacs. Everyone has them. They stay forever.

Music stays in a body, even when much else is gone. The bones save it till last.

This I know.

Postlude

The "Mass of the Bells" surprised my mother.

She was eighty-five. I noticed that Meredith had written a mass, but it was out of print. I wrote to Rosemary Willson. I sent an early draft of this manuscript to her and asked about the Mass.

Rosemary was pleased I was writing the book. She mailed me her copy of the music, inscribed it to my mother. Meredith would have done that.

It was not lost on my mother that Meredith's wife, his third wife, gave her a gift, and of all things, a score for Meredith's Catholic mass. My mother thanked her. It mattered, I could tell. "Rosemary Willson is a fine person, kind and thoughtful," she said. My mother and Rosemary "stood for a few good things," as Marian said in *The Music Man.*

"Mass of the Bells," sent to my mother from Rosemary Willson. (Courtesy of Rosemary Willson)

Years later, the funeral service of Rosemary Sullivan Willson was at Holy Family Church in Mason City, across the alley from our home.

I surprised my father.

He was almost 100 years old by 2003. I'd given him a book: *Music, the Brain and Ecstasy.*

Months later he handed it back to me. The chapters on the ear, the eyes, the touch as it received music he'd underlined.

One sentence he starred.

It became the prelude to my book. And now it is the end.

Simple as science.

For a few moments music makes us larger than we really are, and the world more orderly than it really is. As our brains are thrown into overdrive, we feel our very existence expand and realize that we can be more than we normally are, and that the world is more than it seems. That is cause enough for ecstasy.

Robert Jourdain

Meredith Willson's star on the Hollywood Walk. (Photo: Jean Marinelli; Courtesy of Jean Marinelli)

Jack Quinby, eleven, Beth's grandson, in costume for *Music Man, Junior*, Southview Middle School, Edina, Minnesota. (Photo, Christopher Quinby)

Journals, Mary Beth Sartor, 1948 to 2011.

Scrapbooks, Luella Margaret Recker Sartor.

Letters from Meredith Willson sent to Mabel.

Letters from Meredith Willson sent to Beth.

John Skipper, Reporter, *Mason City Globe Gazette, Meredith Willson; The Unsinkable Music Man,* Savas Publishing Company, El Dorado Hills, California, 2003.

Meredith Willson, *And There I Stood with My Piccolo,* Doubleday & Company, New York, New York, 1948.

Meredith Willson, *Eggs I Have Laid,* Henry Holt and Company, New York, New York, 1955.

Meredith Willson, *But He Doesn't Know the Territory,* G.P. Putnam's Sons, New York, New York, 1958.

Meredith Willson, *Who Did What to Fedalia?* Doubleday & Company, New York, New York, 1952.

Meredith Willson, *The Music Man,* Pyramid Publications, Inc., New York,

Bibliography

Acknowledgements

I am grateful to:

The *Mason City Globe Gazette* for documenting our lives and giving permission to use the photos;

Kristin Buehner for the recent *Globe* stories;

Mason City, my hometown, a town to be from if you can swing it. Growing up, I shared the collective memories and culture with Meredith Willson, the Music Man. Mason City provided the magic, the setting where music could flourish and never die. Now a destination, it is the home of the last-standing Frank Lloyd Wright bank in the world, topped with his pristinely restored hotel; it has his Stockman house near the Rock Glen neighborhood of prairie-style homes; a Meredith Willson museum; a Bil Baird museum, with his lifetime of puppets, including the *Sound of Music* Lonely Goatherd scene. Mason City is an inspired town. It saves what it has been given. And it's quirky creativity . . .

Mabel Kelso, her love of Meredith, her letters, her music;

Meredith Willson, the person. He gave us word pictures of the settings of his life and in his non-judgmental way, gave us the essence of Cy and Ernie, Rini and others. I could bring them to life;

John Skipper for his biography of Meredith. He shuffled it all for a dandy reference;

My parents for agreeing with me—that I had to dance-out—I had to—almost every night pre-television. For ordering a copy of every glossy photo of every news event of my lifetime; my mother for encouraging reading and journals; my father for his love of facts, history; my own family, for helping, always;

My school, a rocking music-box school house, Holy Family, especially to whoever let me out of geography class to take piano;

My book characters, the shouter-outers of the story;

Professor James Schwartz, my Iowa State University journalism professor in the 1960s. He took this manuscript on fifteen years ago when it was 1,400 pages and fed back big-picture critiques. He said I worked best when writing true stories, what really happened, thus the book is non-fiction. He read my book last, his last read. It was on top of the stack by his bed, book-marked. He died last summer;

The Loft Literary Center, Kate St. Vincent Vogl. She stayed with me and spoke clearest. And my classmates at the Loft. Jack Galloway, for loving the opening pages of the book, those Lilac Girls, in his class at St. Catherine's University; Mary Carroll Moore, for the early book edit;

The first Minnesota Festival of the Book, 1989, sponsored by the Friends of the St. Paul Library—it changed my life. I organized dozens of publishers and authors. That's when I knew: I wanted to write a story. Not be an author, not then yet, just write a story. Thank you Scott Walker, for giving me Brenda Ueland's *If You Want to Write*.

Author Susan Allen Toth and her memoir about growing up normal, *Blooming*. She showed me—our letters, her writing—to just write my story. It was fascinating. In real life, I never got close to a girl like the girl in her story, not in my growing up. Her girl was the almost-popular one, with slumber parties, boyfriends, and swimming pools. And she never knew the girl like me, the girl who danced, all the time, never at those parties. Susan's details were so authentic that I knew who my girl was, knew to hold my story real, stand up for it. Nor would I rewrite history by omission. Minstrelsy started our shows in the early 1950s. We worked out way through. I will always enjoy a tambourine, a banjo, the bones, the tap rhythms, the music;

North Star Press of St. Cloud, Inc., Seal, Brandon, and Corinne. They put heart and soul into every book collaboration.